Patriarchs, Prophets and Other Villains

Gender, Theology and Spirituality

Series Editor
Lisa Isherwood, University of Winchester
Marcella Althaus-Reid, University of Edinburgh

Gender, Theology and Spirituality explores the notion that theology and spirituality are gendered activities. It offers the opportunity for analysis of that situation as well as provides space for alternative readings. In addition it questions the notion of gender itself and in so doing pushes the theological boundaries to more materialist and radical readings. The series opens the theological and spiritual floodgates through an honest engagement with embodied knowing and critical praxis.

Gender, Theology and Spirituality brings together international scholars from a range of theological areas who offer cutting edge insights and open up exciting and challenging possibilities and futures in theology.

Published:
Resurrecting Erotic Transgression
Subjecting Ambiguity in Theology
Anita Monro

Forthcoming in the series:

Through Eros to Agape
The Radical Embodiment of Faith
Timothy R. Koch

Unconventional Wisdom
June Boyce-Tillman

Women and Reiki
Energetic/Holistic Healing in Practice
Judith Macpherson

Baby, You are my Religion: Theory, Praxis and Possible Theology of Mid-20th Century Urban Butch Femme Community
Marie Cartier

Radical Otherness
A Socio/theological Investigation
Dave Harris and Lisa Isherwood

Our Cultic Foremothers
Sacred Sexuality and Sexual Hospitality in the Biblical and Related Exegetic Texts
Thalia Gur Klein

For What Sin Was She Slain? A Muslim Feminist Theology
Zayn R. Kassam

Patriarchs, Prophets and Other Villains

Edited by
Lisa Isherwood

LONDON OAKVILLE

Published by
Equinox Publishing Ltd., Unit 6, The Village, 101 Amies St., London SW11 2JW, UK
DBBC, 28 Main Street, Oakville, CT 06779, USA

www.equinoxpub.com

First published 2007

Cover artwork: Megan Clay

British Library Cataloguing-in-Publication Data
A catalogue record for this book is available from the British Library.

ISBN-10 1 84553 130 2 (hardback)
1 84553 131 0 (paperback)

ISBN-13 978 1 84553 130 0 (hardback)
978 1 84553 131 7 (paperback)

Library of Congress Cataloging-in-Publication Data

Patriarchs, prophets and other villains / edited by Lisa Isherwood
p. cm. – (Gender, theology and spirituality)
Includes bibliographical references and index.
ISBN 1-84553-130-2 (hb) – ISBN 1-84553-131-0 (pb)
1. Bible – Criticism, interpretation, etc. 2. Feminist theology. I. Isherwood, Lisa II. Series. BS511.3.P38 2006
220.6 – dc22
2005037992

Typeset by S.J.I. Services, New Delhi
Printed and bound in Great Britain by Lightning Source UK Ltd, Milton Keynes

In loving memory of Asphodel Long,
dear friend and inspiring sister in the struggle

CONTENTS

List of Contributors

Lisa Isherwood
Professor of Feminist Liberation Theologies, University of Winchester, Department of Theology and Religious Studies, Winchester, SO22 4NR, UK.

Asphodel Long (1921 – 2005)†
Goddess activist, Writer, Teacher, Feminist Theologian.

Carol P. Christ
Leader in the academic study of women and religion and the Goddess Movement. Director of Ariadne Institute for the Study of Myth and Ritual (www.goddessariadne.org).

Ruth Mantin
Senior lecturer in Religious Studies at University of Chichester, UK.

Dominique Olney
Received her Master of Philosophy from the College of St Mark & St John, UK, and now works in girls' education in Nicaragua.

Sarah Rogers
Received her Master of Arts from the College of St Mark & St John, UK.

Graham Harvey
Lecturer in Religious Studies, The Open University, Arts Faculty, Walton Hall, Milton Keynes MK7 6AA, UK.

Ken Stone
Professor of Bible, Culture and Hermeneutics, Chicago Theological Seminary, 5757 S. University Avenue, Chicago, IL 60637, USA.

Janet Wootton
Director of Studies for the Congregational Federation, 8 Castlegate, Nottingham, NG1 7AS, UK.

Marcella M. Althaus-Reid
Professor of Contextual Theology, University of Edinburgh, School of Divinity, Mound Place, Edinburgh, EH1 2LX, UK.

Daniel E. Cohen
Freelance Thealogian, Emeritus Reader in Pure Mathematics, School of Mathematical Sciences, Queen Mary University of London, Mile End Road, London E1 4NS, UK.

Thalia Gur-Klein
Completing her PhD at the University of Amsterdam, De Kosterskamp 207491 KR, Delden, The Netherlands.

Renato Lings
Translator/Interpreter, Honorary Research Fellow at The Queen's Foundation, Somerset Road, Edgbaston, Birmingham, B15 2QH, UK.

Preface

Lisa Isherwood

This book started life in a conversation between two friends, one in which they mused on how such a book would be a useful tool for students who need other perspectives and a roller coaster ride for those who are invested in dominant readings of texts for power based utterances of exclusion and individual certainty. We chuckled and felt delighted to be working together. The plan grew and other things got in the way and then, some two years ago, the space became clear and the project started in earnest. Asphodel Long and I were on a roll, contacting friends to talk about articles and agreeing deadlines. Asking ourselves if the time for such a book was still right, have people moved beyond Bible based arguments in theology and religion! How could we ever have imagined that this may be the case? Wondering if we should concentrate on the Hebrew Bible or include the Christian scriptures as well. Our final decision was made because in the Hebrew Bible we saw the initial roots of the exclusion of the Goddess in both Jewish and Christian traditions and we also wished to honour Asphodel's Jewish heritage through attempting to provide creative and alternate ways of reading those scriptures. Asphodel found enthusiasm for this work despite her failing health and as ever was so well supported by friends in the by now difficult task of information gathering. Just as we got to the point of agreeing contributors and contributions Asphodel died and for me the work became urgent.

Asphodel spent much of her life challenging through scholarship the narrow readings dedicated not to truth but to dominance that have plagued academic and religious readings of texts for generations. She understood this book to be a celebration of how far we have come through the possibilities opened by the hermeneutics of suspicion which has fed so many diverse readings and at the same time a moment to reflect on how far we still have to go. It was her belief that we can at least see the path a little more clearly now that we have exciting hermeneutical tools with which to forge forward. We still, however, need the courage and this is perhaps less easily found in these days when the boundaries are becoming more defined and the circles narrowing in the academy. Gathered here are scholars not afraid to pose the hard questions and read into the dark, that is to move into spaces that have been designated as beyond the light of either scholarship or faith. And how they have moved—like blazing meteors dazzling but lighting up the eyes, throwing light into corners and making visible the edges!

We know by now how dominant readings do damage to texts and the integrity of the belief systems they represent and most importantly how they hide and demonize those in the texts that they have no interest in fully understanding or including. Asphodel always felt angry that the first woman to be so treated was Lilith and she spent time attempting to redress the balance. Here is what she had to say.

If matriarchal feminists reread the Bible they can find it a source of fascinating information and inspiration about our powerful foremothers and the Goddesses they worshipped. It also records their put-down, Goddesses and women alike. Lilith is one powerful example of how this process works.

> The land shall become burning pitch. Thorns shall grow over its strongholds. It shall be the haunt of jackals yea there shall the night hag alight and find for herself a resting place. (Isa. 34. 8–14)

Who is this 'night hag'? What is she doing in the biblical Book of Isaiah? The verses describe a state of desolation, due, in the context, to the destruction of Jerusalem by the Babylonians in 587 BCE. God is angry both at the destruction of the place and the exile of the people from it; the verses are also supposed to reflect that this desolation is brought on themselves by people who worshipped other deities. We know that this part of the Bible was written by the scribes in exile at that time and put together later, as an object lesson in what happens to those people who did not adhere to the patriarchal monotheism that was the religion of the ruling classes.

The word in Hebrew which is translated by night hag is Lilith. It is the only time in the Bible that the word Lilith appears. The translation night hag comes from the Revised Standard Version. The more familiar King James Bible (authorized version) translates Lilith as 'screech owl'. A look at other Bible translations shows that the New English Bible (NEB) gives night-jar. The Revised Version (RV) of 1881 uses night monster; the Latin Vulgate of the fourth century CE from which most Christian translations stem says Lamia—who are the Hellenistic 'dirty goddesses'. Moffat (American) produces 'vampires' (plural). None of them give her real name, Lilith. Perhaps they are afraid to use it. The patriarchal world turned Lilith into a monster, strangling new born babies and sucking their blood; a demoness howling in the desert and in the night, making men impotent, causing cattle to die and generally being the personification of evil. In medieval times, the Christian church called her Mother of the Witches, and projected on to women all these feared so-called attributes of Lilith. Christians united with Jews and Muslims in their fear of her.

Here is a charm against Lilith as a 'Striga', a witch, dated 1531 C.E.

Black Striga, black and black
Blood shall eat and blood shall drink;
Like an ox she shall bellow
Like a bear she shall growl
Like a wolf she shall crush.

There is a linguistic connection in Hebrew between Striga and hystera—womb. Once again the power of women and their wombs are connected, what deep anxieties men must feel that they misrepresent women in such a way.

The question comes up since Lilith is only referred to once, in Hebrew, in the Bible. Why all this fear of her, why this emphasis on her demonic character? I want to say that in studying our mother Lilith, I see in what happened to her an exact parallel with what has happened to women in patriarchy.

We have several sources of information about Lilith, the archaeological records and pictures from the ancient Near East; Jewish rabbinical and medieval literature as well as the Kabalistic writings, an Arabic pool of Lilith legends and many Christian church references, mainly connected with the persecution of the witches.

Yet the secret of Lilith is revealed for me, right at the beginning in her name.[1] All the rest flows from that. The various translations help us to deduce what is being hidden from us, while the misogynistic stories are designed to put her down—literally—into the worst and furthest place the male mind can dream up. Lilith is connected with two root words—Layil, Hebrew for night, and Lil, Sumerian (c. 3000 BCE) for wind or breath. Traditionally, until the information from Sumer came to light, Lilith was always derived from 'night', but today scholars insist that it is more correct to use Lil. This Sumerian word meant breath, or spirit, and was borrowed by the Babylonians for the same use, becoming Lillitu. One of their chief deities, En-Lil is Lord of the Lilim, a host of ghostly spirits flying around.

I suggest that Lilith is the first and original 'breath of life'. In the Bible (Gen. 2:7) God breathes the breath of life into the human being formed of dust, and this being 'became a living soul'. Words in many languages which double as wind and spirit indicate the creation process, the turning of inanimate matter into animate (anemos is Greek for wind). Another Greek word for both wind and spirit is pneuma, used impartially for air—as in pneumatic—or in a philosophical sense as breath, spirit, or soul. The biblical Hebrew 'ruach' is used both as the spirit of God and a mighty wind (Gen. 1:2 and 1 Kgs 19:11).

So, I believe her to be the Lady of the Air, of the living breath, that gives life to us all. It seems to me, reading from her records and her symbols, that she is also an early Wisdom Goddess, also responsible for creation and for outer and inner knowledge. Lady of the Air is Lady of Knowledge. I look to some legends for this information, the first from Sumer, then from early Judaism, and lastly from Arabic literature. In addition, there is a relief of her, from Northern Syria, dated about 2000 BCE which tells us a great deal.

The Sumerian Gilgamesh Epic[2] includes the story of the hero Gilgamesh and the Huluppu tree. In this legend we already see some patriarchal influence, where the goddess Inanna insists on a throne being made for her from this special tree (it may have been

1. S.H. Langdon, *The Mythology of All Races* (New York: Cooper Square Publishers, Inc, Vol. 5, 1964), pp. 361–62.

2. S.N. Kramer, *Gilgamesh and the Huluppu-tree*, (Chicago, 1938; cf. S.N. Kramer, *Sumerian Mythology*, 1944), pp. 30–32. See also Gilgamesh epic in Tablet 12.

a willow) and the hero is eager to cut it down in order to do this. But in the tree are three beings—a bird at the crown, a 'snake who knows no charm' at the base, and in the centre, Lilith had built herself a house. She is called a 'desolate maid'. When Gilgamesh chops down the tree, all these beings leave it, and Lilith flies off to the desert.

The Jewish legends have been the subject of intense inspiration to feminists. In the beginning, (though not in the Bible) Lilith (female) and Adam (a man) are made from the same and equal dust. They engage in sexual intercourse but Lilith objects to the missionary position saying, 'I am made of the same earth, why should I be treated as inferior?' She escapes from Adam by uttering the magic name of god and flies away to the desert. God sends three angels to bring her back but she refuses. So, in her place Eve is made from Adam's rib to be subordinate to him forever. In both legends, Lilith flies off to the desert where she is free. Note that Lilith knows the magic name of god (which is hidden from Adam), and God cannot compel her, but can only ask, and she can refuse—and does so.[3]

Arabic legends show Alilat (a form of Lilith) as the daughter of Allah and Goddess of the night, and her symbol is an owl. She is also recorded as Mother of the Queen of Sheba, who is so wise she can even test the Master of Wisdom—Solomon—with riddles, and win. A relief inscribed with her name has been found in Northern Syria, and dates to about 2000 BCE. It shows a beautiful naked woman with bird's legs and talons, huge wings and a crown; she is attended by two owls, and stands on two lions (possibly lionesses). The symbols that come with Lilith as well as the translations in the Bible tell a story that has to be connected with Wisdom. The owl universally is a wisdom bird; Alilat has been identified with Athena, ancient Wisdom Goddess; she is also of the night, as is the owl and it is in the dark of the womb and the earth that all nature germinates; and in the dark of the mind, ideas are born, before they spring into the light.

The snake in the huluppu tree reminds us of the serpent in the Garden of Eden; there the serpent was coiled around the Tree of Knowledge of Good and Evil and scholars remind us that this was not moral knowledge—it was knowledge of magic in its different forms.

3. See fifth responses to King Nebuchadnezzar in the 'Alphabet of Ben Sira', trans. Norman Bronznick (with David Stern & Mark Jay Mirsky) (Stern 90).

We may also ask ourselves, from the Jewish legend, how did Lilith and not Adam, know the magic name of God? I suggest it is because she is the original Wisdom Goddess who was with God from the beginning (Prov. 8.22) She was the creation principle with him 'When he established the heavens I was there'. She is the serpent of Wisdom who offers to her sister Eve her own knowledge. Both are punished by the patriarchy for their innate power.

But wisdom comes through again later. Though not called Lilith, but by the Hebrew word for Wisdom, Hochma, she appears in the Book of the Wisdom of Solomon (c. 200 BCE),

> Though she is but one, she can do all things, and while remaining in herself she renews all things... she reaches mightily from one end of the world to the other, and she orders all things well (Book of Wisdom of Solomon, 7:27 8:1)

In Chapter 10 of the same book, Wisdom is credited with 'protecting the first formed father of the world' and with the saving of the world from its own stupidities.

The statement of her reaching mightily from one end of the world to the other recalls her tremendous wings. She is spirit of the wind and of the air, Lady of Knowledge and Wisdom. In Jewish lore, the Shekinah the female divine presence over the ark of God also has huge far-reaching wings. Later, Hochma becomes the Greek Sophia, Lady of Wisdom, and in the Gnostic picture, the creatrix, while to many of the early Christians she was pneuma—the Holy Spirit.

A legend from the Mandean Gnostics reveals that Lilith knows 'the secrets of darkness and light, and unites heaven and hell'. Her aspect is that of Wisdom. Although history downgraded and poisoned her, occasionally someone calls on the older myths and begins to reinstate her. The Kabalistic Zohar [focuses on Lilith in several passages. In the Zohar 3.19a for example, she appears as Adam's first wife, but in a further]text 'she has dominion over all instinctual natural beings over every living being that creepeth'. Some Kabalists went further: 'Lilith is a ladder on which one can ascend to the rungs of prophecy,' says one; he makes the connection with the tree of knowledge of good and evil. Another document sees her actually as the bride of god.[4]

The vestiges of Lilith as a Wisdom Goddess cling through all the scurrility about strangling babies, and being a night demoness and

4. Zohar 3.69a.

queen of evil. There is some possibility that the emphasis on her negative role in childbirth may be a reversal of an earlier time, when like Artemis and Astarte, she was Goddess of childbirth and assisted women in labour.

Many feminists have been interested to concentrate on her autonomy, her freeing herself sexually from Adam on the grounds of equality; others have become involved with darkness and in getting into the dark side, the dark of the moon, and the shadow side of our natures. We renew ourselves by accepting it and experiencing it. I feel at one with these insights, but for me Lilith goes further.

In addition to all these, She is the spirit that gives life, the wind or breath of life; She is the Wisdom Goddess who creates, renews, protects and makes knowledge available so that we do not perish through our own ignorance. She is the Goddess who knows the 'magic name of god' because it is her own. She is the powerful creatrix. Lady of Wisdom and Knowledge, Lady of the Air and of Breath, the original Mother Goddess.

Patriarchy has turned her into queen of the demons, killer of children, particularly to be feared by mothers in childbirth. And that sums it up; instead of the creatrix they have made her the destroyer. The symbol of women's wisdom and power, she has become a source of evil to be feared most particularly by women. She represents to us our innermost herstory. In reclaiming Her, we throw off and pour away forever the poison about ourselves, our so-called inferiority, our evil inner selves, our guilt. On reclaiming Lilith we reclaim the breath of life, that emerges as we give birth to our children, to our works of all kind, we reclaim our Wisdom, our knowledge, our power, our autonomy.

So here we see just what can be done with counter readings at which Asphodel was so gifted. From the realms of the demon emerges the breath of all life, the Wisdom Goddess and the empowerer of women. Not a reading that would sit well with those who wish to see a hierarchical world. But a reading that demands the reader takes off the blinkers of cultural normality and takes seriously their own ability to see and perceive – to read with eyes wide open and lenses peeled of preconceptions.

The Book

The first four chapters of this book deal with the way in which the female aspects of the divine have given way under relentless male interpretation and misrepresentation, yet how there still remains a trace, a thread that can be woven into a tapestry of rebellion and reclaiming that will empower women. Asphodel Long reclaims the asherah and shows how the female divine still lurks in the male traditions of Judaism waiting to be seen for who she is, while Carol Christ reminds us that we need a female language for the divine since how we speak also affects how we image the world. If we continue to hold on to the male language then we also get the male God and the male world, one in which dominating male power persists. She offers a challenge to liberation theologians who perhaps unwittingly claim something of this dominating God in using the Exodus stories as a starting point for much of the theology of liberation. A timely challenge and one for which I am immensely grateful. Ruth Mantin urges us to give up male monotheism and encourages us to embrace the sacrality that emerges once that vice-like grip is shrugged off. The villain of the piece for her is that so-called great prophetic achievement, the imposition of the belief in one God. Dominique Olney examines how through the torafaction of Wisdom Ben Sira places her in the hands of men, literally as the scrolls of the law, a placement that goes against her inner being, her striving for expansion not a closing down through law. Olney argues for the renewed dignity of Lady Wisdom and the release once again of her vitality in open and free space.

The next six chapters deal with people from the Hebrew Scriptures and look again to examine if they are indeed as they have been portrayed or whether there are other readings that give a different picture. Daniel Cohen provides us with a midrash on Gen. 3:6; 12 which enables us to look again at the foundational texts for the oppression and exclusion of women. He illustrates that only when we have looked again can the story really begin! Sarah Rogers looks at the complex character of her namesake, Sarah, in order to discern something of the ways in which the oppressed can also be oppressors. Is Sarah a villain or a sad victim of powers she can never overcome? Graham Harvey casts a pagan eye over Huldah's scroll and asks whose story and what story are we presented with. The story, he feels, marks another movement in the rejection of polytheism and the female divine. Janet Wootton takes on a giant of a figure when she engages with King David and finds that what we actually have is a monstrous figure who has loomed in an unhelpful way over both Jewish and Christian traditions. With ken Stone we move into rather adventurous territory, the homoerotic, sadomasochistic relationship between Jeremiah and God. Stone wonderfully demonstrates that if we read with unclouded eyes, that is if we allow real life to impact on our readings then we open up new and very challenging possibilities within the text. Marcella Althaus-Reid follows on with a search for the queer Sophia-Wisdom, another adventurous piece that takes as a guide the post-colonial Rahab. Althaus-Reid suggests as a hermeneutic, the passion for cruising and opens up the text accordingly.

The next three chapters engage with ways in which texts may be read that challenge traditional conceptions. My own piece takes a reflective look at the Song of Songs, a text that has traditionally been used as the basis for celibacy. I question this and see instead a very solid foundation for a challenge to heteropatriarchal systems based in the body of a sexually empowered women naming and embodying her desires. Thalia Gur Klein examines the tradition of sexual hospitality in the Hebrew Bible and in so doing of course raises eyebrows, was there really such a thing? Further, she asks if this is yet another use of women for male pleasure or was it in fact a matriarchal act of rebellion. The book closes with Renato Lings taking a long look at the texts of Sodom and how they have been manipulated to exclude and punish. This is a good article to close on as it illustrates so well what the book has been about, the manipulation and misreading of texts for the purpose of power and domination, for the moulding of society through exclusions.

So, Asphodel, here it is, that book we plotted, thirteen chapters of it, a very good number! Shalom my friend.

Chapter 1

ASHERAH, THE TREE OF LIFE AND THE MENORAH: CONTINUITY OF A GODDESS SYMBOL IN JUDAISM?

Asphodel Long†

That there might be a connection, rooted in the Hebrew Bible, between the female figure there named Asherah, the Garden of Eden's Tree of Life and the Menorah (the seven branched candlestick of Jewish life and ritual) occurred to me when [1] I was writing a study of the biblical divine female figure of Wisdom—Hochma in Hebrew, Sophia in Greek. To some extent it appeared that Hochma was the alter ego of God presented in the feminine gender. In doing this work I looked at other female divine figures in the Hebrew Bible, of whom Asherah was certainly the most prominent. Where Hochma, Wisdom, encapsulated the comprehension of creation and the brilliance of order and the intellect, it seemed that Asherah stood for the concept of life, its physicality, its sacrality, its cyclical renewal within nature and the hope by the human beings who worshipped her that such renewal was some sort of symbol of eternal life. It seemed of particular interest that this female divine figure was always associated with trees. LXX translated the word Asherah into Greek as also, grove, or also, groves, or occasionally by dendra, trees; the Vulgate in Latin provided lucus or nemus, a grove or a wood. These translations lead to the consequent loss of Asherah's name and knowledge of her existence to English language readers of the Bible over some 400 years.

I noticed then the possibility that the special tree, the Tree of Life, might act as a signal concerning the presence of this divine

† This article is published posthumously.

1. Asphodel Long, *In a Chariot Drawn by Lions: The Search for the Female in Deity* (London: The Women's Press, 1992).

female being. The familiar Gen. 3:24 tells us that the human being (ha- adam) was driven out of the Garden of Eden and God placed the cherubim with a flaming sword which turned every way, to guard the way to the Tree of Life. On the other hand, Prov. 3:18 tells us of female Wisdom 'she shall be a tree of life to all who lay hold on her'. The contrast here was striking. For the J writer of Genesis, the Tree of Life was denied when our foreparents had gained knowledge of good and evil, yet the Wisdom writer at approximately the same period commended it to the seeker as divine female wisdom. The questions raised were linked. Is Gen. 3:24 an expression of the prohibition of worship of a goddess figure who might be Asherah? And is Prov. 3:18 a relic of the popular religious veneration of the female in deity?[2]

The distinguished scholar Peter Ackroyd has suggested that the hostile portrayal of goddesses in the Hebrew Bible, was part of a polemic. Its aim was to discredit any cult of goddesses and to classify them as alien rather than part of the Hebrew popular religion.[3] From there it was a short step to the ideas of feminist theologians which provided the encouragement to pursue the study further. I have been particularly struck with Rosemary Ruether's formulation which calls upon us to find a remedy for the age old exclusion of women from the norms of divinity and of humanity,[4] and with Elisabeth Schüssler Fiorenza's methodology for so doing. This, following Ricoeur, she has named the hermeneutics of suspicion. We are not to be intimidated by the androcentricity of the texts but must search for the female who has been obscured.[5] In my case, I have been seeking not so much the stories of the women in the Hebrew scriptures but whether a female dimension of deity is to be found there.

One solution to this question was proposed three decades ago by Phyllis Trible who has discussed at length the many female characteristics of God in the Hebrew Bible. She linked them first with Gen. 1:26: 'God created the human being in his own image, male and female created he them'; and then, with the cognate

2. Long, *In a Chariot*, pp. 130–31.

3. Peter Akroyd, 'Goddesses, Women and Jezebel' in A. Cameron and A. Kuhrt (eds.), *Images of Women in Antiquity* (London: Croom Helm, 1983).

4. Rosemary Radford Ruether, *Sexism and God Talk: Towards a Feminist Theology* (London: SCM Press, 1983), pp. 14–19.

5. Elisabeth Schüssler Fiorenza, *Bread Not Stone*, (Boston: Beacon Press, 1984).

Hebrew words for compassion (rahamim), and for the womb, rehem.[6] This had a great value to those seeking a female dimension, but within tradition, of keeping a monotheistic stance intact. However, Trible's work does not satisfy the many questions that arise from archaeological finds, chief of which is iconographic and linguistic evidence for a proposition summed up by archaeologist Ze'ev Meshel in the question, 'Did Yahweh have a consort?' and by the title of fellow archaeologist, Richard Petteys, more recent book 'Asherah Goddess of Israel'.

What do We Mean by the Asherah?

There are 40 references to Asherah in the Hebrew Bible, almost all couched in hostile terms. Forms of the name include the singular Asherah, or plural either Asherim or Asheroth. The form Ashtoreth is also found, containing the vowels of the Hebrew word bosheth meaning shame, put in by later redactors.

A few texts from RSV translation will provide a touch of their flavour. Deut. 12.2 calls upon the people to 'tear down their altars, dash in pieces their pillars and burn their Asherim with fire.' Deut. 16:21 commands them not to plant any living tree as an Asherah beside the altar of the Lord. Judg. 6:25-26 not only insists that the Asherah which the Hebrews have built beside the altar of Baal be cut down but also it must provide the wood to make a burnt offering of the bull that was used to pull down the shrine. There are also references to the Asherah as an image in the temple of Yahweh:(2 Kgs 21:7) while the account of Josiah's reform recounts the high priests actions in bringing out not only the vessels made for Asherah in addition to those made for Baal and the host of heaven but also the Asherah itself from the house of the Lord. The text (2 Kgs 23:6-7) tells how he burned it and beat it to dust and cast the dust upon the graves of the common people. 1 Kgs 18:19 refers to 400 prophets of Asherah alongside those of the Canaanite god, Baal.

The association of Asherah with trees in the Hebrew Bible is very strong. For example, she is found under trees (1 Kgs 14:23; 2 Kgs 17:10), is made of wood by human beings (1 Kgs 14:15, 2 Kgs 16:3-4) and is erected by human beings (2 Kgs 17:1). The Asherah often occurs in conjunction with shrines on high places, which may

6. Phyllis Trible, *God and the Rhetoric of Sexuality* (Philadelphia: Fortress Press, 1978), p. 33.

also be to other gods such as Baal, and frequently is mentioned in association with the host of heaven. Richard Pettey[7] has catalogued each reference and produced tables showing all combinations of Asherah with images, pillars, high places and altars. Using these he argued that Asherah, always associated with the worship of a deity whether JHWH or Baal, is a cultic object used along with the altars, high places and pillars in the service of such deities which included Jahweh (this is also the position of widely quoted biblical exegete Saul Olyan).[8] It is rather surprising considering the numerous references to trees in connection with Asherah that Pettey does not include them in his formula. To the question—was Asherah a Goddess of the Israelites? he answers both no and yes. Certainly no, he says, the biblical authors were unanimous in their abhorrence of Asherah worship, but, yes, she was without doubt popularly accepted as the goddess of Israel. One thing is certain: that the Asherah with attendant asherim has many forms but is never far from trees or the wood of trees. First you would look on every high hill and under every green tree, (e.g. Jer. 2:20, Jer. 3:6, Isa. 57:5). There you may discover that she is also associated with sexual activities. In the words of the biblical writers, the people of Israel who worshipped her there bowed down playing the harlot, or burned with lust among the oaks. We will return to this subject later. It will however, be seen immediately that Asherah was a vital force in the life of the people of Israel, and indeed Raphael Patai in his study of the Hebrew goddess has calculated that 'the statue of Asherah was present in the temple for no less than 236 years, two-thirds of the time the Solomonic temple stood in Jerusalem.' This worship, he asserts, was part of the legitimate religion approved and led by the king the court and the priesthood'.[9] So those seeking Asherah would find her in groves and on the hills, and in the temple of JHWH itself. The question now to be answered is:

What Would You Find?

We see that it is difficult to define Asherah. She is female and something divine that people worship. She appears to be made of

7. Richard Pettey, *Asherah, Goddess of Israel* (New York: Lang, 1990), pp. 153–54.
8. S.M. Olyan, *Asherah & the Cult of Yahweh in Israel* (Atlanta: Scholars' Press, 1988).
9. Raphael Patai, *The Hebrew Goddess* (Detroit: Wayne State University, 1990), p. 38.

wood. She is a living tree that can be planted and cut down, or, she is erected and made by human beings; she stands both in the temple of the Lord and at the shrine of Baal; she is connected with pillars and, in some texts, with the mysterious host of heaven. There are many asherim yet there is one who is worshipped in the temple of Yahweh. She has 400 priestesses serving her. She is worshipped on high hills and under green trees. She is referred to in the singular and in the plural.

Answers to what has often been called the puzzle of Asherah have been attempted for hundreds of years. The most ancient commentators whose works are still extant are the rabbis who wrote the Mishnah, the Oral Law, in about the second and third centuries of this era. The Mishnah's definition of an Asherah is any tree worshipped by a heathen, or any tree which is worshipped. The great Rabbi Akibah said, 'wherever thou findest a high mountain or a lofty hill and a green tree know that an idol is there.'[10] Trees described by the rabbis as being an asherah or part of an asherah include grapevines, pomegranates, walnuts, myrtles and willows.[11] From this it will be seen that these early lawmakers denied Asherah as part of the Hebrew religion but recognized her as a divinity worshipped by the 'heathen', and treated her as a living tree or living part of a tree.

Their testimony was made in exile and under persecution from the Romans, but still within community memory of a former Israel which though a tributary state to Rome, was able most of the time to order its own religious affairs, and to contain the vast memory of its long religious life. Because of this I am inclined to take their view very seriously even though some modern scholars do not agree with them.

John Day, one of the current leaders in the field of ancient Near Eastern studies, expresses a majority consensus when he declares that no serious scholar today believes the Asherah was a living tree.[12] A minority opinion in favour comes from the French scholar, Andre Lemaire. Day points out that in the late 19th and early 20th century before the major discovery at ancient Ugarit in Northern Syria, (today called Ras Shamra), of Canaanite material (which we

10. H. Danby, *The Mishnah* (Oxford: Oxford University Press, 1933), p. 441.

11. Danby, *The Mishnah*, p. 176.

12. John Day, 'Asherah in the Hebrew Bible and North Semitic Literature', Journal of Biblical Studies 5.3, pp. 395–408.

shall be examining a little later on) three main views obtained concerning the identity of biblical Asherah. The German school believed she was the goddess Astarte or her symbol; the British school led by William Robertson Smith, the centenary of whose death was commemorated by a distinguished gathering at his alma mater, Aberdeen University, thought that Asherah was not the name of a deity but of a sacred symbol, a wooden pole, such as a maypole used as a cult object. This is still the position of a few scholars, notably Saul Olyan, and Baruch Margalit. It is conceded, that this symbol might be a faint echo of a previous Canaanite deity.

John Day's third category is that Asherah is both a sacred object and a goddess, and this reading he believes is now mostly accepted and most consistent with the evidence.[13] Ruth Hestrin, of the Israel Museum in Jerusalem, has gone further and built this into an extremely satisfactory solution to the conundrum.[14] She states that the goddess Asherah is represented in the Bible by three of her manifestations—as an image representing the goddess herself, as a green tree, and as the asherim, tree trunks. She points out that this interpretation fits well with that of the rabbis' statement in the Mishnah. The major reason for the substantial recognition of Asherah as a goddess and for the current explosion of interest in her status and function is the discovery of texts and iconographic material in the territories now Syria, Palestine, Sinai and Israel.

We will look at four major discoveries: In the first Asherah may be recognized as a pre-biblical Canaanite goddess in her own right; in the second and third we have Israelite depictions and inscriptions linking Yahweh and Asherah, while in the fourth, pictures of her connect her closely with those of the Tree of Life.

The Ras Shamra Texts

In 1929, a substantial discovery was made in Northern Syria, of texts dating to the Bronze age of about 1400 BCE. They contained a cycle of divine myths of the Canaanite people. From them, we learn that chief among the gods were El, the father god, and his consort, the Lady Athirat (Ugaritic version of Hebrew Asherah). Asherah's titles included Creatress of all the Gods, and Mistress of Sexual

13. Day, 'Asherah in the Hebrew Bible', p. 398.

14. Ruth Hestrin, 'Understanding Asherah: Exploring Semitic Iconography', Biblical Archaeology Review Vol. xvii No. 5, pp. 50–59.

Rejoicing. She was also called rbt ym which has been variously translated as Lady who walks on the sea, or perhaps, She who walks on the dragon—both suggested by Albright in 1940. A contemporary Hebrew scholar, Baruch Margalit,[15] remarks the fact that this interpretation of the divine name Athirat/Asherah endured for nearly half a century is a measure of its appeal as well as the unparalleled authority of its author. However, he yields to linguistic objections raised by other scholars and eventually agrees with John Day that probably the simpler solution, Lady of the Sea, is a preferred alternative. It is often remarked that this title would suit a deity of the Canaanites who lived on the coastline. Later the Israelites took over the higher inland countryside, and this title of Asherah faded from use among them.

The Ras Shamra material shows Asherah to be a powerful deity: she procures a palace for the god Baal when he is unable to do so himself; she is in some conflict with El, who asks Am I a slave that I must do her bidding? but indeed he finds he must; Frank M. Cross in his groundbreaking 'Canaanite Myth and Hebrew Epic' designates her 'as the primary wife of El' and as such the 'Creatress of creatures' as well as' the creatress of the gods'.[16] Her function he believes is as a mother goddess.

Baruch Margalit proposes[17] a different reading of her name: it is 'she who walks behind', and, he declares, this describes a wife. His interpretation is idiosyncratic and there is little support for it by other scholars. In fact, a quite different appreciation of Asherah's position in the Canaanite world comes to the fore when it is realized that she is also addressed as Qudsu, holy, and identified with a goddess of that name who was well-known in Egypt as a goddess of love at the time of the Phoenician or Canaanite influence there. Mark Smith[18] points to passages in the Ras Shamra texts that may be relative to the equating of Qudsu with Asherah: in both of them nudity and lovemaking is inferred. In fact, it is usually conceded that Asherah/Athirat and Qudsu are identical deities, whose major function is to do with sexuality and the prosperity of the land and

15. Baruch Margalit, 'The Meaning and Significance of Asherah', Vetus Testa Mentum 40, 1990, pp. 264–97.

16. F.M. Cross, Canaanite Myth and Hebrew Epic (Harvard: Harvard University Press, 1973), p. 32.

17. Margalit, 'Meaning and Significance', p. 269.

18. Mark Smith, The Early History of God: Jahweh and the Other Deities in Ancient Israel (San Francisco, Harper and Row, 1990), p. 269.

people, arising from it. Such a goddess is a potent deity in her own right, and we may presume that although she appears as a consort of El, ideas of a kind of wifehood that means walking behind, are in the commentator's mind rather than in the text.

An example of the interchangeability of the tree and the goddess is suggested by the ancient Near Eastern scholar, John Gray.[19] Referring to a relief on an ivory casket found at Minet el Beida, in a neighbouring mound to Ras Shamra and of equivalent date, he writes 'it depicts the Mother Goddess offering heads of corn to two rampant caprids (animals of the goat family). This is a significant sculpture as it seems a variant on the motif of two caprids similarly flanking a date palm found most abundantly in the vicinity of Tel el Ajjud, Palestine. The Minet-el-Beida sculpture suggests that the tree corresponds to the Mother Goddess and is in fact the 'Tree of Life.'We shall see later other examples of this interchangeablity and identification of tree and goddess.

Kuntillet Ajrud and Khirbet el Qom

The second and third of our categories that have persuaded many scholars to regard biblical Asherah as a goddess in her own right consist of shrines bearing texts and pictures. Archaeologist Ze'ev Meshel disclosed in 1979 that he had discovered a rock shelter at Kuntillet Ajrud in Sinai, possibly used by travellers on cross country routes.[20] It contained drawings and inscriptions both on the walls and on pithoi, large storage jars. They showed a seated female on a throne playing a musical instrument, portrayals of a cow and her calf and numerous other figures, some in procession. In his communication publishing his findings he asked: 'Did YHWK have a consort?' This arresting question was based on two inscriptions, which read as an appeal for blessings from' Jhwh and his Asherah' or 'Yhwh and Asherah'. A similar inscription found at Khirbet El Qom—presumed site of the biblical Makkedah—reinforces the problems.

Judith Hadley[21] of Cambridge has examined this and suggests the reading: Blessed be Uriyahu by Yahweh. For from his enemies,

19. John Gray, 'Ugarit' in Winton Thomas, (ed.), *Archaeology and Old Testament Studies*, (Oxford: Clarendon Press, 1967), p. 123.

20. Ze'ev Meshel, 'Did Jahweh Have a Consort?' Biblical Archaeology Review 1979, pp. 24-36.

21. Judith Hadley, The Khirbet El Qom Inscription, Vetus Testamentum, Vol. XXXVII No. 1, 1987, pp. 50-62,

by his [YHWHs] Asherah, he Yhwh saved him [again the term Asherata is used.]

Hadley discusses the linguistic problems in some detail; the question returns: do the words actually mean 'his' Asherah, or Asherah in her own right? Hadley comes to the conclusion that in this instance, Yhwh remains the subject of the blessing, but it is carried out by 'his Asherah'. Other scholars provide different understandings: for example, the meaning of Asherah in the context might be 'holy place' a reading which links with previous attempts to define Asherah in terms of a grove or shrine. There is also consensus for 'a wooden cult object representing the goddess'or by contrast it is translated as: I blessed Uriyahu to Yahweh and from his enemies Oh Asherata save him, where Asherata is an invocation to the named goddess herself. There is also the question of whether the seated female figure and the depiction of a sacred tree and a cow with her calf may themselves be portrayals of the goddess. It is impossible here to outline the many complexities of the various scholarly arguments, but it can safely be stated that the divine figure of Yhwh is associated with either a cult object or a divine and female personage. Opinion on which of these seems to be equally divided; but even assuming that 'cult object' is the more accurate interpretation the questions remain of what function that object performed, and whether it was a representation of the goddess. It is clear that positive identification of Asherah as a Hebrew goddess at least in some circles in ancient Israel is much enhanced by these finds.

The Cult Stand at Taanach

The fourth of our archaeological indications of the nature of Asherah takes the form of a pottery stand uncovered at Tel Taanach in Israel, identified as a cult stand or an object used in ritual and worship. Ruth Hestrin has described this object extensively and discussed its possible religious background. It is dated to the 10th century BCE and is remarkable for the number and subject of the scenes that decorate it. Hestrin [22] describes them as follows:

> In the lowest register a crudely shaped naked woman flanked by two standing lions is represented … the second register has an opening in

22. Hestrin, 'Understanding Asherah', pp. 61–77.

> the centre flanked by two sphinxes with a lion's body, bird's wings and a female head. Two round protuberances are seen between the legs. The faces resemble that of the naked woman. A sacred tree is represented in the centre of the third register composed of a heavy central trunk from which sprout symmetrically three pairs of curling branches. Two ibexes stand on their hind legs in an antithetical position ... flanking this group are two lionesses almost identical to those in the lowest register.

Notice particularly the shape of the sacred tree and the number of branches—you will see that the trunk plus the branches make it seven-fold. Analysing the decorative material on the cult stand, Hestrin comes to the conclusion that two of the registers show an Asherah, once as a naked woman, and once represented by her symbol, the tree. The very fact that the lions in the registers are almost identical in shape and position indicate, she says, that they belong to the same deity. Representations of a nude goddess flanked by lions and holding snakes and lotus blossoms are known widely in the ancient Near East. In particular, as already mentioned, those uncovered in Ugarit and Minet-el-Beida show similar themes, as do portrayals of Qudshu from Egypt.

Iconographic evidence alone can only suggest an identification between the goddess Asherah-Qudshu and a sacred tree; but support for such an identification is considerable when seen in relation to our textual material. John Day, discussing what he calls the sacred Asherah pole—that is, a pole from a sacred tree and taking on its significance, writes: 'It may be that the sacred Asherah pole had the form of a stylized tree. The evidence for this I would seek in Hos. 14:9 There the prophet makes Yahweh declare: 'Ephraim what has he still to do with idols? It is I who answer and look after him. I am like a luxuriant cypress, from me comes your fruit'. Day continues: 'The bold comparison of Yhwh with a tree, unique in the Hebrew Bible juxtaposed with the condemnation of idolatry has suggested to many scholars that Hosea is polemicizing against idolatry associated with Canaanite tree symbolism. Could this be a polemic against Asherah? A number of scholars have believed that it is'.[23]

The implications of this suggestion of Day's are far-reaching, and for me they extend as far as the Garden of Eden. The narrative there tells us that the tree forbidden was of knowledge of good

23. Day, 'Asherah in the Hebrew Bible', p. 404.

and evil; but when humans ate its fruit, they were then denied access to the tree of life. Although this had not been forbidden originally, Gen. 3:22 has God saying that the human beings having eaten of the forbidden tree might next 'take of the tree of life, and eat and live for ever'.

It is time to look further at the Tree of Life.

The Tree of Life

The idea of a Tree of Life is a concept held by many peoples of different cultures. Roger Cook has surveyed this phenomenon from Ygdrasil,'the great tree which is the Scandinavian axis of the world' and which links the underworld, middle earth and the heavenly land of the gods; to the ... cosmic Bhodi tree under which the Buddha gained enlightenment. Through varying cultures and times the Tree of Life has been a symbol both of this world and a world of the divine. It represents the theme of rebirth, along with the union of opposites.[24] In one instance the great tree is said to shake, bringing about the destruction of the gods and the world. However, concealed within its trunk are the seeds of the world's renewal in the form of a man and a woman from whose union a new race will appear to re-populate the world.

Cook writes:

> the full breasted tree divinity is one of the many epiphanies or divine manifestations of the Great Mother Goddess known in mythology the world over. As the Earth Mother (Tellus Mater) she embodies the regenerative powers contained in the earth and the waters ... (she is) a perpetual source of cosmic fertility. Woman and Tree alike embody this Great Earth Mother for both are visible manifestations of her fruitfulness.[25]

Whether we agree or not with Cook's description of one universal great goddess, there is no doubt of the association between sacred trees, fertility and a female dimension of the divine. All are involved in the continuation and nurture of life in this world and sometimes in the next. Fertility, in the sense of the continuation and sustenance of the earth and of people is celebrated sexually in the shade of the Tree, or grove; this has been the practice in many cultures among

24. Roger Cook, *The Tree of Life* (London: Thames and Hudson, 1974), pp. 25-26.
25. Cook, *The Tree of Life*, p. 13.

them the people of Israel as we know from our biblical texts. There, as elsewhere, the power of life giving and life sustaining is associated not only with the Tree of Life but very often is one of the attributes of the female divine.

An account of the mythology of the sacred tree is given by Yarden who connects it closely with the Menorah as we shall see later. Yarden describes an ancient myth of 'the cosmic or World Tree usually conceived at the centre of the earth … with its roots in the Underworld … and crown in Heaven. He surveys the extent of this myth in the ancient Near Eastern world and its echoes in the biblical texts. He records that 'representations of sacred trees or their branches appear on even the oldest finds'. He surveys the extent of this myth in the ancient Near Eastern world and its echoes in the biblical texts and records that 'representations of sacred trees or their branches appear on even the oldest finds'.[26]

In this connection, we will look to the distinguished biblical scholar Carol Meyers, whom I will later be introducing in connection with the Menorah. In an account of ancient Near Eastern iconography she writes 'it is hardly an exaggeration to indicate that the sacredness of vegetation and trees has been a recurrent and integral theme in a wide range of cultures spanning most areas of the globe and most epochs of human history … the sacred quality of trees lies in the fact of their embodiment of the life principle'.[27] She speaks of 'the widespread association of vegetal life with the generative power of the divinity', resulting in the common phenomenon of the manifestation of deity within or at certain trees which would be especially favoured; these trees would lead the worshipper in the direction of the divinity. Furthermore the divinity revealed in the tree is also the source of the hoped-for life after death … thus the theophany motif of the sacred tree becomes blended inextricably with the concept of life eternal. The Tree of Life, in the sense of immortal life, becomes an inseparable aspect of the regenerative principle contained within plant life'. Here we have clearly set out the relationship between the tree which gives us the daily fruit of our life, and its relationship with divinity and with

26. L. Yarden, *The Tree of Light: A Study of the Menorah* (Ithaca, N.Y.: Cornell University Press, 1971), p. 35.

27. Carol Meyers, *The Tabernacle Menorah* (Missoula, Mt.: The Scholars' Press, 1976), p. 96.

eternal life. We also can understand from this some of the relationship of fertility practices to the sacred.

Howard Wallace in a Ph.D dissertation entitled 'The Eden Narrative' analyses the different meanings of the word life in ancient Near Eastern literature. Looking at the Babylonian epics of the third millennium BCE which contain accounts of various heroes of that period who attempted to find eternal life, he comments that it is mostly said to be available from plants or leaves. For example, the hero Gilgamesh at one point finds a plant which might have provided what he sought but it is stolen from him by a serpent. Another hero Adapa, through a mistaken decision does not partake of the food and water of life actually offered to him. The divine Ishtar in her descent to the Underworld, in the Sumerian version of the story is given the plant of life. Albright has described how Gilgamesh reaches the goddess Siduri-Sabatu. She is seated under a vine in the Paradise garden which is described as of 'dazzling beauty'. The vine is its centrepiece. Siduri-Sabatu is addressed as Goddess of Wisdom, Genius of Life, and referred to as 'Keeper of the Fruit of Life'. He asks her for the gift of eternal life but she refuses; Wallace writes: The aspect of 'life' in these stories changes from one to the other,(but) the various aspects are all part of the broader concept of life in all its abundance; it is worthy to note that the gaining of divine qualities of life is associated with ... eating or drinking some substance which possesses the magical powers to grant this gift'. Wallace makes the point that usually the substance needed will be procured from a tree.[28]

He compares these texts with Psalm 1, which declares of someone who seeks wisdom: 'he will be like a tree transplanted by channels of water which gives its fruit in season whose leaf does not wither.' There we may understand a Tree of Life that is both temporal and eternal. Its fruit brings abundance in this world but its unwithering qualities bring it into eternal life. Wallace then discusses the Hebrew words for life and sees a possible connection between life—the Hebrew word hayyim, and Eve—Hebrew word Hayya. He proposes a strong association between the two. Can Eve, called the Mother of all living, be identified as the Tree of Life itself? Wallace cites a fertility motif as the connecting link between the two. He sees a strong association between Eve, the Tree of Life and Asherah,

28. Howard Wallace, *The Eden Narrative* (Missoula, Mt.: The Scholars' Press, 1985), p. 114.

creatress of the gods, and writes 'it is not impossible that a tree which is associated with fertility and the mother goddess figure on one level of a story could take on other life-giving aspects, also a divine gift at another level, especially when we remember the broad spectrum covered by the word "life"'.

The biblical writers lived with the evidences around them of sacred fertility rituals on every high hill and under every green tree in honour of the goddess Asherah. It is not impossible that Wallace's identification of Eve in this way could account for the hostility shown to her and the malediction set upon what might be thought to be the joyful human condition of sexuality and reproduction. Wallace's identification of Eve, with Asherah and with the Tree of Life, may be deemed by some to be a walk along the wild side of speculation, yet its resonances with the polemics of the material are strong.

Thus, the ancient monotheistic heritage of the religious system that became traditional Judaism, where the deity is always expressed in the masculine gender, is challenged by current archaeological and textual evidence. This suggests that a goddess or goddesses were worshipped not as part of a residue of foreign cult, but in her own right in the Hebrew religion. She would be associated with all that is meant by life and symbolized by the Tree of Life: an indwelling Deity who was the source of not only food, sexuality, reproduction, at a mundane level, but also wisdom and possibly the promise of immortal life. The high hills, green trees and groves where she was worshipped were expressions of herself; parts of trees were made into images of her or set up as poles in her honour. Traditionalists might still argue that all these forms of worship were extraneous to the Hebrew religion and were in fact 'heathen'; but the current evidence is mounting against them. It is reinforced by a concept of the Tree of Life that has been part of normative Judaism for a millennium and a half: part of normative Judaism but hidden from more than half of Judaism's adherents. I refer to the Kabbalah.

This is the mystical system practised until recently only by an elite few, who must be male and married and over forty years of age. It was kept secret from everyone else, notably women. It is the Kabbalah, now more available to those wishing to study it, no matter their sex and age. At its heart stands a Tree of Life. Surrounding the Tree in all its glory is a divine female entity, named the Shekinah, the dwelling place of God. The nearest that the traditional commentators came to the feminine Shekinah was to say it represented the community of Israel, historically in a marriage relationship with God. But distinguished Kabbalah scholar, Gershon Scholem, found differently. He writes: 'the Shekinah becomes an aspect of God that is a quasi-independent feminine element within him … the necessary discovery of the female element with God … regarded with the utmost misgiving by non-Kabbalistic sources was a mystic conception of the feminine principle'. The Shekhina reflects her own and God's glory, she is the Face of God and she envelopes the Tree in her shining light. She is sometimes represented as a Paradise Garden full of luxurious trees.[29] The Tree of Life in itself, is the image of God's creation, it offers a depiction of what Cook has called 'the mysterious relationship between the invisible transcendent god and the visible world of creation'.[30] The image used is that of an inverted tree, descending from heaven to earth. Its branches are emanations—called sephiroth; they represent the divine powers and spheres through which the human being can work towards the mystical divine. It is impossible here to address this subject with any but the briefest of glances; it has been the basis of a Western tradition of esoteric religious magical working, has been related to the continuous underground hermetic tradition and today continues to fascinate new generations of seekers with its profoundities. It has been and is understood as a most powerful symbol of divine glory. We cannot avoid the connection of this Kabbalistic Tree, an ongoing conception from early rabbinical times to its first publication in the 13th century of our era, with the sacred trees we have been addressing. Certainly there appears to be a large time lag, but Kabbalists will affirm that their material can be traced continuously to biblical times. The divine female element was re-created, in the understanding of many of the Kabbalists, to become the Shekinah. It is not too fanciful to propose that in her is a resonance of Asherah, whose name and presence became obscured but never lost. We will now look at the connections of this material with the Menorah.

29. Gershon Scholem, *The Kabbalah and its Symbolism* (New York: Schocken, 1969), p. 58.

30. Cook, *The Tree of Life*, p. 18.

The Menorah

While the Kabbala was practised by men in the synagogues away from the domestic hearth, there was—and is—in their homes, presided over by the woman, a powerful symbol of that same Tree of Life which was the heart of their study. This is the Menorah. Cook describes it as 'an important ... Jewish symbol related to the cosmic tree'. We first hear of it in Exod. 25: 31-40.

> You shall make a lamp-stand of pure gold ... its cups its capitals and its flowers shall be of one piece with it. And there shall be six branches going out of its sides, three branches of the lampstand out of one side of it and three branches out of the other side of it; three cups made like almonds, each with its capitals and flower, on the one branch, and three cups each with its capitals and flower on the other branch—so for the six branches going out from the lampstand.

This lampstand was the desert Tabernacle Menorah guarding and throwing light towards the Ark of the Covenant.

Note that its cups were to be shaped in the form of almonds, which themselves are precursors of returning life to the trees in spring, being the first tree to flower before even its leaves have opened. Carol Meyers today a distinguished theologian made the Tabernacle Menorah her Ph.D dissertation in 1974. She addresses the relationship between God and the Trees of the garden, and offers the perception:

> in the primeval cycle of Genesis, the primacy of God separate from nature is the clear message The mythological forces represented by the life-giving nature of plant life ... are confronted ... in a direct way ... nevertheless there is not a radical and permanent breaking off of such ideas. The power of the underlying mythic ideas was enormous and is not to be under estimated. It evidently lay beneath the surface ready to materialise for a long time during Israel's history.[31]

Here Meyers points to the continuity of ideas hidden perhaps within Hebrew monotheism that support the concept of the Genesis Eden narrative as polemic.

When she turns to the Menorah of Exodus, the Tabernacle Menorah, she examines in detail its relation to the iconography and texts concerning sacred trees in the ancient Near East. She writes that her study 'has shown that the tabernacle menorah in form and detail belongs to the conventional way for the sanctity of vegetable

31. Meyers, *The Tabernacle Menorah*, p. 133.

life to be depicted'.[32] She declares that it has long been recognized that because of the language employed to describe the Menorah and because of its appearance as a thickened stem or shaft from which its branches project that the whole shape strongly resembles a stylized tree. Meyers cites S.A. Cook who pointed this out some time ago, largely on the basis of its representation in later Jewish art. He would, she says, have laid it down that the candlestick and the tree inevitably tend to merge into one another. Goodenough also suggests this, pointing out that the vision of Zachariah (4:1–14) with trees flanking the Menorah perhaps preserves the original meaning of plant form imbued with sanctity. She argues:

> A consideration of some of the details of such forms has revealed that there is a close morphological connection between arboreal expressions on ancient seals and monuments and the branched form assumed by the superstructure, as it were, of the tabernacle Menorah (whose form) is exactly (that) taken by the quintessential stylized tree or branch in the Mesopotamian, Aegean, and Syro-Palestinian religions. Whereas there are various modes for expressing stylized plant life throughout Mesopotamian history it is precisely in the Late Bronze Age that a specific six plus one axis form not only comes to dominate but is also disseminated throughout the Eastern Mediterranean island and coastal areas'.[33]

Referring to the sanctity of the vegetable and plant life symbolized, she declares that it 'involves both the fertility theme of the tree and the immortality concept'. She calls attention to the variations in design of the Menorahs of the first and second Temples, and quotes first century Josephus' description of the latter: 'facing the table, near the South Wall, stood a candelabrum of cast gold ... it was made up of globules, and lilies, pomegranates and little bowls ... it terminated in seven branches, regularly disposed in a row. Each branch bore one lamp'. The tree and plant allusions are clear here, as they also are in a Talmudic description which she quotes: 'the cups were like Alexandrian goblets, the knops like Cretan apples, and the flowers like blossoms around the capitals of columns'.[34]

The material that she presents is in line with the views of earlier Jewish scholars in this century concerning the relationship of the

32. Meyers, *The Tabernacle Menorah*, p. 134.

33. E.R. Goodenough, *Jewish Symbols in the Greco-Roman World* (Toronto: Pantheon, 1965), p. 135.

34. Goodenough, *Jewish Symbols*, p. 38.

Menorah to the Kabbalistic Tree of Life. For example, Menahem Recanati, calls attention to the vision of Zachariah, where the text of 4:10 reads 'these seven (lamps) are the eyes of God'. He claims that this asserts that God governs by means of the Sephirot emphasized by the seven branches of the Menorah: the divine power is exercised through the Menorah'.

L. Yarden has surveyed the Menorah from its inception until the present. He believes it has enormous significance in 'fundamental conceptions' of (hu)mankind's most fundamental conceptions of Nature, of Life and Death, of Cosmos and God. He connects it with the ancient sacred tree,[35] and then discusses its light as the 'light of God and the Torah'. He shows its ubiquity throughout Jewish history in a series of remarkable pictures of synagogue vessels and decorations from early times until the present.

Present day Kabbalist Ze'ev ben Shimon Halevi argues that in the Menorah we can see a symbol of both the mystical and objective knowledge of the universe conveyed by God to Abraham and to Moses. He writes: 'the construction of (Solomon's) Temple and the seven branched candlestick are both formulations of the Tree of Life'.[36] In an illustration of the Menorah as the Tree of Life he shows how its stem and branches indicate the different Sephiroth (emanations of God) which to the Kabbalist are the basis of study of eternal wisdom. Words shown at each candle flame are the names of each Sephira.

If we now look at the Menorah in the religious life of Judaism it is clear that while it has a mystical significance which can lead the adept to the throne of the divine, yet throughout the whole history of Judaism it has taken the form of a practical symbol of everyday religious life. It is kept in the synagogue and in the home. Each winter a special version of it, with nine, not seven branches comes into use for nine days. This is at Chanukah, the winter festival of lights, commemorating the miracle of preservation of the oil for the lights in the Jerusalem temple in the 2nd century BCE when Judas Macabeus and his brethren led a successful revolt against their imperial persecutors (1 & 2 Maccabees).

Depictions of the Menorah are universal in Jewish history. A huge portrayal of it is shown on the triumphal arch of Titus in Rome,

35. Yarden, *The Tree of Light*, pp. 18–40.

36. Shimon Halevi, *The Tree of Life* (Bath: Gateway Books, 1991) p. 18.

emphasizing the plight of the Jews losing their home and going into slavery in 70 CE, after the destruction of Jerusalem and the temple. Art historian Heinrich Strauss has called attention to the menorah on walls of ancient and medieval synagogues from Asia Minor to Spain as well as to those many in the modern era. He points to its depiction on coins, amulets and jewels of all kinds throughout the lands of the dispersion of the Jews, being particularly noticeable on Persian artefacts. Scribblings of menorahs by Jewish prisoners awaiting execution can be seen on the walls of Roman catacombs, such as beneath the Villa Torlonia. Nearly two thousand years later, similar designs were scratched at Auschwitz and Therienstadt death camps, and when the memorial to the Warsaw Ghetto fighters was unveiled in 1963, two huge Menorahs were seen to be its most significant element.

The Menorah is a homely, as well as a sacred symbol, familiar to all Jewish families and a part of their life as it has been over the centuries. It is unlikely that the ordinary family, and particularly the women of the house, would be aware of any sacred significance other than its appearance in the story of Exodus and its identification with the Chanukah lights. There is certainly no idea whatever in normative Judaism that this candlestick could be an image or symbol of, or could in any way resonate with, the goddess Asherah whom the biblical writers and traditional Judaism so abominate. Yet it appears that such a concept is not impossible.

I have suggested that the Hebrew religion contains a female divine figure, Asherah, who may have been the consort of God, Yhwh, and also was interchangeable with the Tree of Life. This latter is represented by the Menorah, the seven branched candlestick, a religious symbol in Judaism whose connection with the female aspect of divinity has been lost. Until the archaeological finds of this century it was generally supposed that the forty texts in the Hebrew Bible concerning Asherah, referred to wooden cult objects connected with earlier Near Eastern goddesses, associated with trees. To perceive in the biblical texts, any reference to the figure of Asherah as a Goddess in her own right, and certainly as a goddess of the Hebrews was condemned.

It was clear that the original description of an Asherah as alien to the Hebrew religion could not be sustained; she was certainly a Canaanite goddess; and it was possible that she was a Hebrew goddess. Further it had been observed that a sacred or cosmic tree

attended by animals was a constant theme in ancient Near Eastern iconography. The cult stand of Taanach gave major indications that the tree could be replaced by, and was interchangeable with, a female figure conjectured to be a goddess, with some evidence that she might be Asherah. The Tree of Life was generally considered to be the dwelling place of the divine, source of fruitfulness, and nourished not only life here in this world, but held the hope of immortality. This background to the Eden story has led to scholarly enquiries concerning its polemic origin. Could the texts have been written as rhetoric against worship of a goddess, who was likely to be Asherah?

Alongside this theme there runs a parallel concept where a stylized version of the Tree of Life is created in the form of the seven branched candlestick—the Menorah described in the Book of Exodus. This stood in the first Jerusalem temple and a similar model was placed in the second. Eventually models abounded and came to be a symbol of the Hebrew people. At a later date such replicas were connected with the Maccabean struggles, and continue to hold that identity, as well as that of the Tree of Life.

As time went on, the idea of a divine female figure at the core of Judaism was totally forgotten except within the Kabbalah, a secret mystical form of the religion. Central to this system is the Tree of Life concept, where the ten emanations are enveloped in the glory of the divine female Shekinah. Praxis within the Kabbalah included identification of the Tree of Life with the Menorah. I have suggested that we may reasonably perceive resonances between the Menorah and the biblical figure of Asherah, herself very possibly connected with the Tree of Life.

Reference has also been made to the Eden story and scholarly commentators who believe that it was composed as a polemic against the worship of Asherah. Referring back to my original question: Was the story of the denial of the Tree of Life to humans in Gen. 3:24 a prohibition of worship of the goddess Asherah? It is suggested that an affirmative answer may respectably be given. Finally raising these questions is an expression of the profound shift that feminist theology makes to our thinking. As a Jewish woman myself, I was until very recently quite unaware of the heritage I have outlined, and I find it inspiring and liberating. I am particularly moved by the Menorah, since now I am able to see in it a reminder that in my background religion of strict monotheism a female aspect or dimension or symbol of the divine may have been present from the beginning. Although Jewish memories of her significance became distorted and eventually faded, yet a symbol of her has been continually present in our homes. I feel that to be a reinforcement of great strength and inspiration since it helps restore to women their full personhood of humanity and divinity.

Chapter 2

THE ROAD NOT TAKEN: THE REJECTION OF GODDESSES IN JUDAISM AND CHRISTIANITY

Carol P. Christ

The road not taken referred to in the title of this paper is the incorporation of female language for God into Christian and Jewish worship, prayer and liturgy, a subject that was dear to the heart of Asphodel Long, to whom the essays in this volume are dedicated. The cover of the original edition of Long's book, *In a Chariot Drawn by Lions: The Search for the Female in Deity*, boasts that the book is 'Exploding the great myth that God is male.'[1] Yet despite the work of Asphodel Long and others, the 'great myth' is alive and well and functioning in most Christian and Jewish congregations—including those led by women. In *Introducing Thealogy*, Melissa Raphael concludes that the feminist project to change the face of God within received traditions has for the most part failed, stating that 'most female rabbis and priests ... for the sake of peace within their congregations, find themselves able to make only minor adjustments to the received patriarchal model of God held by the majority of their congregants.'[2] My discussions with Jewish and Christian feminists confirm this. Recently a friend who is a retired Episcopal priest told me that in her experience, younger women priests consider the issue of inclusive God language to be uninteresting and unimportant.[3] My question is why is this so? *Is the God of Judaism and Christianity as they have developed and been transmitted 'really' a male after all?*

1. Asphodel Long, *In a Chariot Drawn by Lions: The Search for the Female in Diety* (London: The Women's Press, Ltd.), 1992.

2. Melissa Raphael, *Introducing Thealogy* (Sheffield: Sheffield Academic Press, 1999), p. 52.

3. Conversation with Marjean Bailey.

In 1971 at the first meeting of women theologians at Alverno College, another woman and I drafted a position paper on God the Mother.[4] Inspired by Mary Daly whose 'After the Death of God the Father'[5] had recently been published, we argued that one of the most important changes feminists could make in religion would be to begin to speak of God the Mother alongside God the Father. Our paper was met with stunning silence, and it was not selected by the conference organizers for distribution.[6] I found this puzzling. Like other Christians (I was baptized Presbyterian but was a practicing Roman Catholic at the time), I 'knew' that God was not really a male, and it seemed to me quite obvious that God's love for the world was 'like' that of my own mother and grandmothers for me and my brothers. Naively, I assumed that it would be a relatively simple matter to insert female God language into liturgy and prayer in both Judaism and Christianity. *After all, God was not really a male. Or was he?*

When I first began to teach Women and Religion in 1973, I discovered Raphael Patai's *The Hebrew Goddess*.[7] Patai argued that the Goddess had been worshipped in the temple of Solomon for more than 200 years. He said that the Hebrew Bible as we know it is not a fair and accurate telling of the history of ancient Hebrew religion. Rather, the Bible that has come down to us was edited by 'monotheistically oriented authors and/or editors' who 'strove to suppress, eliminate, and replace' all evidence that the ancient Hebrews had worshipped the Goddess or Goddesses alongside Yahweh, the well-known male God of the Bible.[8] Patai's evidence for this astonishing claim was four-fold:

1. The evidence of the Bible itself, especially the ubiquitous condemnations of worship of divinities other than Yahweh;
2. Archaeological evidence of female 'figurines' found in the lands of Israel and Judah;

4. I no longer have a copy of this paper, nor do I remember the name of the woman (who was from the Midwest) who wrote it with me.

5. See Mary Daly, 'After the Death of God the Father: Women's Liberation and the Transformation of Christian Consciousness' in Carol P. Christ and Judith Plaskow, (eds.), *Womanspirit Rising: A Feminist Reader in Religion* (New York: Harper and Row, 1979), pp. 52–62; originally published in *Commonweal* (March 12, 1971).

6. Although my paper on Karl Barth was.

7. Raphael Patai, *The Hebrew Goddess*, (KTAV Publishing House, Inc. [no place given], 1967).

8. Patai, *The Hebrew Goddess*, p. 31.

Mythological and archaeological evidence from nearby ancient Near Eastern cultures; and finally

4. Literary sources from post-biblical Judaism.[9] Asphodel Long's work can be read as an extended feminist midrash on Patai, adding much new evidence and clearly articulating the feminist implications of the discovery of the Goddess within Jewish and Christian traditions.

For me, Patai's work provided the warrant for reintroducing female God language and even the word 'Goddess' into Christian and Jewish worship. Patai had shown that God the Mother and Goddess were not the creation of feminist desire and longing, nor were they newcomers on the scene. Quite the contrary, Goddesses had been part of the faith of 'our' mothers and fathers at the beginning of ancient Hebrew religion. And thus, I thought (as did Asphodel), Goddess could be reintroduced into contemporary Jewish and Christian understandings of God. Current research, I thought, would relativize the Bible as the sole source of authority for the faiths of our ancestors. We could go back to the earlier Hebrew religion that the authors or editors of the Bible had (falsely and wrongly, I thought) condemned. Once we recovered the lost religious views of our ancestors, I thought, the path to reintroducing God the Mother and Goddess back into Judaism and Christianity would be a simple one. *Yet this has not been the case. I wonder why.*

As I see it now, the fact that feminists have succeeded in making 'only minor adjustments' to the received patriarchal image of God is testimony to the power of God as a dominant male other in the biblical imaginary. To be fair, a few changes have been made in the prayer books and lectionaries of the most progressive branches of Judaism and Christianity. The most common of such changes is to excise the ubiquitous 'He' and 'His' from translations of the Bible and/or from the languages of prayer and worship. Such changes remove the most blatant offense of male God language. On the one hand, they allow some feminists who otherwise might have left the church or synagogue to feel comfortable in communal worship. On the other, they do not require those who 'know' God as a dominant male other to change their understanding of 'His' power and glory.

I would argue that the reason feminists can make only 'minor adjustments' to the received imaginary is that to go any farther is

9. Patai, *The Hebrew Goddess*, p. 31.

to challenge the image of God as an image of dominant male power that most congregants find not only acceptable, but also comforting. These congregants (and some feminists may be among them) want to believe that 'someone is in charge,' and for them, that someone is appropriately called our 'Lord' and 'King,' the 'Ruler' of heaven and earth. I would argue further that the notion that 'someone is in charge' is very much bound up with traditional notions of biblical authority. To make more than 'minor adjustments' in biblical imagery is not only to challenge people's understanding of God as a dominant male other, but also to pull the rug out from under whatever notions of 'authority' individuals and communities attach to the Bible. The notion of biblical 'authority,' I would argue is very much connected to the idea of God as Lord and King. You cannot change the image of God as a dominant other without challenging the authority of the Bible in radical ways.[10]

In *The Coming of Lilith*,[11] Jewish feminist theologian Judith Plaskow, challenges other feminists to question the authority of the Bible and traditions. While acknowledging that religious traditions and communities are profoundly ambiguous, many spiritual feminists still want to argue that there is a 'core' of unambiguous 'truth' within them. For some, this core is to be found in ethical monotheism or in the Exodus traditions and the prophets, for others, in Gal. 3:28 ('there is no more Jew or Greek, slave or free, male or female'), or in Jesus' alleged feminism. Plaskow resists this temptation, arguing that there is no unambiguous source of truth within Jewish (and by extension other) religious traditions. Non-progressive uses made of both the Bible and traditions show that the progressive's core is not a given, while the existence of progressive strands within traditions shows that conservative understandings also are not givens, for they have been and can be challenged from within tradition. Plaskow urges Jewish (and by extension) Christian feminists to clearly affirm that 'we are to be our own authorities—not against God, not without God, but also

10. I discuss the 'theological error' of belief in infallible revelation in my recent book, *She Who Changes: Re-imagining the Divine in the World* (New York: Palgrave Macmillan, 2003). Infallible revelation is not an exclusively Roman Catholic doctrine; some sort of belief in infallible revelation is found in most understandings of the 'authority' of Bible, tradition, or clergy.

11. Judith Plaskow, *The Coming of Lilith* (Boston: Beacon Press, 2005).

not in such a way that we dodge our responsibility to create the structures of meaning we need to live our lives.'[12]

I would argue that most Jewish and Christian feminists have avoided this challenge through selective readings of biblical and other inherited traditions. Progressive Jews and Christian liberation theologians have stated, for example, that there is a liberating message to be found in the Exodus traditions and in the prophets. The God of Exodus freed the Hebrew slaves, it is argued, thus issuing a call for the liberation of all captives. The God of the prophets called upon the people of Israel to care for the poor and the widow, thus enjoining all of us to care for the dispossessed in our midst. The notion that divine power cares for the dispossessed and wants their liberation is profoundly inspiring. It is well-known that feminists have adapted the Exodus and prophetic traditions to their own ends, arguing that divine power cares for bruised and battered women and calls for the liberation of all women, especially poor women, the poorest of the poor. It is widely recognized that such feminist interpretations of the Bible and tradition have empowered women around the world.

However, it is less widely understood that many progressive Jewish and Christian interpretations of Exodus as a liberating metaphor fail to question the image of God as a dominant other in the Bible and related understandings of divine authority enshrined in traditions. Consider the following passage from Exodus:

> And the people of Israel groaned under their bondage, and cried out for help, and their cry under bondage came up to God. (Exod. 2:23)

A progressive Jewish or Christian reading of this text would stress that the God of Exodus hears the cries of the oppressed and acts to secure their liberation. A feminist midrash might suggest that because God is on the side of oppressed women, God inspires and supports women's struggles for liberation. So far so good, but what about this passage?

> I will sing to the LORD, for he has triumphed gloriously;
> the horse and his rider he has thrown into the sea.
> The LORD is my strength and my song,
> And he has become my salvation;
> this is my father's God, and I will praise him;
> my father's God and I will exalt him.

12. Plaskow, *The Coming of Lilith*, p. 127.

> The LORD is a man of war;
> The LORD is his name. (Exod. 15: 1-3)

If progressive readings of the Exodus tradition fail to criticize this text, they have also done nothing to challenge the notion of God as a dominant male other who is appropriately called 'my father's God,' 'the LORD' and 'a man of war.' The God of this text is a dominant male other, the biggest bully of all, capable of defeating all the other bullies in the world. No doubt such an image of God has a certain appeal to the oppressed. But it is also an image of God that has been used to oppress. It is an image of God that valorizes power as dominance or power over, power that is achieved through violence. Indeed, such a God is appropriately imaged as Lord and King and Ruler, and 'his' continuing appeal may be one of the reasons that the feminist project of changing the image of God as a dominant male other has not succeeded.

To question the imagery of God as a dominant other in texts that progressive Jews and Christian liberation theologians have cited as core texts, is to question the authority of what is called the core tradition. The progressive or liberation agenda is often presented as the 'true' or 'truest' understanding of Judaism or Christianity, because it is based in a cherished or core biblical text or set of texts. In other words, it is often asserted (with varying degrees of methodological clarity) that Exodus traditions tell us that God is on the side of the oppressed, that God will vindicate the oppressed, and that the warrant for this understanding of God is the authority of the Bible. Three things are being said or implied here:

1. God is on the side of the oppressed;
2. God vindicates through force and violence;
3. There is a core tradition within the Bible that functions as unambiguous authority.

I am suggesting that items 2 and 3—from a feminist point of view at least—ought to be seen as incompatible with item 1. But to the extent that this contradiction is not recognized, it is easy to see why it is so difficult to convince even progressive church and synagogue communities to change the traditional image of God as a dominant other. The association of divinity with domination is consciously or unconsciously reinforced when it is asserted that God saves the oppressed through force and violence, and when the Bible itself is presented as an authority that cannot or need not be challenged.

Thus far I have suggested that the feminist project of changing our image of God as a dominant male other is hampered by the powerful appeal of notions of God as a dominating other and of the Bible as authority within even some of the most progressive understandings of Judaism and Christianity. But there is another reason as well. This is an effort to 'suppress, eliminate, and replace' the Goddess by the authors and/or editors of the *Bible*.

> For Solomon went after Ashtoreth the Goddess of the Sidonians; and after Milcom the abomination of the Ammonites. (1 Kgs 11: 5)

> My people inquire of a thing of wood,
> and their staff gives them oracles.
> For a spirit of harlotry has led them astray,
> and they have played the harlot.
> They sacrifice on the tops of the mountains,
> and make offerings upon the hills,
> under oak, poplar, and terebrinth,
> because their shade is good. (Hos. 4: 12–13)

The passage from Kings is the first of a long litany that accuses the kings of Israel and Judah of apostasy because they worshipped other Goddesses and Gods in addition to Yahweh. In it, the consonants of the name of the Goddess Asherah are combined with the vowels from the word 'bosheth,' meaning abomination. There is no room left for asking if Solomon, known as the wisest of kings, might have been following the way of wisdom when he set up an altar to Asherah in the temple. The passage from Hosea continues the 'tradition' of vilifying those who worship other Goddesses and Gods alongside Yahweh. The prophet is both unfair and nasty in his consideration of the religious practices of (apparently large) numbers of the people of ancient Israel and Judah. Their rituals are slandered as 'harlotry.' They are accused of 'inquiring of a thing of wood' when in fact they must have been honoring the Goddess Asherah in the form of a carved wooden statue, a pole, or a living tree. They were probably honoring the cycles of birth, death, and regeneration in sacred places within the natural world (marked by mountaintops and large trees), but they are accused of doing nothing more than 'looking for shade.'

As Judith Plaskow has stated, in passages such as these the biblical authors do not display even the most elementary forms of decency when dealing with people whose religious practices are different from their own. This tradition of slander has come down to

Christians and Jews as the condemnation of 'paganism' and 'idolatry.' As Plaskow notes, the religious practices condemned by the writers of biblical history and by prophets involved the celebration of Goddesses, the female body, sexuality, and nature. Thus feminists who wish to reintroduce into Judaism or Christianity images of God-She or Goddess that value the female body, sexuality, and connection to nature will inevitably be accused of 'reverting' to paganism. Judith Plaskow has taken a brave and important first step in encouraging Jews to become critical of 'anti-paganism' within Judaism.[13] Christians too have inherited anti-paganism, but (as far as I am aware) have yet to engage in open criticism of Christian anti-paganism and anti-'idolatry.'

Asphodel Long believed (as I did) that telling the history of the suppressed Goddesses within Judaism and Christianity would open the door for Christians and Jews to reclaim the divine as female. But obviously, this is a road not (yet) taken. I suggest that the reason for this is that Christian and Jewish feminists and other Christians and Jews have not confronted the anti-paganism at the heart of monotheism. Until they do, I suspect, they will remain in its thrall, and they will not succeed in changing the image of God as a dominating male other. Rather, they will continue to willfully or unconsciously misunderstand the Goddess and the healing She can bring to their traditions. In the remainder of this essay I will address some of these misunderstandings.

As I have argued in my widely reprinted essay, 'Why Women Need the Goddess' and later in *Rebirth of the Goddess*, Goddess is a symbol of the divine as female and therefore of femaleness as divine or in the image of divinity. Re-imagining divine power as Goddess has important psychological *and* political consequences.[14] The first and most important of these is that the symbol of Goddess affirms

13. See, 'Jewish Anti-Paganism' in Plaskow, *The Coming of Lilith*, pp. 110–13.

14. 'Why Women Need the Goddess' was originally presented to a small seminar at the American Academy of Religion meetings in 1977 and then presented to a crowd of more than 500 at the Great Goddess Re-emerging Conference at the University of Santa Cruz in the spring of 1978. It was first published in *Heresies* 5 (1978), and reprinted in *Womanspirit Rising* (San Francisco: Harper and Row, 1979), pp. 279–300, which sold over 100,000 copies, in *The Politics of Women's Spirituality* which has probably sold at least as many copies, and in scores of other anthologies. Given that this essay and others are readily available, there is no valid intellectual reason for the repeated statement that the Goddess movement is apolitical. Also see, Carol Christ, *Rebirth of the Goddess* (New York: Routledge, 1998 [1997]).

the legitimacy and beneficence of female power—including the female will and the female body. This is psychologically and politically critical for women who have been raised in cultures where we have been taught that we must always be subservient to male power—in the family, in society, in the world. As Mary Daly so aptly noted, when God is imaged exclusively as male, then the male is God.[15] If women are to gain the power to resist our oppression, then we need, as Alice Walker put it, to get the old white man off our eyeballs—and out of our body-minds. The uncritical hagiographizing provoked by the death of John Paul II in both religious and secular quarters testifies to the fact that the mystification of dominant male power continues to shape the societies in which we live.[16]

To re-imagine the divine as female does not simply replace the exclusively male God with an exclusively female one, nor patriarchy with matriarchy, though this charge is frequently repeated. Feminist re-imaginings of God challenge all images and understandings of divine power as domination or power over, renaming divine power as power with—inspiration, sympathy, and love.[17] This means that we must question the ways in which divine power has traditionally been understood as omnipotent, omniscient, unchanging, and unsympathetic or nonrelational power.[18] In addition, traditional images of God as male have been understood through dualisms in which a male God is identified with the unchanging, the rational, the conscious, the soul, the absolute, and the infinite, while femaleness (and sin) have been identified with the changing, the irrational, the unconscious, the body, finitude, and nature. Thus when we re-imagine the divine as female we begin to re-imagine the 'despised other'—not only the female, but also the changing, the nonrational, the body, finitude, and nature as part of the divine. This does not mean that the old dualisms are simply inverted, and thus that any positive values associated with maleness or rationality

15. See, Mary Daly, *Beyond God the Father* (Boston: Beacon Press, 1973).

16. In Greece, where I live, television news covered the dying, death, lying-in-state, and burial of the pope in excruciating detail, always followed by someone speaking of what a great pope he was, never mentioning that it was under his leadership that the question of women priests was dismissed, that he stifled dissent and packed the house of cardinals with yes-men, or that he opposed homosexuality, etc.

17. I argue this in *She Who Changes*.

18. I discuss these issues more fully in *She Who Changes*.

are denied.[19] Nor does advocating female images for divine power mean that there is no place for (non-dominant) images of God as male in prayer and worship in mixed gender communities.

Contemporary Goddess spirituality is often criticized for not providing roles for men or male imagery of the divine. Yet there are feminist Goddess groups—including the Reclaiming movement founded by Starhawk and others—that are open to men and that have re-imagined male imagery for the divine.[20] On the other hand, many women practice feminist Goddess spirituality in groups that are for women only and that use exclusively or primarily female imagery for the divine power. Yet most of the women in such groups have no particular antipathy for men as such—many of them are or were married or have male lovers or male children. Nor do they believe that Goddess worship should always and everywhere exclude men. In the best of all possible worlds, we would all be feminists and images of Goddess as well as non-dominating images of God would be widely accepted. Like that found in the Womanchurch movement or in Jewish Women's Seder movement, the Goddess movement's separatism is for the most part practical rather than ideological: women often find it easier to explore and express their emerging spiritualities with other feminist women.

Within Western interpretive frameworks influenced by patriarchy in late antiquity and in Christianity, Goddesses were identified exclusively with fertility and reproduction. It is hard even for feminists to get beyond this mindset, because it is so deeply engrained. Yet it diminishes the powers that Goddesses once had. In prepatriarchal cultures, as Marija Gimbutas has shown, Goddesses were symbolic of all the creative powers in the universe, not only the power to give birth to children and crops, but also the creativity that led to the invention of agriculture, weaving, pottery-making, poetry, song, and writing itself.[21] Some non-feminist advocates of the re-emergence of the Goddess (including Jung and some of his followers) identify the Goddess primarily with the 'negative' or despised side of the classical dualisms such as the body, nature, the unconscious, and the irrational. Some Jungians still consider rational consciousness to be 'male' and the unconscious to

19. These issues are discussed in *Rebirth of the Goddess*.

20. See, www.reclaiming.org.

21. See, Marija Gimbutas, *The Language of the Goddess* (San Francisco: Harper & Row, 1989).

be 'female.' In contrast, Goddess feminists call for a transformation of dualistic habits of thought, critique any and all understandings of divine power as power over, and advocate embodied thinking (which includes both rational and other than rational elements).[22]

It is sometimes said that focusing attention on changing our images of divine power is the privilege of elite white women who have the time and energy to deal with so-called 'psychological' issues. Poor women and women of color, it is said, do not have the time to devote to 'psychological' issues, but must focus on survival and 'political' resistance to more obvious sources of oppression. Yet I first heard God imaged as female in the words of a black woman in Ntozake Shange's play *For colored girls who have considered suicide/when the rainbow is enuf*. This woman had just narrated the murder of her children by their father who held them out the window and threatened to drop them if she did not take him back. Ntozake Shange was criticized for bringing up issues that could divide the black community at a time when (it was said) it needed to hold together against the racism of white society. I suspect that Shange was not unaware of this potential criticism of her work when she chose to tell a 'black girl's story' as truthfully as she could. Shange felt that black women's liberation depended on freeing black women from the mystification of male power that made it seem right for them to suffer abuse from men. She also felt that re-imagining the divine in a black female body—in her words, 'I found God in myself and I loved her/I loved her fiercely' [23] —would help black women to gain power and control over their own bodies and their own lives. Audre Lorde invoked African Goddesses in her poetry as symbols of black female power.[24] Alice Walker has identified herself as a pagan who worships Mother Earth.[25] In *The Color Purple*, she showed how Celie's image of God as an old white man contributed to her accepting her abuse.[26] Like Shange, Walker was accused of dividing the race by mentioning black men's abuse of black women. Alice Walker's gutsy definition of womanism inspires womanist theology, yet Walker's embrace of a female God

22. See, Christ, *Rebirth of the Goddess*, chapter 2.

23. Ntozake Shange, *For colored girls who have considered suicide/when the rainbow is enuf*.

24. See, Alexis De Veaux, *Warrior Poet* (New York: W.W. Norton, 2004).

25. 'The Only Reason You Want to Go to Heaven', Alice Walker, *Anything We Love Can Be Saved* (New York: Ballantine Books, 1997), pp. 25-26.

26. Alice Walker, *The Color Purple* (New York: Pocket Books, 1983).

and paganism is erased when it is stated that 'the Goddess' is a 'psychological' issue exclusively relevant to white women.

Re-imagining the male image of God as female is to challenge the hegemony of male power as domination or power over—power which is exercised over women, men, and other beings in the web of life. To create alternatives to the image of male power as domination is a deeply political issue—one that is relevant to all women of every color and of every culture—and to men and to all living things. The image of God as a dominant male other functions to make male domination seem to be the most natural form of power. Thus it is not surprising that feminist images of Goddess and God-She provoke resistance within every community where they are introduced. To question God-He is to remove the veil that shrouds the mystification of male power. For most people, both women and men, rich and poor, this will be deeply threatening.

Indeed, for all that Goddess has been said to be a white women's issue, in white churches and synagogues in the USA, Canada, Great Britain, Australia, and New Zealand God continues to be invoked as male, as Father, Lord, and King.[27] As noted earlier, in the most progressive churches and synagogues God-He and God-His may be avoided where possible. But there are few congregations (whether white, black, Hispanic, Asian-Pacific or mixed) in which positive images of the divine as female—God-She, God-Her, God-Sophia, God-Shekhina, God the Mother, God the Daughter, God the Sister, let alone Goddess—can be regularly invoked. Why is this? I suggest that it is because images of God-She and Goddess are deeply upsetting to a status quo of male dominance in religious institutions and in the larger societies in which they are situated. Men who are comfortable with the mystification of male power that justifies their own regular or occasional assumption of dominant roles and behaviors in family and in society will, of course, feel an immediate challenge. But so will women who live within relationships that depend on not challenging—or not openly challenging—the mystification of male power in family and society that allows them to 'keep their men' and 'keep them happy'. In addition, and perhaps even more upsetting to traditional habits of thought, once we begin to imagine alternatives to God as a dominating other, we begin to question assumptions about divine

27. See Raphael, *Introducing Thealogy*, p. 52.

power as omnipotence.[28] But if God is not omnipotent, then is any one individual 'in control' of the world? And if not, who will save us from ourselves—or more to the point perhaps, from President George Bush and his cronies? (The answer to this question is that we must work with the divine power to co-create a better world.) If God-She and Goddess cannot be invoked in Christian and Jewish worship for these and other reasons, then, I suggest, these religions continue to perpetuate the mystification of dominant male power.

The idea that Goddess is a white women's issue may have its source in sociological fact. The Goddess Movement began as and by default has remained—because its insights have not been accepted in religious institutions or in the academy—a grassroots and countercultural feminist movement. Images of Goddess have taken root in the hearts and minds of hundreds of thousands of women and some men who have read books in feminist theology and thealogy (published primarily, but not exclusively, in English in the past twenty-five years) and who have participated in the Goddess Movement inspired by them (which is strongest in English-speaking countries, including the United States, Canada, Great Britain, Australia, and New Zealand). It is true that the women who consider themselves part of these movements tend to be fairly well-educated and are primarily—but not exclusively—white. To say that the Goddess Movement is only white ignores the participation of nonwhite women in it from its beginnings.[29] The greater numbers

28. I discuss omnipotence as a theological mistake inspired by the notion of God as a male dominant other in *She Who Changes*.

29. The Goddess group I participated in for a decade in the late seventies and eighties was co-led by Latina E. Carmen Torres and often visited by a well-known black ecofeminist. Also see, Sabrina Sojourner, 'In the House of Yemanja: The Goddess Heritage of Black Women,' in Gloria Wade-Gales (ed.), *My Soul is a Witness* (Boston: Beacon Press, 1995), Luisah Teish, *Jambalaya* (San Francisco: HarperSanFrancisco, 1985) and *Carnival of the Spirit* (San Francisco: HarperSanFrancisco, 1994) and Paula Gunn Allen, *The Sacred Hoop* (Boston: Beacon Press, 1986); Tracey E. Hucks, '"Burning with a Flame in America": African American Women in African-Derived Traditions,' *Journal of Feminist Studies in Religion* 17/2 (fall 2001), pp. 89–106, Arisika Razak, '"I Found God in Myself": Sacred Images of African and African-American Women' and Miri Hunter Haruach, '"You Acting Womanish": The Queen of Sheba as an Ancestral Grandmother,' both presented at the 2002 meetings of the American Academy of Religion; the founding of a Goddess Movement in Korea by Chung Hyun Kyung following the publication of several books on the Goddess published in Korean, also discussed at the 2002 AAR, the new column in *SageWoman* magazine by Stephanie Rose Bird; artists such as Earthlyn Manuel and AfraShe Asungi.

of white women in the movement may have more to do with conditions of access than anything else. Goddess feminists are not necessarily middle class, if this means they all have careers in which they can make a lot of money, though most are living above the poverty level.[30] Because it celebrates female power, the Goddess Movement is attractive to lesbians, but also to other women both married and single, to all who have freed or are freeing themselves from the mystification of male power.

It is not true (as is so often said) that the largely white women members of the Goddess Movement are apolitical—content to reap (shall we say) the rewards of white supremacy and colonialism. To the contrary, Starhawk, the most well-known twentieth and twenty-first century advocate of the Goddess is also a leader in the anti-globalization movement, while Charlene Spretnak is a leader in the Green political movement in the United States.[31] Other members of the Goddess Movement are active in a wide variety of feminist, ecological, and social justice causes.[32] Nor is it true (as is sometimes stated) that the 'Goddess is white'. Though some members of the Goddess Movement have focused on Celtic, Greek, or Old European Goddesses, Goddess traditions can be found in every land—Goddesses are white, black, brown, yellow, and red. Many white women have been exploring non-white Goddesses or traditions, while others, wary of colonial appropriation, support and seek to learn from non-white women who reclaim Goddess traditions rooted in their own cultures.

The sociological fact that the members of the Goddess movement are primarily white, educated, and not living below the poverty level should not be taken to mean that Goddess can have no relevance to poor women or to women of color. In a world where women and girls of every color and in almost every culture suffer incest, battery, rape, involuntary infection with AIDS, and murder at the hands of men every minute of every day, can challenging the mystification of male power be only a white women's issue? In a

30. Starhawk asserts that many members of the Reclaiming Movement should be considered lower middle class, Marguerite Rigoliosso, 'Interview with Starhawk,' *Feminist Theology* 13.2, p. 178.

31. See Starhawk, *Webs of Power* (New York: Harper Row, 2003) and Frijof Capra and Charlene Spretnak, *Green Politics* (New York: Dutton, 1984).

32. See Kathryn Rountree, *Embracing the Witch and the Goddess* (London: Routledge, 2003).

world where a born-again white male Christian president of the United States collaborates with the male hierarchy of the Roman Catholic Church and traditional male Muslim clerics to withhold birth control and access to abortion from poor women around the world, can challenging the mystification of male power inherent in images of God be only a psychological issue? In a world where Christian, Jewish, and Muslim leaders raise the call to war 'in the name of God,' can challenging the mystification of power as domination inherent in (male) images of God be of concern only to white women? In a world that stands on the brink of nuclear and ecological destruction, can re-imagining the divine in the body and the world be only a psychological issue?

Yet the same criticisms of the Goddess and the Goddess Movement continue to be reiterated by Christian, Jewish, and secular feminists—with no recognition or apparent knowledge that some of them are factually untrue (for example that Goddess feminists are not political) or that others have been responded to time and again (for example that Goddess feminism replaces a male dominant God with a female dominant Goddess). Could it be that as Judith Plaskow wrote, 'The deep resistance called forth by [the Goddess's] naming indicates that the needs that she answered are still with us.'[33] In other words, is dismissing the Goddess Movement a way to avoid the challenge that the image of the Goddess represents to the mystifications of male power that continue to operate in recognized and unrecognized ways within Christianity, Judaism, and the larger world of which they are a part? And if so, is a radical dimension of the feminist challenge to traditional religions being sidestepped? At what cost? Asphodel Long believed that with knowledge comes the power to transform traditions. I agree with her, and I hope that the day when Goddess can be named as a liberating power within inherited Western religious traditions will occur within the lifetimes of those who read this essay.

33. 'The Right Question Is Theological', in Susannah Heschel (ed.), *On Being a Jewish Feminist* (New York: Schocken Books, 1983), p. 230.

Chapter 3

'Dealing with a Jealous God': Letting go of Monotheism and 'Doing' Sacrality

Ruth Mantin

According to mainstream Judaism and Christianity, one of the greatest achievements of the prophets and patriarchs was to instil a belief in One God. (e.g. Exod. 20.5) The rejection of polytheism and iconic representation was what distinguished the Hebrew people from their cultural milieu. It is proclaimed that such remarkable insight and moral superiority confirms that the history of this people from nomadic tribes to Near-Eastern nation-state was guided by a sacred hand and resulted in the supreme revelation of the divine. Integral to most forms of Christian theology is the notion that monotheism, like the God it proclaims, sits at the apex of a hierarchical triangle, with all other forms of belief spreading beneath and 'idolatrous' polytheism at the very bottom of the heap. In more radical forms of theo/alogy, however, such an assumption is being seriously challenged. We recognize that history is written by winners. The biblical literature portrays 'lapses' into the debased and degenerate worship of 'foreign' deities as the occasional digression from the path of following Israel's One God. Such departure from true worship is constantly associated with licentiousness, promiscuity and 'deviant' sexual behaviour. The language of abuse used to denigrate those unworthy gods and goddesses negated by exclusive monotheism makes it clear what is to be 'othered' by this jealous god—female autonomy and non-hegemonic sexualities.

The biblical account of a sure progression from polytheism to monotheism is now being interrogated. Instead, a growing number of scholars are recognizing that a wide variety of options remained a feature of ancient Israel's religious landscape throughout its history. They are demonstrating that the received account of Israel's religious journey negates the account of the many 'Yahwisms' and 'Judaisms' which contributed to its narratives of the sacred.[1] Scholars can read the clues left by the text itself, despite the shaping of an editorial process which attempted to deny the plurality of religious expression in Israel's history. Other deities are therefore demoted or disguised. Some become the subordinate members of 'Yahweh's' celestial court, some are reduced to cultic objects used in the worship of 'Yahweh', others are turned into mere abstract qualities.[2] Significant among these deities is the enigmatic Goddess Asherah. Her persistent presence in the biblical texts, witnessed by forty different references, is denied by the redactors' attempt to render her invisible through her metamorphosis into a 'grove' of trees or 'wooden pole'. Scholars are, nevertheless, having to come to terms with the convincing evidence that 'an Asherah' was not only to be found 'on every high hill and under every green tree (e.g. Jer. 2:20, Jer. 3:6, Isa. 57:5) but was actually resident in the Solomonic temple for over 200 years.[3] The results of archaeology have provided further evidence of a more complex and ambiguous religious culture than the one presented by traditional theological accounts. Most famous and intriguing are the inscriptions which speak of YHWH and his Asherah'[4]. These allow a glimpse into the possibilities of a religious awareness in which male and female were incorporated into images of divinity. [5] Asphodel Long's germinal work, *In a*

1. E.g. Diana V. Edelman, (ed.), *The Triumph of Elohim: from Yahwisms to Judaisms* (Kampen: Pharos, 1995) presents a collection of essays which reassess traditional assumptions about the process leading to the emergence of monotheistic belief systems in the ancient Near East. They draw on recent developments in biblical, historical and archaeological studies.

2. Edelman, *The Triumph of Elohim*, pp. 16–17.

3. This claim was first made by Raphael Patai in his groundbreaking book, *The Hebrew Goddess* (Detroit, MI: Wayne State University Press, 1990).

4. E.g. Herbert Niehr, 'The rise of YHWH in Judahite and Israelite Religion: Methodological and Religio-Historical Aspects' in Edelman, *The Triumph of Elohim*. Niehr provides a careful account of these inscriptions and other archaeological and textual evidence which give some insight into the rich variety of religious traditions in ancient Israel. Asphodel Long also discusses these in A. Long, *In a Chariot Drawn by Lions: The Search for the Female in Deity* (London: Women's Press 1992), pp. 128–29 and pp. 10–12.

5. It is also being recognized that such multiplicity continued into the development of 'Judaism'. Scholarship of the last few decades has revealed the pluriform nature of the Judaism of the Second Temple era. Indeed, a significant number of

Chariot Drawn by Lions,[6] undertook the search for this hidden Female in Deity, exposing the many means by which She is hidden and exploring the far-reaching implications of her re-discovery. Long underlined the pattern of oppression which was sanctioned by a narrative of divine monotheism expressed solely in the male gender. She delighted in catching glimpses of Asherah, who, despite the powerful attempts to slander and suppress her, could still be encountered in the Jewish tradition through the Tree of Life and who was constantly present in the reassuring glow of the menorah.[7] The (re)emergence of contemporary Paganism and of the Goddess movement, (of which Long was regarded to be the prominent leader in Britain), witnesses the desire to recognize plurality in divinity and to re-sacralize the material world.[8] As a Jewish feminist, Judith Plaskow has alerted her own tradition, in view of its own experience

scholars maintain the need to recognize the existence of not just different types of Judaism but of several 'Judaisms'. One of the first Jewish scholars to coin this term is Jacob Neusner e.g. T*orah Through the Ages: A Short History of Judaism* (London: SCM Press, 1990), pp. 168–74. The emergence of rabbinic Judaism out of the rubble of the second temple brought a notion of 'normative' Judaism. Echoes of a more diverse phenomenon remained, however, and, it is argued, continued to exert influence on Jewish religious life through traditions such as Gnosticism, Kabbalah and Hasidism. Philip Davies, 'Scenes from the Early History of Judaism in Edelman, *The Triumph of Elohim*, p. 145 n.1.

6. Long, I*n a Chariot Drawn by Lions*.

7. Long, A*sherah, The Tree of Life and the Menorah* (Neath UK: BISFT, 1998).

8. The relationships between Paganism, witchcraft, 'Wicca' and feminism in the Goddess Movement are complex ones and cannot properly be explored here. The relationships between them have been explored in a series of studies over the last twenty-five years, e.g. Margot Adler, *Drawing Down the Moon: Witches, Druids, Goddess-Worshippers and Other Pagans in America Today* (Boston: Beacon Press, 1979); Carol P. Christ, *Rebirth of the Goddess – Finding Meaning in Feminist Spirituality* (Reading, Massachusetts: Addison Wesley; *Feminist Theology*, 1997); Graham Harvey *Listening Peoples: Speaking Earth* (London: Hurst & Co., 1997); Ursula King, *Women and Spirituality: Voices of Protest and Promise* (London: Macmillan Educational, 1989); Asphodel Long, 'The Goddess Movement in Britain, *Feminist Theology* 5, 1994, pp. 11–39; Melissa Raphael *Introducing Thealogy: Discourse on the Goddess* (Sheffield: Sheffield Academic Press, 1999); Starhawk *The Spiral Dance: A Rebirth of the Ancient Religion of The Great Goddess* (San Francisco: Harper & Collins 1979). Kathryn Rountree, *Embracing the Witch and Goddess* (London: Routledge, 2004). Despite the complexity of these overlapping definitions, the Goddess Movement is, nevertheless, being recognized as a specific and significant feature of contemporary religious expression. Similarly thealogy, reflection on the nature of divinity within a female perspective, is beginning to be acknowledged as a distinctive discipline.

of slander and vilification, to the dangers of demonizing Paganism.[9] At the same time, however, we need to be vigilant against falling into the trap of 'blaming the Jews' for the 'death' of the Goddess or for being responsible for obliterating the possibility of diversity plurality in divinity.[10] There is ample evidence that every established religious tradition has used its narratives of the sacred to 'other' autonomous femininities and non-hegemonic masculinities. I am certainly not accusing Judaism of being responsible for imposing on the dominant world view the paradigm of hierarchical dualism. As Asphodel Long frequently mentioned in conversation, it was almost an accident of history that the religious history of ancient Israel became so influential in the development of Western culture. Only because Christianity, the unlikely offshoot of Judaism(s), became an even more unlikely contender for adoption by the Roman Empire did the metanarrative of monotheism become enmeshed with the radical dualism of classical philosophy. The result however, has provided the blueprint and framework for ensuing patterns of oppression. History is littered with the corpses of those whose wilful obliteration is considered necessary or whose casual annihilation is deemed expedient by narratives of the Absolute and the Other. This, I am arguing, is why we need to access narratives which welcome multiplicity and ambiguities. This is the only way that we can sustain the complex patterns of relationship upon which all forms of life depend. For this reason, I underline the importance of a growing tendency to que(e)ry dominant theologies, expressed through feminist thealogies and queer theologies.

The powerful and destructive impact of the image of male monotheism on the social and cultural imaginary was identified most cogently by the pioneers of feminist theo/alogy such as Mary Daly[11] and Carol P. Christ.[12] As a result, they concluded that the term 'God' could not be separated from the hierarchies of domination and oppression it sanctioned. They therefore turned to

9. Judith Plaskow, *Standing Again at Sinai: Judaism from a Feminist Perspective* (San Francisco: Harper & Row, 1991).

10. For e.g., Asphodel Long addressed some of these issues in her article 'Anti-Judaism in Britain', *Journal of Feminist Studies in Religion 7/2*, Fall, 1991.

11. For e.g., Mary Daly, *Beyond God the Father – Toward a Philosophy of Women's Liberation* (Boston: Beacon Press, 1973).

12. For e.g., Carol P. Christ, 'Why Women Need the Goddess: Phenomenological Psychological and Political Reflections' in C. Christ & J. Plaskow (eds.), *Womanspirit Rising: A Reader in Feminist Religion* (San Francisco: Harper Collins, 1979).

Goddess as an enabling expression for narratives of the sacred. Nelle Morton, another fore sister of the Goddess Movement, linked to her rejection of exclusively male imagery a deep distrust of transcendence as a quality of the sacred. This realization led her to abandon 'God' as a dead and redundant symbol. Instead she saw the exorcizing and regenerative possibilities of Goddess-talk as metaphoric process, moving beyond any attempt to reify the divine.[13] As feminist thealogy has travelled, the non-realist aspects of Goddess-talk have been discussed and debated by participants in and commentators on the Goddess movement.[14] I am arguing here for further recognition of the possibilities for non-realist thealogical discourse to transform the religious and cultural imaginary. I am proposing a radical, post-realist approach to 'Goddess-talk', which offers the potential for refiguring expressions of spirituality and of the sacred in a post-metaphysical, postmodern context which has much to share with the insights offered by queer theory.

The issue of monotheism in the Goddess Movement does, however, remain a contentious issue. Most commentators on and within the Goddess Movement refer to *the* Goddess but the issue of whether this relates to one deity or many is an area of debate. Many Goddess feminists understand the paradigm shift generated by Goddess-talk to challenge a monotheistic worldview in which one supreme deity replicates and sanctions hierarchical power structure. For such thealogians therefore, monotheism is the antithesis of Goddess spirituality. When thealogians draw on a mythology provided by female images of the divine they have access to a multiplicity of Goddess names and images. For many this plurality is a vital feature of what Goddess-talk offers and some Goddess scholars argue that thealogy should speak in terms of Goddesses rather than the Goddess.[15] At the same time, however,

13. Nelle Morton, *The Journey is Home* (Boston: Beacon Press, 1985).

14. For e.g., Asphodel Long discusses the nature of Goddess in Asphodel Long, *'The Goddess Movement in Britain'* and Asphodel Long, 'The One or the Many: The Great Goddess Revisited', *Feminist Theology* 15, 1997. Carol P. Christ addresses this issue in *Rebirth of the Goddess* and in *She who Changes: Re-Imagining the Divine in the World* (New York: Palgrave, 2003), where she applies Process philosophy to thealogy in order to affirm the changing, relational nature of Goddess, whilst maintaining her reality as a personal presence. The realist nature of Goddess is also debated by Melissa Raphael and Beverley Clack in Deborah Sawyer, and Diane Collier (eds.), *Is There a Future for Feminist Theology?* (Sheffield: Sheffield Academic Press, 1999).

15. For e.g., Emily Culpepper, 'Contemporary Goddess Thealogy: A Sympathetic Critique' in Clarissa Atkinson, Margaret Miles, and Constance Buchanan (eds.), *'Shaping*

the 'one or many' debate in thealogy is related both to the issue of matriarchal prehistory and to disputes about the realist nature of Goddess-talk.[16] A narrative which presents the possibility of a universal Goddess-centred worldview which predates patriarchy can be seen to be linked to an understanding of the Goddess as monotheistic but revealed in many aspects. At the same time, however, the notion of plurality is central to the resacralization envisioned by thealogy. Goddess, as the sacred immanent in the natural world, expresses the teeming biodiversity of all forms of life and death. Furthermore, in expressing the sacred as female, Goddess embodies the change, flux and lateral systems of women's experience as opposed to the singular, linear quest of the heroic male.

A further, crucial factor of these debates is the argument that to distinguish between the 'one' and the 'many' is to collude with a framework of binary oppositions which is challenged by a thealogical worldview. Asphodel Long, for instance, argued that the use of the phrase 'the Goddess' has never implied monotheistic assumptions.[17] The narratives of many Goddess feminists reinforce this opinion. A typical example is provided by a respondent in Cynthia Eller's influential survey of Goddess spirituality in America.

> I don't make those kind of distinctions that you hear about, they don't make any sense to me. You can say it's the Great Goddess, and that's one Goddess, but she's also all of the many goddesses, and that's true. And she's everywhere. She's immanent in everything, in the sparkle of the sun on the sea, and even in an animistic concept. I think certain objects can embody force and power. So I worship the Great Goddess, and I'm polytheist and pantheist and monotheist too.[18]

At the same time, Long also voiced her concern about a perceived move towards 'Goddess fundamentalism' which seemed to replicate

New Visions: Gender and Values in American Culture' (Ann Arbor MI.: University of Michigan Press, 1987), pp. 50–60. Christine Downing, *The Goddess: Mythological Images of the Feminine* (New York: Crossroad, 1990); Harvey, *Speaking Peoples, Listening Earth.*

16. It could be argued that a realist/non-realist debate is more apparent in British thealogical circles (e.g. the debate between Melissa Raphael and Beverley Clack in Deborah Sawyer and Diane Collier (eds.), *Is There a Future for Feminist Theology?* (Sheffield: Sheffield Academic Press, 1999), whereas in America the focus is on issues of Matriarchal prehistory.

17. Long, 'The One or the Many?'

18. Cynthia Eller, *Living in the Lap of the Goddess: The Feminist Spirituality Movement in America* (Boston: Beacon Press, 1993), pp.132–33.

male monotheism in its presentation of one, universal, unchanging Cosmic Mother.

In general, however, fluidity of thought, which speaks in terms of the singular and the plural as mutually inclusive, is characteristic of the narratives of women who identify themselves as Goddess feminists.[19] Thealogy's ability to embrace diversity and ambiguity makes it difficult to define but also provides it with the capacity to respond to challenges of a postmodern world. On the other hand, it could be argued that thealogy's roots are placed firmly within feminism as an emancipatory movement and are therefore inherently related to modernist ideals of progress and liberation. The possible tensions between the postmodern and modernist aspects of Goddess feminism have been identified by Melissa Raphael.[20] In my own journey, I have encountered such tensions, but have found myself travelling in a different direction from the one taken by Raphael. With Raphael, I would argue that the Goddess Movement can offer enormous potential for the refiguration of narratives of the sacred. I am sure, however, that much of that potential has still to be realized and that Goddess-talk offers the opportunity to carry further the metaphoric process set in motion by thealogical challenges to dominant discourse. Feminist thealogies can give voice to attempts to move away from static, reified and transcendent images of the divine in order to offer post-metaphysical and post-realist expressions of the sacred which welcome notions of plurality and ambiguity.

The move to recognize difference and diversity in the realm of divinity parallels the significant shifts which are de-stabilising notions of the fixed, unified self. A growing number of feminists are recognizing the socio-political implications of scrutinizing Cartesian assumptions about the subject. Despite the understandable reluctance of some feminists to relinquish a notion of the female Self, denied to women for so long, many welcome the changing

19. This was illustrated by the responses of women with whom I was in conversation as part of the research for my doctoral thesis. Ruth Mantin, *Thealogies in Process: The Role of Goddess – Talk in Feminist Spirituality* (unpublished, Southampton, 2002).

20. For e.g., Melissa Raphael, *Thealogy and Embodiment: The Post-Patriarchal Reconstruction of Female Sacrality* (Sheffield: Sheffield Academic Press, 1996); Raphael, *Introducing Thealogy;* Melissa Raphael, 'Monotheism in Contemporary Feminist Goddess Religion: A Betrayal of Early Thealogical Non-Realism?' in Sawyer & Collier (eds.) *Is There a Future for Feminist Theology?*

understanding of the subject which underpins postmodernist and poststructural theory. They can distinguish the connection between the presentation of a Cartesian, unified, self-authenticating subject and the patterns of domination inherent in the Enlightenment project. Rosi Braidotti has constructed her philosophical framework around her conviction that 'the gesture that binds a fractured self to the performative illusion of unity, mastery and self-transparence' is an act of powerful violence and 'terrifying stupidity'.[21] Braidotti maintains that for feminists to welcome the 'death of the subject' need not mean falling into relativism or political despair. She notes that, because of the hold that modernist assumptions still have on philosophical discourse, the challenge lies in thinking about processes rather than concepts.[22] This calls for new images and myths or, as she prefers, figurations.[23] These are needed to generate a social imaginary which can cope ethically and creatively with on-going transformations and can free difference from the negative charge which dominant philosophies have built into it'.[24] In order to address this task, she employs the image of the nomadic subject.[25] This mythic figure expresses the ability to travel between categories and identities. The image of nomadic subjectivity is many layered, allowing affirmation of movement, whilst maintaining the possibilities of community, commonality and situatedness. While recognizing the value of employing the image of nomadic consciousness, I would want to underline Braidotti's reminder of the figurative nature of the language being used here. Braidotti distinguishes the nomadic state from that of enforced exile[26] and doesn't attempt to disguise the harsh realities of lived nomadic experience or ignore the ethical challenges they present.[27] Braidotti also acknowledges that her figuration is inspired by the experience

21. Rosi Braidotti, *Nomadic Subjects-Embodiment and Sexual Difference in Contemporary Feminist Theory* (New York: Columbia University Press, 1994), p. 12.

22. Rosi Braidotti, *Metamorphoses: Towards a Materialist Theory of Becoming* (Oxford: Polity, 2002) p. 1.

23. Braidotti, *Nomadic Subjects*, p. 4.

24. Braidotti, *Metamorphoses*, pp. 4–5 and 267.

25. Braidotti's use of this image is obviously influenced by her teacher, Deleuze. She does, however, develop her understanding of nomadic subjectivity in a distinctive way and, whilst acknowledging her debt to Deleuze, is critical of his work, especially its androcentric assumptions. (e.g. Braidotti, *Nomadic Subjects*, pp. 111–23).

26. For e.g., Braidotti, *Nomadic Subjects*, pp. 21–27.

27. For e.g., Braidotti, *Metamorphoses*, p. 3.

of some peoples or cultures which are literally nomadic, but maintains that,

> the nomadism in question here refers to the kind of critical consciousness that resists settling into socially coded modes of thought and behaviour. ... It is the subversion of set conventions that defines the nomadic state, not the literal act of travelling.[28]

Braidotti also contrasts the relationship that nomadic communities have with the land upon which they travel to an approach which wants to regard identity—or any other entity—as something which can be 'possessed'.

> Identity is retrospective; representing it entails that we can draw accurate maps, indeed, but only of where we have been and consequently no longer are. Nomadic cartographies need to be redrafted constantly; as such they are structurally opposed to fixity and therefore to rapacious appropriation.[29]

Like Morton, Daly and Christ, Braidotti recognizes the power of language and images. She values a 'visionary epistemology' which recognizes that a new image has the 'capacity to offer us ordinary access to extraordinary thinking'.[30] She echoes Donna Haraway's call for 'ecstatic speakers' and 'heteroglossia'.[31] Braidotti endorses, as an example of such heteroglossia, Haraway's image of the cyborg.[32] This she welcomes as an enabling figuration whose hybrid nature gives expression to the many contemporary challenges presented to the opposing distinctions structuring the Western self. Haraway famously concludes her manifesto for cyborgs by claiming that she would rather be a cyborg than a goddess.[33] Like Braidotti, she suspects the ability of any 'metaphysical' discourse to deal with the current 'threat of an informatics of domination'.[34] At the same time, Braidotti in a characteristically provocative manner, recognizes the narratives of the sacred still hold sway over much of Western thought when she notes that

28. Braidotti, *Nomadic Subjects*, p. 5.
29. Braidotti, *Nomadic Subjects*, p. 51.
30. Braidotti, *Nomadic Subjects*, p. 8.
31. Braidotti, *Nomadic Subjects*, p. 8.
32. Donna Haraway, 'A Manifesto for Cyborgs: Science Technology and Socialist Feminism in the 80s' in L. Nicholson (ed.), *Feminism/Postmodernism* (London: Routledge, 1990), pp. 190–233.
33. Haraway, A *Manifesto for Cyborgs*, p. 223.
34. Haraway, *A Manifesto for Cyborgs*, p. 204.

> God may be dead but the stench of his rotting corpse pervades all of Western culture.[35]

I therefore echo the argument of feminist thealogians that the influence of God-talk is too pervasive to ignore—it must be refigured. I also wish to challenge the assumptions of Braidotti and Haraway that goddesses are chained to a nostalgia for essential unity. On the contrary, I maintain that Goddesses can provide a range of transgressive hybrids to symbolize the process of transformation through unstable categories. Goddesses can reflect a nomadic consciousness. Their connections with shape-shifters make it much more difficult to fix them within a system and their relationships with monsters allow them to include rather than marginalize the other. I therefore maintain that Goddess-talk can function as heteroglossia.

When examining Braidotti's call for the figuration of nomadic subjectivity, it is worth noting that integral to the dominant Israelite metanarrative of exclusive monotheism is the sacred history of a people led from tribal nomadism to the exalted status of a settled people in the land given by God (e.g. Deut. 26:5–9). A nomadic consciousness recognizes that we wander through a multiplicity of identities. Those who wish to deny this nomadic subjectivity do so by asserting 'this is what *I* am—and *not* 'that'. Those whose attitude towards their identity is the same as their attitude to 'their' land. 'This identity/land is *mine*. I draw the lines of the map, regardless of what other identities I deny in the process. I claim this, I possess this and it must be defended against those who would 'take it from me' regardless of whether they were there all along. This is an attitude which parallels that exposed so skilfully by Michael Prior in his book, *The Bible and Colonialism*. Prior was shocked into examining the ways in which biblical narratives sanction colonial exploitation when he was working in Israel and was faced with a response to the Exodus narrative from the perspective of *Palestinian* Christians. One of the powerful and devastating narratives that the Exodus story legitimizes is the myth of the empty land. When the 'settlers' take the land it is wide, empty space, despite the fact that *there are already people living there*. In the same way, I would argue, we can have a myth of the absent identities. We are all made

35. Rosi Braidotti, '*The Body as Metaphor: Seduced and Abandoned: The Body in the Virtual World*', video recording (London: ICA, 1995).

up of many possibilities. We can have a colonial attitude about our own subjectivity. The most dangerous of such examples are those who maintain that they are *only* male, *only* white and *only* straight. Judith Butler also gives voice to this when she identifies the ways in which a modernist model of subjectivity condones colonial assumptions by complying with a construct of the subject which operates through 'the exclusion of those who fail to conform to unspoken normative requirements of the subject'. [36]

The priestly tradition which wrote into its historical memory the linear, progressive triumph of monotheism over the denigrated narratives of religious plurality also designated the nature of 'holiness' (e.g. Lev. 19). To be 'holy' is to keep oneself separate from others. [37] This emphasis on separation also informs the dominant western notion of subjectivity although, again, I am not suggesting that the priestly traditions of ancient Israel can be held solely responsible for this. The Cartesian image of the fixed, unified self, legitimized by a sacred narrative which sanctifies unity and separation casts a powerful influence over western thought. Indeed, Catherine Keller has argued that 'it is a self conceived as separate that has ... projected its grid of fragmentation upon the world'.[38]

When Keller, drawing on process philosophy, explores the possibility of other images to express a mythology of the fluid, multiple, relational self, it is to goddesses that she turns. She explores pre-literary and hermeneutical evidence of ancient, pre-patriarchal goddess traditions which expressed a very different way of knowing and relating, conveyed through symbols of biophilic energy and female sacrality. Keller contrasts these with the dominant myths which celebrate the demonizing and/or domesticating of powerful and autonomous goddesses. Their suppression is part of the 'heroic'

36. Judith Butler, *Gender Trouble: Feminism and the Subversion of Identity* (London: Routledge, 1990), p. 5.

37. It is interesting to note that in his groundbreaking examination of Jesus' teaching, Joachim Jeremias presented a Jesus whose rabbinic teaching deliberately recalled prophetic narratives of inclusion which had been subjugated by the dominant message of superior holiness through separation. For e.g., J. Jeremias, *The Parables of Jesus* (London: SCM Press, 1972). Such a view is largely ignored by mainstream theology but, as Isherwood has shown us, disadvantaged communities continue to draw on an abundant range of images to liberate Christ from the metanarrative of domination. Lisa Isherwood, *Liberating Christ* (Cleveland OH: Pilgrim Press, 1999).

38. Catherine Keller, *From a Broken Web: Separation, Sexism and Self* (Boston: Beacon Press, 1986), p. 161.

male quest for a unified, independent self which has denied connectedness and therefore sustained patterns of alienation and domination. Keller shows how the myths which have determined our symbolic order inform us that true selfhood, the prize of all heroic quests, can only be attained by conquering and exterminating the Other, thereby denying any sense of plurality or relation *in ourselves*.[39]

Travelling from a very different direction and by a different route, Judith Butler has also exposed some of the far-reaching implications of feminist challenges to the fictive unity of the self. These have been presented since her groundbreaking and influential book, *Gender Trouble*.[40] In line with poststructural theory, Butler contrasts the humanist conception of the subject as a substantive person, who is the bearer of various essential and non-essential 'attributes' (of which, gender would be one), with a social theory of gender. Here, gender is understood as a *relation* among socially constituted subjects in an historically specific set of relations. Famously, she develops this argument further, however, to maintain that gender is 'an identity tenuously constituted in time, instituted in an exterior space through a *stylized repetition of acts*'.[41] Butler concludes, therefore, that 'gender', as a constructed identity, is enacted as 'a performative accomplishment'.[42] From Butler's radical challenge to notions of 'gender' have emerged expressions of queer theory which interrogate the perceived boundaries between performative sexualities constructed within the context of a heterosexual matrix.

The move from defining the 'self' as a fixed category that is separate and self-authenticating to a recognition of identity as performative allows, I believe, a similar move to take place in our expression of the divine. As with our identity, we can recognize that divinity is an event, a process. Feminist theo/alogies have envisioned images of the sacred which are embodied and present in the flux and fluidity of lived experience. I, however, welcome further movement in that shift, beyond realist and metaphysical definitions, allowing a notion of sacrality which leaves behind a

39. Keller, *From a Broken Web*, pp. 47-92.

40. Butler, *Gender Trouble*.

41. Butler, *Gender Trouble*, p. 140.

42. Butler, *Gender Trouble*, p. 141.

reliance on self-referential stability. When the metaphysical and Cartesian trappings of immutability have been removed, we are left with an expression of sacrality as process. A vital aspect of this process, however, is that it is *relational*. This was suggested by Daly's configuration of Goddess as Verb at the very beginning of feminist thealogy. Notably, the verb is an intransitive one. It therefore has no object, it does not attempt to define the other. It does have a subject but that subject is not fixed, it is constantly in relation to the verb.[43] Following this movement, sacrality is recognized as a process which releases movement, defies boundaries and enables relationality. Developing theories of subjectivity have led to a change in language which signals important changes in perception. We can speak of 'doing' identities rather than 'having' a self or 'being' a gender. I am asking, therefore, do we need to speak of 'doing' our sacrality rather than 'having' a distant, divine, hierarch?[44] To define the limits, location and nature of the sacred is a political act. If we recognize that sacrality is performative then such an act is no longer the premise of those in power. Our cultural imaginary is framed by narratives of the sacred which posit the power of male monotheism over against the threatening, promiscuous chaos of multiplicity. A jealous God cannot tolerate the competition offered by diversity. The boundaries between the Absolute and the devalued Other are therefore firmly drawn. If we are to foster positive responses to difference we need a transgressive sacrality which questions such boundaries[45] and which incorporates the enabling risk of plurality. I maintain that Goddess-talk has a distinctive role to play in renegotiating re-visioning and refiguring such a paradigm shift.

43. Mary Daly, *Beyond God the Father*. This is not to deny Daly's very serious reservations about postmodern and poststructural trends in feminist thought—a scenario which she has incorporated into her Sado Ritual Syndrome!

44. Richard Grigg also recognized something of this when, as an enthusiastic observer, he attempted to appropriate into mainstream theology the enabling insights of feminist theo/alogy by calling for 'enactment theology'; Richard Grigg, *When God Becomes Goddess: The Transformation of American Religion* (New York: Continuum, 1995).

45. I am grateful to Carol Christ for alerting me to the crucial distinction between boundaries set by those in power and those which are drawn by individuals. Only the former are to be transgressed by performative sacrality. In other cases, blurring boundaries can itself be an act of oppression, as in incidents of sexual harassment and child abuse.

Chapter 4

THE 'TORAFACTION' OF WISDOM IN BEN SIRA[1]

Dominique Olney

Some of the most vibrant pages of the Hebrew Scriptures come out of the Wisdom writings and their way of imaging Lady Wisdom: She makes her first entrance in Prov. 1:20–32, appears further in Proverbs 8 and 9, and then in Job 28; in the Apocrypha she appears in Ecclesiasticus as well as in the Greek book of the Wisdom of Solomon, where, after leaving her unforgettable imprint on chapters 7 and 8, she disappears totally after chapter 10.

The fact that the figure of the feminine divine—endowed with so many features of real women—was chosen to express most clearly the image of God, remains a fascinating puzzle. How could such a gloriously female image walk so blazingly on so many prominently patriarchal pages of the Hebrew Scriptures?

In the words of Asphodel P. Long:

> Everything to do with her is mysterious and paradoxical. In the Bible, she is always female.... She is continually being sought and found, lost and found; she ascends and descends; she finds her place in Israel, she can find no place in Israel. She is the divine female companion of God eternal with him before creation.... She may be married to God or to selected men, and she may be the mother of the created world. Human beings must follow her rules if they are to succeed in this life, and also possibly partake in an afterlife with God. It was she who helped God create the universe and she knows all its secrets. She moves through it and orders it well.[2]

1. By 'Torafaction' I imply transformation with manipulation or exploitation.

2. Asphodel P. Long, 'The Goddess in Judaism: An Historical Perspective' in A. Pirani (ed.), *The Absent Mother: Restoring the Goddess to Judaism and Christianity* (New York: HarperCollins Publishers, 1991), p.46.

With Ecclesiasticus, a new phase in Hebrew Wisdom writings begins. While relying on the text of Proverbs, Sira transformed Personified Wisdom and by chapter 24 he has disappeared her into the Torah. It is this transformation ('Torafaction') I wish to explore here, within its historical and social context in order to assess the influence this merging had on Sira's theology in particular, and on Jewish theology in general. With this union, Wisdom's femaleness and the way it was manipulated take on a crucial meaning. The analysis of this 'torafaction' provides valuable insight for understanding how theodicy can affect human behaviour and the well-being of any community—whether in the past, present or future.[3]

There can be little doubt that Sira's aim was to present the Law in as attractive a guise as possible, using all available metaphorical imagery to make her irresistible: Israel was the chosen one, the only one worthy of receiving Wisdom on her soil. However, he did not reject all aspects of foreign cultures. Egyptian imagery and a certain degree of Hellenism permeate his work—although few theological or philosophical concepts seem directly hijacked from Greek thought. In 38.12, for example, he advises Jews not to despise or fear Greek medical progress but to 'give the physician his place, for the Lord created him'.

The partly autobiographical form of the book announces a break with the universal type of instruction for which the wisdom writers made neither personal claim nor pretence of exclusivity. This new factor reflects a deep transformation within the wisdom tradition: although his predecessors demonstrated an awareness of humankind's dependence on the will of God, they never claimed to reveal that will to their pupils until Ben Sira. While the authority of his precursors was entirely based on human experience, his, he considered, was downloaded from God. While they felt they had no right to the exclusive possession of wisdom; he was conscious of holding a position of honour and privilege within his community:

> ... he who devotes himself to the study of the law of the Most High
> will seek out the wisdom of all the ancients,

3. The Torah, while interpreted by many Christians as a set of restrictive laws, represents for Jews something quintessential to life: 'Just as oil gives light to the world, so too do the words of the Torah give light to the world' (Deuteronomy Rabbah 7.3) - cited in W. D. Davies, *Paul and Rabbinic Judaism: Some Rabbinic Elements in Pauline Theology*, rev. edn., (London: SPCK, 1965), p. 148.

> and will be concerned with prophecies;
> he will preserve the discourse of notable men
> and penetrate the subtleties of parables; (39:1–2)

Ben Sira's predecessors dispensed an instruction that was available to any ordinary intelligent person, but he addressed himself specifically to the people of Israel. Their traditional instruction comprised both received knowledge and their own experience of life; his teaching, though derived from these same traditional sources, was constantly measured and checked against God's commandments. Their knowledge of the world was knowledge (within the limits of human possibility) of the nature of wisdom, and constituted both the authority of the teacher and the content of his teaching. Thus the good life was something which could be taught, communicated by one man to another without any need for divine revelation. It was basically no more than common sense; but Sira's knowledge was not—as far as he was concerned—confined within the limits of human possibility: he spoke on behalf of God, therefore reliance on his own knowledge and experience of the world was always suspect, neither proper nor sufficient. This is not to say that the predecessors felt no need or love for God, on the contrary their self-confidence and feeling of harmony within a world they felt at one with reflects an unshakable trust and faith in a God they knew themselves to be part of. They were in constant communion and co-union with their God, Sira was in constant dependency of his God.

A comparison of the Book of Proverbs with that of Ben Sira gives an immediate insight into Wisdom thinking. The two books are both so alike and so vividly different that a close comparison of key passages reveals a bold, striking, transformation. Both works are presented as the teaching of a father/teacher to his son/pupil (on rare occasions, 'sons'). They provide the reader (son or pupil) principally with prudential sayings whose aims are to enable the young person to achieve a state of wisdom. These sayings draw on much accumulated human experience, Jewish and foreign, and are interspersed with the sages' reflection on Divine Wisdom or creation, as well as with hymns in which She actually speaks in the first person. Much of Ben Sira reads like Proverbs—indeed sometimes the transference of text is practically direct. Yet the reader soon realizes that there are some fundamental differences. As the most striking factor resides in the transformation of Lady Wisdom herself, it is tempting to ask oneself to what extent this is not at the source of all other differences.

From the very first chapter Ben Sira introduces two leitmotivs: 'All wisdom comes from the Lord and is with him for ever' (v.1), and 'there is One who is wise, greatly to be feared' (v.8). This is then taken up in verse 11, the first of ten sentences to sing the refrain of 'the fear of the Lord (is...)'. By the end of chapter one, the 'fear of the Lord' theme has been relentlessly hammered on the brain of the reader. In fact, by the end of verse one they have already guessed that the free-flowing, independent Wisdom discovered in Proverbs had lost her freedom and independence. That She 'comes from' and 'is with' Yahweh is not a new concept but it is presented as such: Wisdom's dependence on Yahweh has to be absolutely clear and unequivocal. The first time we hear of Wisdom in Proverbs she is standing in the street, teaching of her own free will; she is introduced by the teacher, not so much as God's Wisdom or as acting on God's behalf, but as a fully independent feminine divine character. In the mind of the people teaching and listening in those days, her partnership with God was implied, but there is no doubt either that the 'I' of Wisdom is a consistently free 'I'. Within Prov. 1:20–33, the 'fear of the Lord' expressed in verse 29 is very much out of place in this hymn of self-appraisal retracing Wisdom's desperate attempt to save a humankind she fiercely loves. Similarly in Proverbs 2, verses 5–8 seem to interrupt the train of thought within the chapter, and this recurs throughout the Book. McKane's opinion that the 'fear of Yahweh' is totally alien to the mentality of Proverbs has to be taken seriously. The very least that can be said is that this theme of the fear of the Lord never seems to quite fit the text of Proverbs. The whole of Ben Sira on the other hand, seems constructed in order to give this very theme the maximum punch; this fear of the Lord is the root (v.20) and the beginning (v.14) of wisdom, it delights the heart (v.18), brings blessings at the time of death (v.13); it is Wisdom's crown (v.18) and its full measure (v.17). So from Sira's chapter 1 the whole situation is reversed and it is now the 'fear of the Lord' which becomes the anchor and the norm. This is the first step taken by Sira to nationalize wisdom. For Whybray[4] however, this was the wisdom teachers' ultimate aim: having rendered their tradition of didactic discourses both less

4. R.N. Whybray, *Wisdom in Proverbs* (London: SCM Press, 1965), pp. 92–93.

'foreign' and more attractive by the addition of the feminine wisdom passages, they made a conscious effort to merge this wisdom into mainstream Yahwism, making her *Yahweh's* wisdom. But against this interpretation it becomes more logical to see in this merging (if it took place at all) a will to change Yahwism in order to make it more adaptable and more attractive as well as to inject it with the energetic boost of a skilful, mature trust in humanity's capacity to take its destiny firmly in hand. Indeed, the writers of Proverbs are worlds apart from Ben Sira's later and unmistakable wish to nationalize wisdom; their whole ethos, their obvious trust in their ability to solve their own problems, their whole attitude to life contradicts Whybray's opinion.

It is also in chapter one that Ben Sira presents his view of Wisdom. In 1:2-6, Sira echoes both Proverbs' understanding of a cosmic Wisdom who was created by God 'before all things...' and Job's vision of her mysterious, ungraspable presence: 'who can count the sand of the sea...' (implied: God knows). Verse 19 recounts God's search for—and establishment of—Wisdom, in parallel with Job 28:27. Thus Ben Sira juxtaposes the various texts which describe Wisdom's beginnings.

Proverbs 8	*Job 28*	*Sira 1*
The Lord created me at the beginning of his work, the first of his acts of old. (v.22)		Wisdom was created before all things.... (v.4)
	The deep says, "it is not in me" and the sea says, "it is not with me." (v.14)	The sand of the sea, the drops of rain, and the days of eternity—who can count them? (v.2)
	It is hid from the eyes of all living ... (v.21)	
	When he made a decree for the rain, and a way for the lightning of the thunder; then he saw it and declared it, he established it and searched it out. (vv.26–7)	He saw her and apportioned her, he rained down knowledge and discerning comprehension, ... (v.19)

This gives good insight into the thinking mechanisms of the wisdom writers who instead of locking a concept into a definition, thereby limiting the concept itself and restricting its possible evolution, chose to steer clear of all well-defined, clear-cut explanations. Von Rad comments on this trait:

> ...the relevant statement is not limited (defined), but remains open and in the balance and is simply joined to the one next following. The statements which we would like to differentiate sharply almost merge with each other. In this way, however, the author can achieve what he wishes; he circles round the phenomenon in the totality in which it can be experienced by man and which removes it still further from a precise, conceptual definition because, no matter how much one tries to define it, it becomes lost again in mystery.[5]

Ancient wisdom relished contradictions. By presenting various aspects of the same truth they safeguarded the mystery of life and creation and the environment of trying to make sense of it. Thus the study of wisdom never became simplistic but forced readers into perpetual challenge. No thought was too daring, even that of a direct accusation and challenge to God (Job). Ben Sira however breaks off this tradition. He juxtaposes past understandings of Wisdom not in order to sharpen readers' acuity but rather to cast wisdom into his own mould. She is poured into a perfectly designed container which marries exactly the 'fear of the Lord'. She can now be used to illustrate a theology which feels the urge to maintain humanity in a monotonous, non-inquisitive state of piety and fear. We are far away from the Proverbs-type of humankind who is not only encouraged to be inquisitive but positively taught that life can be pure delight. We are even further away from the Job-type of humankind who turns inquisitiveness into the most pregnant theological tool and pushes integrity to the edges of sanity.

It is in chapter 24 that Ben Sira achieves the fusion between Hokma and Torah, as well as the merging of old and new religious concepts. These new developments have been introduced since the beginning of the book, especially through the Wisdom hymns (1:1–10, 4:11–19 and 6:18–37); however it is only with chapter 24 that the full extent of this fusion, and the theological transformation that flows from it, become apparent. This key chapter holds the central position of

5. Gerhard von Rad, *Wisdom in Israel*, trans. J. D. Martin (London: SCM Press, 1972), p. 242.

Ben Sira's writings and concentrates all his theological thoughts as well as providing some of the most beautiful imagery of Wisdom ever written—a magnificent tomb-stone?

Von Rad states rightly that for Ben Sira, the norms of behaviour are inferred from the didactic wisdom tradition or from the store of experience of the elders, rather than from the Torah.[6] However he denies the importance—and overlooks the consequences—of this new alliance between nomism and wisdom: this reality of the Torah-Wisdom union does have some effect on the didactic passages, although admittedly, in this area, its influence is so subtle that it does not seem to have attracted notice. And yet in parallel with the Torah-Wisdom marriage comes the development of a narrow-minded dualism foreign to the zestful, piquant Wisdom texts of the past:

> Good is the opposite of evil,
> and life the opposite of death;
> so the sinner is the opposite of the godly.
> Look upon all the works of the Most High;
> they likewise are in pairs,
> one the opposite of the other. (33:14–15)

What has happened to the wise people's insatiable curiosity, daring intellectual appetite and acute awareness of complexity?

This narrow-mindedness reflected itself in Ben Sira's creation theology. A community's creation theology always mirrors its people's behaviour and beliefs; it deeply influences the way that community views itself and its God. It is not surprising therefore, that when wisdom theology flowed through Ben Sira's community, it underwent a transformation of its understanding of God, Wisdom and Humankind, each in their individuality as well as in their interrelationship. It is in chapter 16:24–18:14 that Ben Sira illustrates this new concept of the creation of the world. His doctrine of God's absolute control of the universe follows a step by step logical progress:

– Verses 16:24–28 recount God's control of the universe, all has been 'disposed in an eternal order', and has been fixed 'for all times.' This is closer to the Egyptian environment of an order frozen in its eternal perfection, than to the chaos-friendly Hebrew beginnings.

6. Von Rad, *Wisdom in Israel*, p. 144.

- Verses 16:29–30 recount God's control over the earth, reminding the reader that all the living creatures he created have to return into the ground.
- Verses 17:1–11 recount God's control over man 'created from the earth', and as God is in control of man, so is man of the earth and all its creatures. As man has to fear God, animals have to fear man. Job had learned that he was, with humankind, within and part of God's universe; Sira placed humanity either 'under' the rule of God or ruling 'over' part of creation.

As noted by Snaith,[7] although Ben Sira remained close to the Genesis account of the creation of the universe, he did adapt and change the text freely, alluding to Stoic concepts[8] as well as using wisdom images and language when appropriate. The most striking reversal into wisdom language occurs in 17:7:

> He filled them with knowledge and understanding,
> and showed them good and evil.

Snaith notices: 'Scriptural quotation ended, the author ignores Gen. 2:17, where man's possession of "the knowledge of good and evil" is against God's will, but refers rather to the intuitive *discernment* that wisdom teachers tried to develop in their pupils.'[9] Ben Sira instinctively reverted to wisdom tradition when dealing with the concept of good and evil: the notion that Wisdom encouraged people to learn and find out about good and evil was so deeply engrained in those who had a place within the Wisdom Tradition that it overruled the Scriptures!

- verses 17:11–17 recount God's control over his 'chosen people': from verse 11 Ben Sira starts to build a mental dividing wall between humanity and Israel. Little by little, he adds details and controls language in order to bring his reader to the obvious conclusion that God 'chose Israel to be his own possession' (v.17). The old wisdom teachers would have agreed with Ben Sira that God gave humanity knowledge (or rather, they would have thought, the *ability* to develop knowledge), but never would

7. John G. Snaith, *Ecclesiasticus or the Wisdom of Jesus Son of Sirach*, Cambridge Bible Commentary (Cambridge: Cambridge University Press, 1974), p.87.

8. Later editors of Ben Sira have inserted a verse between verses 4 and 6, in keeping with Stoic philosophy: v.5. They obtained the use of the five operations of the Lord: as sixth he distributed to them the gift of mind, and as seventh reason, the interpreter of his operations.

9. Snaith, *Ecclesiasticus*, p. 87.

they have tied their pupils to the concepts of 'life-giving law' (v.11) and the establishment of a 'perpetual covenant' (v.12), replacing thus in one sweep intuitive discernment with piety and repentance—and the main reason for repentance is that one is 'never hidden from his [God's] scrutiny' (v.15). When discussing this transformation of Wisdom into the Book of the Law, Long comments:

> Here there is no symbiosis between the actions of humans and the course of nature. Rather, it is an expression of the division between the Creator and the created; the division remains even for the righteous, for they will be 'rewarded'.[10]

Humankind is no longer the mate of Wisdom, endeavouring to perfect itself to graciously add to the harmony of universe; it has become a guilt-ridden mass with no hope of righteousness, happiness or fulfilment, and has no option—having fully deconstructed its harmonious three-way interrelationship—but to construct for itself the only God it deserves: one who can only pour out sickly compassion on its infinite weakness. This stands worlds apart from Wisdom pouring knowledge on the humankind she loves. Ben Sira in these passages, sits on the same benches as Job's friends and equals their most narrow-minded speeches, adding a pinch of the pessimistic streaks of Qoheleth without mentioning any of his redeeming philosophical thoughts.

How can von Rad put forward the argument that Ben Sira's 'thoughts about the correlation between fear of God and wisdom are no different from those of teachers in earlier centuries.'[11] Surely, it is crucial not to ignore the consequences of such a development. The fear of God is now well on the way to replacing instruction as the fundamental element of wisdom: it has become the very essence and beginning of Wisdom, as expressed in v.14. This obsessive refrain is further developed in chapter 2, where it becomes clear that humanity's well-being and happiness no longer rest on a community of mature human beings who continuously re-learn to think in harmony with the laws of the universe, using past and present, foreign and local experiential knowledge. Now Wisdom is sinking under the weight of piety, and humankind is advised—

10. Asphodel P. Long, *In a Chariot Drawn by Lions* (London: The Women's Press, 1992), p.32.

11. Von Rad, *Wisdom in Israel*, p.245.

instead of developing acuity and intelligent sensitivity—to cower and repent in front of God, to wait for his mercy (v.7), to hope for good things (v.9), to trust in the Lord's compassion as 'he forgives sins and saves in time of affliction' (v.11), to seek his approval (v.14), and to fall into his hands (v.18).

Trust in people's ability to solve their problems has been replaced with admission and acceptance of their helplessly sinful nature. Independence and maturity have been replaced with dependence and guilt.

In chapter 24, far more than in the previous ones, Ben Sira gives Wisdom a fully transcendent, fully immanent status. She is introduced in all her radiant glory: glory among 'her people' and glory 'in the assembly of the Most High' (vv. 1–2). Many have seen a Jewish response to the threat posed by Hellenistic cults to Isis (Maat) in Ben Sira's painting of Wisdom as coming forth 'from the mouth' of Yahweh and 'covering the earth like a mist, involved with the making of the 'circuit of the vault of heaven' and walking in the depth of the sea and the width of the earth (vv. 3–6); but Hengel makes the point that by then, these no longer represented a serious threat. He argues that it is much more towards the philosophy of the Stoics we should turn to for analogies:

> Ben Sira was probably no longer aware of the original mythological features in his wisdom hymn in chapter 24, and regarded wisdom more as a kind of *'world reason'* emanating from God, which filled and permeated the whole creation and finds the culmination of its task in making man a rational being (1.9f., 19; cf.17.7). For him, the working of wisdom and God's creative action formed an inseparable unity. Thus 'wisdom' in Ben Sira could be understood analogously to the Stoic 'Logos', which permeates and shapes the cosmos.[12]

Despite these echoing consonances, the numerous resonances linking this text to the imagery and tradition of the Hebrew Scriptures form the backbone of the score. And this takes place from the very beginning of the hymn: Wisdom covering the earth like a mist (v.3) brings back memories of Gen. 1:2 and 2:6; her 'dwelling in high places', her 'throne' and 'pillar of cloud' (v.4) immediately transport us in the presence of Yahweh. McKinlay comments: 'This is a striking cluster of traditionally separate images

12. Martin Hengel, *Judaism and Hellenism* (London : SCM Press, 1974), vol. 1, pp. 159–60.

which present a wisdom.... taking on a Yahweh guise.'[13] Verses 5 and 6 echo Proverbs 8:27–28 in which God established the heaven and drew a circle on the face of the deep in the presence of Wisdom, but in Sira's adaptation, Wisdom herself is the creator of the universe and she takes an interest in the whole of mankind. By the end of v.6 therefore we have been presented with a free-flowing and ungraspable Wisdom through vocabulary that images immensity and majesty, universality, constant mobility and changeability. With vv.7–12 however, the universe is suddenly imploded down to one small dot: the land of Jacob, and Wisdom is imaged as being restricted within closed boundaries; in Zion, in Jerusalem, in Jacob, in Israel is her only choice of resting place. McKinlay draws our attention to the repetition of the word 'in', which 'emphasizes the settlement and links the details together, making a unity of the passage.' She notes further on that 'This is her goal; this is a place and a role for Wisdom....'[14]

Wisdom's initial free and fluid mobility as the all-embracing lover-creator of the universe is instantly frozen into servile obedience just as her boundary-free territory is instantly collapsed into one small area. Wisdom used to belong to everyone. The only condition attached to possessing her was the intensive and relentless search for knowledge and awareness of self, others and creation. Also, the way of possessing—maybe thanks to thinkers such as Job—was never jealous grabbing for one's own benefit (this was the false wisdom of Job's friends) but receiving and letting go. The possessiveness conceived by Ben Sira is different: it is about taking and retaining, keeping safe from others; it is about not letting go. It is the one last step before Baruch's blood-chilling cry: 'Why, O Israel, did you give away your Wisdom to foreign lands?' Ben Sira weaves Wisdom in a tight web, shrinking her domain in a few verses from the universe (v.2) to the earth (v.3) then to Israel's territory (v.7) and a wilderness tent (v.8), and last to a city (v.11) and the tabernacle in the Temple. The irony is that within this deuteronomic, Yahwistic, masculine terminology is inserted the echo of Prov. 8:22–23:

> From eternity, in the beginning, he created me,
> and for eternity I shall not cease to exist. (Sir. 24:9).

13. McKinlay, Judith E., *Gendering Wisdom The Host: Biblical Invitations to Eat and Drink* (Sheffield: Sheffield Academic Press, 1996), p. 137.

14. McKinlay, *Gendering Wisdom*, p. 138.

In Prov. 8:22-23 we had heard Wisdom's song:

> The Lord created me at the beginning of his work,
> the first of his acts of old.
> Ages ago I was set up,
> at the first, before the beginning of the earth.

This is the opening of the hymn to the creation of the world which ends with the remarkably peaceful yet so powerful image of Wisdom who was daily God's delight, 'rejoicing before him always, rejoicing in his inhabited world and delighting in the sons of men.' (Prov. 8:30-31). The irony is all the more biting since Sira's verse 9 just precedes Yahweh's placing Wisdom inside the tabernacle. Wisdom has become the Torah and for eternity her role will be to serve, to minister before her master. The free-flowing, all-loving and embracing partnership between God, Wisdom and humankind have been siphoned, spiralled into three separate entities unable to interact freely: a cowering, sinful humankind, a God who gives commands, and Wisdom who obeys orders. The oneness of mutuality has cracked three ways within this ever-closer identification of Wisdom with Israel. This was probably the price to pay for the safeguarding of the faith and life of a small defenceless people caught between large and powerful empires: 'The universal hostess is now the hostess of Israel, and even the hostess's task has been redefined for a cultic/priestly Wisdom.'[15]

Having established Wisdom's cultic role, Sira embarks on some of the most poetic verses in the book and perhaps in the whole of Wisdom literature. Through the lushness of vegetal metaphors he retraces the ever-changing grace and the constantly renewing beauty of Wisdom's presence within a harmonious order. This is no longer the cosmic, universal Wisdom of the beginning of chapter 24, but Wisdom immanent in earth and plant-life, bringing us back to the Garden of Eden imagery: McKinlay comments rightly that 'the listing of the various trees could suggest the prolific life-producing of Wisdom, earlier described in Proverbs as the Tree of Life.'[16] These verses appeal to all the senses, as each tree named by Wisdom has its own many properties: the reader can see the beauty and grace of their various shapes and the colour of their flowers (vv.13,14), she can feel the cool and protective shade of their 'glorious

15. McKinlay, *Gendering Wisdom*, p. 139.
16. McKinlay, *Gendering Wisdom*, p. 140.

and graceful branches' (v.16) and inhale their fragrant odours (v.15), she is empowered by the strength, the stability of their roots, their majestic trunks and feels regenerated by the continuous cycle of nature which they carry forward from bud to blossom to fruit.

To close this orgy of sheer lushness Wisdom sums up the enchantment and charm she offers so naturally and bountifully: 'Like a vine I caused loveliness to bud, and my blossoms became glorious and abundant fruit.' (24:17)

It is significant that Ben Sira, before losing her into Torah, commingles Wisdom's two complementary sides: in 24:3–6 it is as the divine (co-)creator of the universe that we meet her; more than ever before, she affirms her infinite deftness and craftsmanship, her all-embracing understanding and her harmonious participation and interacting within the order of creation. Yet in 24:13–17 it is as the cyclical and perpetually renewing life-giving source of feminine fertility that she appears to us. This brings to mind Asphodel Long's research on the links between the Goddess Asherah, the Tree of Life, and the Menorah:

> Where Hochma, Wisdom, encapsulated the comprehension of creation and the brilliance of order and the intellect, it seemed that Asherah stood for the concept of life, its physicality, its sacrality, its cyclical renewal within nature and the hope by the human beings who worshipped her that such renewal was some sort of symbol of eternal life.[17]

By the time Ben Sira wrote his book it is highly unlikely that he would have drawn a conscious link between Wisdom, the Tree of Life and Asherah; however his tree imagery is so powerfully evocative of all that Asherah must have stood for that it reverberates like an ancient echo of the goddess. Is there not after all, something infinitely comforting in the 'humanly-graspable' image of Wisdom settling down into the very soil of the earth, and from within that soil, growing in strength, beauty and abundance? An image all the more powerful since it combines vigorous growth with stability, infinite grace with fragile life-sustaining renewal, feminine intimacy and joy with vegetal lushness and generosity.[18] Alain Fournier-Bidoz expresses well to what extent this new garden of Eden represented a vision of abundance and joy, intimacy and fertility in Sira's mind:

17. Long, *Asherah*, p. 1.

18. The growing danger of annihilation felt on the political scene can also explain the need, not only for comfort but also for boosting Israel's confidence in her destiny.

> ... l'arbre y est vu comme la source inépuisable de la fertilité cosmique et, de ce fait, souvent lié à une divinité féminine. Cet arbre cosmique, symbole de l'univers crée et de l'immortalité, pousse souvent au milieu d'un espace sacré, où ciel et terre se rejoignent et dont il incorpore la sacralité.[19]

> Here the tree appears as the inexhaustible spring of cosmic fertility and is therefore often linked to a feminine divinity. This cosmic tree, symbol of the created universe and of immortality, often grows as the centre of a sacred space, where sky and earth meet and whose sacredness it embodies.

To Fournier-Bidoz therefore, the link with a 'feminine divinity' was as obvious as the link with the Tree of Life—embodiment of sacrality—which grows within a sacred space where earth and sky meet. This whole passage (24:13–17), with its proliferation of trees, is strongly reminiscent of the Tree of Life so often mentioned in Proverbs (e.g., Prov. 3:18; 11:30) and as in Proverbs, there is never the least doubt that this divine tree could bring anything but harmony and good. It is in fact the very symbol combining masculine strength and rectilinear stability with feminine curvability. In Sira's vision, Wisdom is well-rooted in the soil of Israel and her portion of land nourishes trees whose fruits are there in abundance to be eaten: Wisdom still distributes her wealth without counting, and nothing she offers can ever bring death or evil. In a way, she rehabilitates Eve who could be thought of as the first being to feel the Promethean urge to obtain knowledge whatever the consequences or costs.[20] However there are no forbidden trees on Wisdom's territory, and the notion that within nature itself there could be evil was nonsense to the writers of Wisdom literature; on that score Sira fits the delimitation of that literature.

For him however, this abundant and joyful fertility which is Wisdom's gift to humanity is irrevocably tied in with the Temple; it is in a subtly subliminal way that he implies Wisdom's transparent yet quite unbreakable connection with the Temple and its cultic

19. Alain Fourniez-Bidoz, 'L'Arbre et la Demeure: Siracide XXIV' 10–17, *Vetus Testamentum*, 34,1 (1984), p. 5.

20. 'The prominent role of the female rather than the male in the wisdom aspects of the Eden tale is a little-noticed feature of the narrative. It is the woman, and not the man, who perceives the desirability of procuring wisdom. ... the close connection between woman and wisdom in the Bible is surely present in the creation narrative, although it is hardly limited to the beginning of Genesis.' Carol Meyers, *Discovering Eve: Ancient Israelite Women in Context* (Oxford: Oxford University Press, 1988), p. 91.

life. The trees mentioned in verses 13 and 14 all have some links with the Temple building or life; the spices and perfumes, McKinlay reminds us, commonly used by lovers, are also the ingredients used in the anointing oil and Temple incense (Exod. 30:22-38). So we have a two-layered text throughout the Wisdom hymns of chapter 24: through the channel of Wisdom tradition, the reader's subconscious is bombarded with discreet but constant allusions to the priestly tradition: the top layer of the text, while it exudes abundance and joy, feminine intimacy and fertility, rests on a Yahwistic foundation of cultic routine and sacred historical background. The ties between Wisdom and Yahwism are of two types: within the hymns themselves they come through in transparency, presumably in order not to damage Wisdom's irresistible feminine appeal, but in the construction of the paragraphs within the chapter, the wisdom hymns are unequivocally inserted into an explicitly Yahwistic frame:

Wisdom is introduced as being in the 'assembly of the Most High':

- *Hymn 1:* (vv.2-6) Wisdom's cosmic origin and role as creator of the universe. Wisdom is ordered by the Creator of all things to make [her] dwelling in Jacob and minister to Yahweh.
- *Hymn 2:* (vv.13-17) Wisdom's Garden of Eden's paradise.
- *Hymn 3:* (vv.19-22) Wisdom's call to eat and drink her produce.

Reminder that 'All this' is the book of the covenant of the Most High God, the Law which Moses commanded us as an inheritance for the congregations of Jacob (Deut. 33:4).

This could be conceived as one of the major turning points in man's understanding of Wisdom since she now has become Torah.[21] The language in vv.25-29 is Wisdom's, so is the imagery: after describing the 'joyous lushness and prolific life-producing bounty of trees', Wisdom exalts the sacred power of great rivers, adding

21. While Philo wrote at a later date, his understanding of the Torah is already apparent in Ecclesiasticus although in a far less developed state: it was 'a source of instruction in specific conduct, an inspired formulation of God's purposes for the beginner, and for the vast majority of men who never get beyond the beginner's stage. It was binding upon the man of higher experience in so far as he had still to live among his fellows.... [for the man of higher experience] The great value of the Torah was ... that it gave an exposition of the nature of God and of the mystic way to Him. ... He still dedicated his life to the Law revealed by Moses, but to him that Law was the unwritten Logos of God.' Erwin R. Goodenough, *By Light, Light: The Mystic Gospel of Hellenistic Judaism* (New Haven, CT: Yale University Press, 1935), p. 93.

the potent symbolism of water to that of trees before launching into the last hymn of chapter 24—again full of Wisdom imagery. This time however, Wisdom's words and imagery belong wholly to Torah. It is no longer Wisdom who speaks although it sounds like her. The international, universal and cosmic Wisdom, the wisdom of mystery, ungraspable and known by God only, even woman Wisdom standing in the market place, shouting to shake off people's apathy, had all in turn brought the Jews to a fountain of spiritual and intellectual energy; Sira carried on with the tradition, adapting his vision to the needs of his contemporaries. Spiritual, moral, physical survival was possibly at stake. His need was for a Wisdom that would give back the dream of the Garden of Eden to the Jews, both as their own Jewish rightful inheritance, but also as the microcosmic projection of the cosmic garden of God. For Sira, the Law into which he merged Wisdom was one with the cosmic order that was both the means and the material necessary for the creation and continuation of the universe. It was also microcosmically contained in each page, each word, each letter of the Torah: a scribe making a mistake on one single letter of the text of the Torah would be committing a crime affecting the balance of the universe.[22] Hengel, when discussing this issue, looks at texts from the first and second centuries CE which indicate clearly that by then, some of the Rabbis at least actually believed and taught that without the Torah—and the people of Israel to uphold it—the world would not exist. 'R.Bannaya expressed the ultimate consequence (towards AD 200): the world was created for the sake of the Torah'.[23] Having zoomed in from the universe (24:5-6) down to Jerusalem and confined Wisdom in a restricted space (24:8-12), Ben Sira proceeds then to stretch space and project it back into infinity. The precision of the clearly defined contours and walled-in boundaries of the Temple, named towns and countries surrounding the territory of Israel vanish. From verse 14 onwards, the confining *in* disappears totally and the reader is catapulted into the blurred natural spaces of growing trees, spreading their branches upwards and filling the atmosphere with sweet aroma and beauty.

> Alone I have made the circuit of the vault of heaven
> and have walked in the depth of the abyss (v.5)

22. Hengel, *Hellenism and Judaism*, pp. 169-75.
23. Hengel, *Hellenism and Judaism*, p. 172, and n. 433 (vol. 2).

> In the holy tabernacle I ministered before him,
> and so I was established in Zion. (vv.10–11)
>
> I grew tall like ....
> I spread a pleasant odour ...
>
> ...I spread out my branches ...
> ...I caused loveliness to bud ... (vv.13–17)

Fournier-Bidoz comments thus:

> ... l'insistance n'est plus sur l'espace, mais sur le processus même d'extension, ce fait de la vitalité inépuisable et séduisante de la sagesse. Ainsi les vv.15–17, privés de localisation nette, exposent avec lyrisme la capacité de la Sagesse à remplir tout l'espace possible. Non seulement elle établit sa demeure en Israel, comme le lui ordonnait son Créateur, mais elle grandit, s'étend, fait montre d'un merveilleux déploiement.[24]
>
> The emphasis no longer rests on space but on the very process of expansion, mark of the inexhaustible and seductive vitality of wisdom. Thus v.15–17, deprived of any clear location, express with lyricism wisdom's ability to fill all possible space, not only does she establish her roots in Israel as ordered by her creator, but she grows stretches and unfolds in a wondrous way.

This contracting and expanding of the space in which Wisdom moves operates in parallel with the contracting and expanding of time: there is a striking contrast between Wisdom presented as belonging outside of time (v.9), having the whole of eternity as a backcloth to her actions, and her new role as servant in the Temple, ministering to God and therefore constrained within cultic time-keeping!

Fournier-Bidoz explores and marvels at the way Sira engineered this double movement within the discourse of Wisdom, giving emphasis to the fundamental axle of space and time, while painting an horizon which spanned the totality of the universe. Within the space-time dimension, Ben Sira played ceaselessly with the notions of mobility and immobility. Mobility through on-going creation, cyclical processes, symbolized by the cycle of the seasons, the earth fertility and the feminine divine. Immobility through man-made artificial spaces symbolised by the Temple, centre of cultic life devized by man in an effort to re-invent or re-enact the natural cycle of life, and by the house, sanctuary offering protection and well-being within a safe and stationary compound.

24. Fournier-Bidoz, 'L'Arbre et la Demeure', p. 2.

But surely this very process of expansion and change which is at the core of Wisdom's unquenchable vitality is—from now on—seriously jeopardized; even if one agrees up to a point with them, Fournier-Bidoz and von Rad, while they provide a remarkably sound analysis of the texts, do not however look beyond that analysis onto the long-term consequences of Ben Sira's thoughts. Once Wisdom can be located 'in', she is in danger of becoming man's possession—or rather man is in danger of thinking himself capable of owning her and thereby of losing her.

Fournier-Bidoz echoes Ben Sira's marvelling at the fact that Wisdom has established her resting place on the soil of Israel 'as she was ordered by her Creator'—a detail which seems to delight them both—and that from there, she grows and unfolds beautifully, moving ever outwards to encompass space itself. Because of their hypnotic beauty these images can be as energizing as they can be destructive. If Wisdom is reduced to the role of mediator between Yahweh and his people at the exclusivity of the rest of humankind, projecting the one up into perfect but remote transcendence and the other down into baseness and imperfection, the three-way perpetual movement of graceful, dance-like complementarity linking Yahweh, Wisdom and Humanity is dead.

And yet, what will be remembered of Ben Sira's Book is not so much the dissolving of Wisdom into the Torah but the memory, sometimes almost erased yet lingering on like a dream, of the lushness and beauty of a regained garden of Paradise whose trees reflect the immanence of a Wisdom-God who nurtures and loves humanity. Although they represent a minority within the texts of the Hebrew Scriptures the undiluted potency of their feminine imaging ripples through the whole Book, offering the reader brief but memorable icons of God as mother, sister, lover, Shekinah.

All the contradictions and tensions that come alive through the language of Sira, projecting divine radiance on one side and sterilized dualism on the other, have found no better expression than in the words of Asphodel Long when as a child she touched on the ambivalence of a reality that may well have moulded women and men from the beginnings of time, and may well carry on moulding them till the end of time.

> When I was a child, sitting in the gallery of an Orthodox synagogue, I always felt embarrassed that men ... should be carrying in their arms an object which seemed to me to be a half life-size woman, or a girl

like myself, and dressing and undressing it, and that this should be the most sacred part of the service... The Scroll of the Law, the Torah—loved, venerated, the object of the most sacred attention, is the Lady Wisdom; the very words, even letters, are holy. Yet in this religion, where God may not be given an image and is totally separate from humanity, the Law is presented not just as a book or even a scroll in itself; it is arranged to resemble a female figure; one that can be carried and cradled in one's arms and where the ceremony of undressing and dressing must indeed evoke echoes, no matter how repressed, of the sexual act. Such sexual overtones are certainly present in a Jewish understanding of the relationship of God and Israel and God and the Sacred Presence of God—the Shekinah.[25]

25. Long, *In a Chariot*, p. 176.

Chapter 5

SARAH: VILLAIN OR PATRIARCHAL PAWN?

Sarah Rogers

Sarah, wife of Abraham, lived in approximately 2000 B.C.[1] While substantial evidence of her existence remains untraceable outside of the texts within the Hebrew Scriptures where she is mentioned,[2] archaeological findings allow us to glean some facts about the type of life she would have led. Sarah is an ideal subject for this book as she presents us with a complex range of issues and we are left wondering just how she is a passive victim and just how she is a villain.

Through a re-visioning of the issues presented in Sarah's story, we can find value in diversity: internally and externally.

Sarah's subordinate status would not have given her the option of creating a life, in which we would say, self-realization figured substantially enough for her, to flourish.[3] The reasons for this lie in the constrictions patriarchy placed on her gender. However, we have no way of knowing whether she was discontent within this framework. Parts of Sarah's story seem horrific in a modern context; her abuse of Hagar (Gen. 16:6) is just one example. From our contemporary perspective, the interpretation we may choose to make of Sarah's subjectivity could be that she was diminished because 'Israel's patriarchal society during those centuries in which the Pentateuch was produced understood the father—that is, the adult male head of the family—as possessing both power and

1. G. Ernest Wright, *Biblical Archaeology* (London: Butler and Tanner Ltd., 1962), p. 43.

2. Wright, *Biblical Archaeology*, p. 40.

3. This is a term which Grace Jantzen gave a lecture on that I attended at Woodbrooke in May, 2001. It describes a woman's capacity for wholeness.

prestige'.[4] The abductions which Sarah experienced evidence the fact that any sexual 'transgression was not understood as violation of the woman in question'.[5] Sarah paid a price for being who she was. That price was the ultimate denial of a woman's right to pursue and realize her own subjectivity. Re-visioning Sarah's story aids us to learn about our own subjectivity, the process of which can inspire us towards right relation.[6]

The Hebrew Scriptures were written from a male perspective about a male-dominated world which speaks 'of events and activities engaged in primarily or exclusively by males (war, cult and government) and of a jealously singular God who is described and addressed in terms normally used for males.'[7] Gen. 20:12 cites Sarai as the daughter of Terah. She would most likely have been an Amorite,[8] though her precise lineage is impossible to trace because the patriarchal system which dominated the society within which Sarah would have lived employed a male-centred form of genealogy.[9] In Sarah's day there was a custom for each tribe to be attributed to the patriarch who had 'originated it.'[10] We are able to trace her roots back to Mesopotamia through findings, mainly about Abraham, and the world which they both inhabited. The Genesis texts cite Abraham as leading the migration into Canaan and archaeological evidence has confirmed that customs which were presupposed in the Genesis texts did exist in Haran.

The custom of a barren woman providing her mate with a fertile female described by the Nuzu documents aligns more substantially with Sarah's story. In Genesis 16 Sarah tells Abraham to sleep with her maidservant, Hagar, in hopes of a future heir. At Nuzu a childless wife was under obligation to provide her husband with a concubine. This parallels the traditions of early Israel where it was believed that a 'wife who did not produce children for her husband was not

4. Alice L. Laffey, *Wives Harlots and Concubines: The Old Testament in Feminist Perspective* (Philadelphia, USA: Fortress Press, 1998; London: SPCK, 1990), p. 16.

5. Laffey, *Wives Harlots and Concubines*, p. 16.

6. See, Carter Heyward, *Staying Power* (Cleveland, OH: The Pilgrim Press, 1995), pp. 7–9.

7. Phyllis Bird, 'Images of Women in the Old Testament' in Rosemary Radford Ruether (ed.), *Religion and Sexism* (New York: Simon and Schuster, 1974), pp. 41–42.

8. Wright, *Biblical Archaeology*, p. 42.

9. Exum, *Fragmented Women* (Valley Forge: Trinity Press, 1983), p. 111.

10. Exum, *Fragmented Women*, p. 40.

fulfilling her duty as a wife. In early Israel it was apparently customary for her to offer him a female slave to bear for her'.[11] Hagar conceived Ishmael and Abraham thereby received his first direct heir. Yet the similarity between the custom described in the Nuzu documents and the saga of Sarah and Abraham stops there.

The complete picture of the issues surrounding the birth of Ishmael is a broad and multi-faceted one, though there are points which illuminate the under-currents surrounding the plot of the narrative. The question of the right lineage is one such issue which betrays the fact that mothers were important, where heredity was concerned. However, if one remembers that the genealogy of the Patriarchal era was patrilineal, it becomes apparent that this area of female power would present a challenge for the narrator. Hence 'what is at stake here is an ideological problem. The Genesis narrators are wrestling with a potential complication, an underlying tension that exists because Israel's ancestry is traced ... also through its mothers. Their problem is to demonstrate that it is the male line of descent that determines Israel's identity, while at the same time affirming the importance of descent from the proper mother.'[12] The conception of Isaac is through Sarah, from whom, we are told, 'kings of peoples' will come (Gen. 17:16). The conception of the Arab world was through Hagar via Ishmael.[13] The racial issues surrounding the differing treatment of the two sons and their mothers carry on over generations. 'The Hebrews had many mixed marriages with Black African people and therefore most of the biblical people would have been quite black. Abraham fathered Black Ishmael.'[14] From the perspective of the patriarchal narrator, Ishmael was not the 'right' son from the 'right' mother[15] to be the founder of Israel because Abraham's first born son resulted from his union with the

11. Bird, 'Images of Women', p. 53.

12. Exum, *Fragmented Women*, p. 110.

13. John Van Setters, 'The Pentateuch', in M. Patrick Graham and Steven L. McKenzie (eds.), *The Hebrew Bible Today and An Introduction to Critical Issues* (Louisville, KY, USA: Westminster John Knox Press, 1998), p. 10.

14. 'Unless we understand the ethnicity of the biblical people, we continue to have a distorted view of the Bible and ourselves.' Barton urges white 'feminists to understand our vulnerability and work in solidarity with us to help rediscover this history. Unless the White feminists consciously reaffirm the non-white skin colour of the biblical people where writings continue to perpetuate the myth that the Bible is about White people.' Barton, *Op.cit.*, pp. 72–73.

15. Exum, *Fragmented Women*, pp. 122, 130.

Egyptian Hagar. Underlying this is the issue of tribalism because Abraham was not white but of Afro-Asiatic origin,[16] although the assumption has often been made that prominent biblical characters are white[17] and such tribalism in the texts may be related to racism in the contemporary world. Isaac the Hebrew, was the 'chosen son' of this narrative who would inherit God's covenant through his Hebrew father, Abraham, on an everlasting basis (Gen. 17:19, 21). By contrast, (Abraham is told that) Ishmael is to be blessed by God and become fruitful, that he will be the father of twelve rulers of a great nation; yet will never be the bearer of the covenant (v. 20). The racial hierarchy between Isaac and Ishmael is further evidenced in the text's depiction of Hagar's mixed-race son as a 'wild donkey of a man' (Gen. 16:12) who will 'live in hostility toward all his brothers' (Gen. 16:12). Ishmael's descendants were to live 'the life of the Bedouin, and they were people who would facilitate the enslaving of Joseph and become one of the neighbours/cousins with whom Israel had a love-hate relationship (cf. Judg. 8:24, Ps. 83:6).'[18] However, the future of the Hebrew Jacob, Isaac's son, is very different: he has his name changed to Israel by God and receives the promise of the land given to Abraham and Isaac as well as a nation and community of nations through his descendants (Gen. 35: 10–12).

The narrative contains fragmented pictures of how the constrictions of the patriarchal world that Hagar and Sarah existed within, distinguished between both gender and race, submerging the women's subjectivity in the process. The central female characters in this saga do not have the freedom to participate in the world in the ways that Abraham and his sons do. Isaac and his father approach the sacrifice without Sarah (Gen. 22). Ishmael, along with all the men in Abraham's household, participate in the all-male bonding ritual[19] of circumcision stipulated by God to be seen as a sign of His covenant with Abraham and Abraham's descendants

16. Barton, *Op.cit.*, p. 73.

17. This is readily evidenced by early and high Renaissance paintings, the Sistine Chapel ceiling being just one example. See H.W. Janson and Dora Jane Janson, *The Picture History of Painting From Cave Painting to Modern Times* (New York: Harry N. Abrams, Inc., 1957), pp. 109–58.

18. John Goldingay, *After Eating the Apricot Men and Women with God* (Carlisle, Cumbria: Solway, an imprint of Paternoster Publishers, 1996), p. 97.

19. See, Exum, *Fragmented Women*, pp. 124–26.

(Gen. 17:10–15, 23–27). Sarah receives an indirect promise of offspring through Abraham and God, but no mention of a covenant with Yahweh comes to Hagar. These women 'are "other" who are also "same", outsiders who are part of the family.'[20] Braidotti, in her book *Nomadic Subjects*, states that the category of other in relation to woman is still very much in existence and is a status which is rooted in assumptions which are enforced by the culture in which European contemporary women live, representing woman 'as being irrational, oversensitive, destined to be a wife and mother. Woman as body, sex, and sin. Woman as "other-than" Man.'[21]

The birth of Isaac displaces both Eliezer and Abraham's first born son, Ishmael (Gen. 21: 9–10). A comparison may be made between the Nuzu documents and the conventions portrayed in the Genesis texts we are looking at, in relation to the subject of the right direct heir. Genesis 15:3 describes Abraham's lament about his lack of direct heirs (to date); Eliezer of Damascus, the son of a servant in his household, would stand to inherit his estate because of the fact that Abraham had no children. Nuzu law recognized both direct and indirect heirs; the latter might be a slave, who was adopted. The indirect heir would have stood to lose his rights if a direct heir was born.[22]

The recurrent theme of the right direct heir places the three main figures of this narrative in a state of compromised-subjectivity, to varying degrees. Of the three central characters, it could be argued that Sarah should be remembered as the person who seems most deficient in a relationship with the divine in God and herself. Abraham plays the part of a witless pawn, though he has the rights which patriarchy grants him for being male and the vision which he gains through his relationship with the Lord. Hagar, though diminished in ways which will be detailed later, also has a relationship with God—the God which she names in Gen. 16:13 as 'the one who sees me'. In Gen. 16:12 the angel of the Lord speaks to Hagar, making her the first woman in the Hebrew Scriptures to receive an apparition[23] in the form of the angel of the Lord. This figure speaks to her, using her name, which neither Abraham nor

20. Exum, *Fragmented Women*, p. 110.

21. Rosi Braidotti, *Nomadic Subjects Embodiment and Sexual Difference in Contemporary Feminist Theory* (New York: Columbia University Press, 1994), p. 235.

22. Direct heirs were known as 'aplu' and indirect, as 'ewirru'.

23. Laffey, *Wives, Harlots and Concubines*, p. 38.

Sarah do. In the course of telling her to return to Sarah and 'submit to her' (Gen. 16:9), the angel directly gives a promise of an abundance of descendants to Hagar in verse 10. It is worth noting that in this respect Hagar receives equal treatment to that of the patriarchs. 'While all the patriarchs of Israel hear such words, Hagar is the only woman ever to receive them. And yet this promise to her lacks the covenant context that is so crucial to the founding fathers.'[24] This factor could have negatively affected Sarah's dealings with Hagar. She lacks the sort of intimacy with God that Hagar and Abraham have. Any information she is granted about God's wishes regarding her, comes to her indirectly (Gen. 17:15–20). By examining Sarah's role in the saga and re-visioning it, we gain a perspective from which to see Sarah's ability to endure her status of 'other'; by using the vehicle of her nomadic quality, we enhance the pursuit of our own subjectivity, the realization of which engenders an ability to see that we are not in exile if we choose to view the whole world as our country. 'To remember is not simply to call to mind or refuse to forget, it is to re-member, to reconstruct a life often broken and distorted by patriarchy for the purpose of releasing its power into our lives.'[25]

One of the consequences of the direct heir theme in Genesis, is the marginalization of the women in the narrative who suffered from this phenomenon in differing ways, as a result of the fact that they were living in a patriarchal society. Sarah dominated Hagar 'on an individual level as patriarchy does on a systemic level,'[26] and Hagar despised her mistress (Gen. 16:4). The quest of a direct heir for Abraham made rivals of Sarah and Hagar. In her treatment of Hagar,[27] Sarah was 'just as dangerous and disheartening as the system, perhaps even more so because of the common bond that is destroyed in the encounter—that of sisterhood.'[28] Their respective motivations were made manifest by the inherent nature of the sort

24. Phyllis Trible, *Texts of Terror Literary-Feminist Readings of Biblical Narratives* (London: SCM Press Ltd, 1992), p. 17.

25. Elizabeth Stuart, *Spitting at Dragons: Towards a Feminist Theology of Sainthood* (London & New York: Mowbray, 1996), p.101.

26. Megan McKenna, *Not Counting Women and Children: Neglected Stories from the Bible* (Kent: Burns & Oates, 1994), p. 186.

27. Gen. 16: 6.

28. McKenna, *Not Counting Women and Children.*

of lives which patriarchy ascribed for them. Hagar was an Egyptian slave[29], while Sarah was her mistress.

Their story continues to incite divided reactions from women, depending on education and economic stability.[30] There are those who can relate to Hagar's oppression: one woman, an 'illegal immigrant from El Salvador', cheered when told of Hagar's negative attitude towards her mistress, once pregnant[31] (Gen. 16:4). She 'said, in her halting English: "Oh, now Sarai gets a taste of her own medicine. Now she knows what it's like to be a slave and be treated like dirt all the time. Serves her right. She doesn't like it—well, we don't either. We don't live just to clean toilets, iron, and clean up after others and to be pushed around." '[32] McKenna states that 'Hagar is like many women who are refugees and immigrants and illegal aliens, barely tolerated or even persecuted and hunted down. She reminds us as well of their sisters, mothers, cousins, and friends, left behind and struggling alone to care for their families because of the death or disappearance of their husbands, brothers and children.'[33] It must not be forgotten that the 'realities of injustice, slavery, oppression, racism, and hatred are still common in the world.'[34]

Hagar, though dominated, was fertile and Sarah, though of privileged status, was sterile for many years. The behaviours which these two women had to adopt, due to their respective circumstances, displaced them both, therein pitting them against each other. 'Competition between two women for one man has thus been historically legitimated as having biblical foundations.'[35] The two female protagonists in this story were not allowed the sort of personal rights which engender feelings of mutuality. Their status of 'other'[36] dictated that they would have had a limited, and different sense of what would be termed by contemporary standards as their subjectivity. Women today have the option to explore their sense of self in ways which can engender mutuality,

29. See Trible, *Texts of Terror*, p. 13.
30. McKenna, *Not Counting Women and Children*, p. 175.
31. McKenna, *Not Counting Women and Children*, p. 175.
32. McKenna, *Not Counting Women and Children*, p. 175.
33. McKenna, *Not Counting Women and Children*, p. 181.
34. McKenna, *Not Counting Women and Children*, p. 181.
35. Laffey, *Wives, Harlots and Concubines*, p. 37.
36. See p. 72 this chapter, with regard to Braidotti.

such as seeing difference in ourselves and others as a positive and potentially bonding issue, rather than as puzzling and/or threatening. 'In her ethical defense of the politics of subjectivity, Cixous speaks of the ability to receive otherness as a new science, a new discourse based on the idea of respectful affinity between self and other. The passion is about belonging to a common matter: life ... it is the way in which self and other can be connected in her new worldview where all living matter is a sensitive web of mutually receptive entities.'[37]

Hagar and Sarah, living as they did under the jurisdictions of patriarchy, would perhaps, not have been receptive to a concept such as interconnectedness because their lives were so controlled. It is questionable whether they would have relinquished their constrictions, given the chance. Sarah was a woman with upper-middle class trappings, such as her servant Hagar, and might have found it difficult to live without them. However, if Sarah's image is re-visioned, she becomes contemporized through her generational quality. It therefore becomes arguable that she might have chosen not to have Isaac. Equally, in such a light, Hagar would have a choice regarding being a surrogate mother. By modern definitions, they were denied any real personal freedom externally and it seems logical that this would have had emotional, psychological and spiritual effects of a negative nature, in terms of their ability to create right relation.[38] It could be argued that Sarah humiliated and banished Hagar (Gen. 21:10) because of her immersion in and co-operation with patriarchy. Such a standpoint would have made the concept of 'the divine in all humans is the capacity to see interconnectedness as the way of being'[39] very foreign indeed. The issues surrounding the interlocking story of Hagar and Sarah are multi-stranded; it is impossible to separate these layers because they are interwoven with one another. Sarah's story gives us an insight into the social prejudice and gender separation under patriarchy.

If there were generations of Sarahs, the issue must be raised of her enduring image. In re-visioning Sarah as the nomadic, bandit-gypsy matriarch, we create a figure which is contemporary in it's nature and one that has stood the test of time.

37. Braidotti, *Nomadic Subjects*, p. 194.

38. Heyward, *Staying Power*.

39. Heyward, *Staying Power*.

Two texts which potentially lend further insight into the religious and political conditions in Syria-Palestine before the Israelite conquest and thus into the world which Sarah and Abraham inhabited, are the Tell el-Amarna tablets.[40] These tablets 'add to our information about the people called the Habiru.'[41] If it is true that Abraham was a ' "sojourner" (*ger*) in the midst of the established peoples of Canaan',[41] it is reasonable to say that he was accompanied by another sojourner—his wife; who was an outsider by the nature of her social positioning, determined by her gender as well as the tribe to which she belonged.[42] She was thus doubly categorized as a foreigner, which becomes ironic in the context of re-visioning her transient lifestyle and sterility. In this light, Sarah the nomad[43] becomes more akin to Daly's wild women, whose country is the whole world. She can not possibly exist outside her world because it is in her. This is re-visioning Sarah. Women 'must attempt to create a symbolic world adequately suited to their perception of reality. This emphasis on women's corpor(e)ality amounts to revalorizing the bodily roots of all subjectivity, although it acquires a sharper edge in feminist politics. It results in the formulation of a new body-politic, that is the stake of specific struggles (contraceptive and abortion rights, campaigns against sexual violence and rape, and so on).'[44]

The Tell el-Amarna tablets describe the Habiru as bandits ... Hardly surprisingly, the name Habiru came to be used generally of enemies or rebels and certainly they spent much of their early history in nomadic wanderings. They were like modern gypsies or migrant workers, many of them moved from place to place with

40. The tablets contain 378 known texts and date in the region of 1400–1360 BCE.

41. Syria-Palestine's earliest name was Canaan. From as early as 3000 BCE, it was populated by immigrants who became highly civilized and was the 'Promised Land of the Patriarchs (Gen. 15: 18, 19). See, Enid B. Mellor, 'The Literatures of the Ancient Near East', in Enid B. Mellor (ed.), *The Cambridge Bible Commentary: The Making of the Old Testament* (London: Cambridge University Press, 1972), p. 23.

42. Abraham is the first person in the Bible to be referred to as Hebrew. (Gen. 14: 13). See, Wright, *Biblical Archaeology*, p. 42.

43. 'The Patriarchal "Hebrews" of the [Hebrew Scriptures] came from the nomadic or semi-nomadic peoples who occupied Northern Mesopotamia before and after 2000 B.C.', Wright, *Biblical Archaeology*, pp. 42, 43.

44. Rosi Braidotti, *Patterns of Dissonance: A Study of Women in Contemporary Philosophy* (Cambridge: Polity Press in Association with Basil Blackwell, 1991), p. 264.

their families and possessions. It is possible to interpret Sarah as having lived the life of a gypsy-bandit; in this light she is both outsider and insider: she who lives within but is forever 'other'.[45] It is questionable whether, like the modern gypsy, Sarah would have experienced social stigmatisation because of her nomadic ways. Contemporary western society 'tolerates' the existence of travellers through the provision of trailer parks, but keeps these parks tucked away from the public.[46] Like the modern Gypsy, Sarah would have been a product of many generations of racially mixed marriage. If parallels can be drawn between the tablets and Sarah's tribal/racial group, and there is question regarding this aspect of her person in relation to the tablets,[47] then parallels can likewise be seen between the time-period in which the text is set and modern society. 'More recently, white women within feminist and Christian feminist circles continue to speak as though theirs is the universal experience. In doing so, they betray their persistent belief in their superiority and sovereignty over women of other races. The truth is, very few black women manage to make it through adulthood without a footlocker of hurtful memories of encounters with white women.'[48] The word 'nigger' is a term which will be familiar to the contemporary reader as a term which originated as an expression of racial abuse and has in recent years been 'taken back', primarily through the civil rights movement[49] and latterly, in the musical movement of Hip-Hop, to demarcate a particular sub-group within the culture. 'Hebrew' was

45. Although scholars formerly thought that there was a close connection between the Habiru and the Hebrews, it is now thought that the connection is indirect. Recent evidence has promoted this shift in opinion. Wright, *Biblical Archaeology*. Please note that there is a discrepancy in spelling of the word 'Apiru'/'Habiru' between Mellor and Wright, respectively.

46. One such 'park' was opened recently in the rear area of Saltram House's grounds—near the dump—in Plymouth. In Camden and Hackney, in London I remember such 'parks' being placed under railway arches. Wood-Green Council in London made a statement towards the celebration of diversity by choosing to allow local gypsies to set up camp in a central part of the area, next to a children's playground.

47. 'Perhaps the most that can be said is that the [Hebrew Scripture] Hebrews belonged to the widespread group for long known in general terms as the Habiru, but that there is no reason to identify them with any specific people mentioned in the Tell el-Amarna or other Near Eastern texts.' Mellor, 'The Literatures of the Ancient Near East', pp. 24, 25.

48. Renita J. Weems, *Just A Sister Away: A Womanist Vision of Women's Relationships in the Bible* (San Diego, CA: LuraMedia, 1988), p. 8.

49. See, *Black Theology and Black Power* (London, Mowbray, 1976).

a somewhat similar term,[50] and occurs thirty-four times in relation to Israelites of the Hebrew Scriptures.[51] Sarah the Hebrew can hence be re-visioned as a gypsy-bandit matriarch. The connotations of such a figure are very different from those of the traditional image of Sarah, sterile wife of Abraham.

Hagar and Sarah

It is apparent that the conception and protection of her family were crucial elements in Sarah's life, though the repercussions of these affairs are largely negative in nature. Sarah lashes out when she sees Ishmael playing with Isaac (Gen. 21:9, 10). She states that she does not want Ishmael to share in Isaac's inheritance, telling Abraham to banish both Ishmael and his mother, Hagar. She refers to Hagar not by name, but as 'that slave woman' (Gen. 21:10). Sarah's abuse of Hagar has, justifiably, been highly criticized by womanist writers.[52] Certainly the issue of racism is obvious in Hagar's story; her social standing and according treatment[53] make it so. The figure of Hagar speaks of the oppressed woman who ultimately finds her way towards freedom. As such she warrants consideration from a feminist 'perspective, which views her as a paradigm of the oppressed woman who has the courage to seek freedom (an odd

50. The term Hebrew may have been 'originally used as an abusive nickname, and was then explained and rationalized in the [Hebrew Scriptures] as coming from Eber, the ancestor of the race (Gen. 10: 24, 11: 14), whose name, from *abar* 'to cross over', is interpreted as 'him from beyond' (the River – that is, the Euphrates.)' Mellor, 'The Literatures of the Ancient Near East', p. 24.

51. Mellor, 'The Literatures of the Ancient Near East'. When the word 'Hebrew' is applied to Israelites in the Hebrew Scriptures, it is usually employed in one of the three following circumstances: '(1) when an Egyptian speaks to an Israelite, (2) when an Israelite identifies himself to an Egyptian, or (3) when the Israelites as a group are named along with some other people or group. An Israelite speaking to one of his own group would not use the term, but in speaking to an Egyptian, he would.' Wright, *Biblical Archaeology*, p. 42.

52. See Renita Weems, 'A Mistress, A Maid and No Mercy' in *idem*, Just a Sister Away: A Womanist Vision of Women's Relationships in the Bible (San Francisco: Lura Media, 1988), pp. 1–19 and Megan McKenna, *Not Counting Women and Children*, pp. 174–89.

53. Weems points out that 'the story of Hagar and Sarai is about more than ethnic prejudice ... In the first place, owning slaves was not unique to the ancient Hebrews ... In the second place, the story of Hagar and Sarai is about the economic stratification of women as much as it is about the ethnic discrimination of one woman against another.' Weems, 'A Mistress, A Maid and No Mercy', p. 9.

reversal of the Exodus paradigm, for here an Egyptian flees oppression by Israel). She becomes the mother of a great nation characterized by its refusal to be submissive.'[54]

Genesis depicts Hagar as a woman who is trapped and abused by patriarchy. She is ordered into submission by both deity and human alike (Gen. 16:9, 21:14). Yet Hagar is a substantial character in the saga. Goldingay proclaims her as 'scripture's first theologian. She theologizes and worships as a woman in pain and sets a pattern for us to follow ... Pain (and specifically women's pain, and perhaps even more specifically the pain of women from the margins) is not an inhibition or an irrelevance to theology or worship. It is their seed.'[55] Trible also, recognizes Hagar as a theologian. She sees Hagar's act of naming the God who talks to her, as uniting 'the diving and human encounter: the God who sees and the God who is seen.'[56] This is referring to Gen. 16:7–15, where Hagar has a conversation with God by a spring in the desert. Trible compares Hagar's exodus with that of the Israelites and draws attention to the fact that unlike Moses, Hagar did not need to call out to God for water.[57] Instead, the Lord's angel found Hagar before he spoke to her (Gen. 16:7–8). These elements form a picture of Hagar which contrasts starkly with the image conjured by the title 'slave woman' which Sarah uses to describe her (Gen. 21:10).

Hagar's story tells a tale of exploitation at the hands of a 'privileged woman'.[58] Sarah's vengeful jealousy of Hagar was reprehensible. It could be argued that Sarah's underlying motivation for her treatment of Hagar was provoked by the marginal positions which patriarchy posited on Sarah and her maidservant made slave,[59] Hagar. 'Both Sarah and Hagar are victims of a patriarchal society that stresses the importance of sons and of a narrative structure that revolves around the promise of a son. Sadly, but not surprisingly in such a context, they make victims of each other.'[60]

54. J. Cheryl Exum, ' "Mother in Israel": A Familiar Story Reconsidered', in Letty M. Russell (ed.), *Feminist Interpretation of the Bible* (Oxford: Basil Blackwell Ltd., 1985), p.77.

55. Goldingay, *After Eating the Apricot*, p. 96.

56. Trible, *Texts of Terror*, p. 18.

57. Trible, *Texts of Terror*, p. 14.

58. Exum, '"Mother in Israel"', p. 77.

59. Trible, *Texts of Terror*, p. 21.

60. Exum, '"Mother in Israel"', p. 77

Patriarchy is guilty of having divided these two women of differing races. 'The hierarchical tree of patriarchy puts men above women, but that is not its only piece of prioritizing ... it has further gradations such as free human being above slave, white above black, employer above employee, landowner above peasant.'[61] In the context of the Genesis texts which concern Hagar and Sarah, it is Sarah the mistress who maintains a superior position in terms of her race, class and marriage. She is a product of patriarchy, unfortunately, and abuses Hagar (Gen. 16:6). Hagar retaliates by running away, with the child fathered by Abraham in her womb (Gen. 16:4–8). There is no mention of physical aggression on Hagar's part, which may well be because of fear of suffering further violence at her mistress' hands. Modern forms of patriarchy still divide women into higher and lower classes according to race and income. It therefore keeps women apart and thus ensures that any potential for female unification is kept severely limited. Exum reminds us that women of 'lower status (Hagar ...) are exploited for the sake of higher class women, which is really for the sake of patriarchy. Patriarchy relies upon women's cooperation, and one of its rewards for cooperation is status.'[62]

Hagar and Sarah were initially placed in a position of social rivalry by the very nature of their unequal power relationship centuries ago but such power relationships continue to exist in the modern Western world. 'None of us is safe from the ravages of a society which makes room for only a chosen few and keeps at bay the vast majority. For those of us who are educated and employed, there is always the potential to be a Sarai; and, lamentably, there are far too many opportunities in a capitalist society for her to surface. Yet most of us are just a paycheck away from Hagar.'[63] If contemporary women are to avoid creating similarly damaging scenarios, they must be aware of two crucial elements: themselves, and where they fit into their worlds. Women have the capacity for realizing that 'nomadic becoming is neither reproduction nor just imitation, but rather emphatic proximity, intensive interconnectedness.'[54] The dictates of patriarchy need not stop us from re-visioning the story of Sarah and Hagar in a way that enhances this capacity. The goal

61. Goldingay, *After Eating the Apricot*, p. 84.

62. Exum, *Fragmented Women*, p. 122.

63. Weems, 'A Mistress, A Maid and No Mercy', p. 11.

64. Braidotti, *Nomadic Subjects*, p. 5.

of this re-visioning is the recognition of the value of our diverse selves in the context of our diverse worlds.

Hagar and Sarah were further set apart by the power issues surrounding the birth of their respective children. Gen. 16:4 cites Hagar as despising her mistress once she was pregnant. Sarah's reaction to this was to 'mistreat' her (Gen. 16:6). 'We know only too well the kinds of violence the Egyptian woman must have been forced to endure: beatings, verbal insults, ridicule, strenuous work, degrading tasks and the like.'[65] For Sarah to have vented her wrath on Hagar in such a fashion, can not be excused; it can however be understood, in the context of Sarah's compromised subjectivity. By this point in the Genesis narrative, Sarah had already been forced to become part of the Pharaoh's harem and had suffered another abduction before she banished Hagar.[66] Although she is said to have been spared any sexual transgression on this occasion, I would imagine that she would have suffered some emotional repercussions. In view of the social systems under which Sarah lived, it is conceivable that she never got a chance to examine the ramifications of these experiences.

What Sarah suffered would be known in the contemporary Western society as an abuse of her person; though like many women who suffer abuse today, she did not have the freedom to declare the wrongs committed against her.[67] As women who's country is the world, we need to realize that we have the ability to know the presence of God 'here and now and the ability to bring about the resurrection. Feminist theology invites us to tell the truth and reminds us that unless we tell our stories we do not learn to value our struggles, celebrate our strengths, comprehend our pain. Without stories we cannot understand ourselves.'

When Sarah banishes Hagar, she commits an act which has the potential to shatter two lives. Sarah and Hagar were caught up in the web of patriarchy which placed them in the situations of opposition, which reaped violent repercussions in both of their lives (Gen. 16 and 21). This web was not one from which they could escape easily; indeed, it was woven well enough to sustain it to the

65. Weems, 'A Mistress, A Maid and No Mercy', p.6.

66. Gen. 20 and 21:8–21, respectively.

67. Sara Tommasi-Rogers, *Journeys Out of the Victim Role: A Feminist Theologian's Personal Reflections on Male Violence* (Plymouth: College of Saint Mark and Saint John, 2000), pp. 18, 19 and 21.

present day. 'Men's wars are most often fought on battlefields with foreign enemies for control of lands and resources; women's wars are fought in their homes with other women, for "control over" the men who are their husbands and the males who will become their sons. The stage is here set for far too much of the history of the last two millennia.'[68] One cannot leave the tale of these two women in Genesis' patriarchal setting; division of women continues to exist, rendering us women unable to achieve justice through unity.[69] The established legal and religious systems controlled Hagar and Sarah's options resulting in each woman leading a life potted with periods of loss. In the course of their movements away from each other, they lost any hope for relation with each other. Instead, the two women were kept occupied by being what can be interpreted as womb-vessels, for both Abraham and the God who selects him as keeper of the covenant.

It is possible, that underlying the banishment of Hagar, in the stated protection of the inheritance of her child (Gen. 21:10), exists Sarah's attempt to protect herself; through maintaining her unique power-base as mother of Abraham's direct heir. While up to this point Sarah's life has been painted as economically difficult, it is noted in Genesis that Abraham was wealthy and had quite an amount of livestock as well as a number of tents (Gen.13: 2, 18). He had also been given a thousand shekels of silver along with more livestock by Abimelech, after Sarah's abduction in Gerar (Gen. 14–

68. Laffey, *Wives, Harlots and Concubines*, p. 37.

69. In my twenty years of working in technical theatre, television and offices, I have seen women vie for position in a variety of gruesome ways: I've worked alongside cliché cases of sleeping with one's boss (a particular young producer did so during her honeymoon and became the series producer in the next series. Her boss was married). I have experienced the stab in the back many times myself and admit to being guilty of having done the same on occasion. Competition among us is fierce because we don't get as many opportunities for advancement as our male colleagues. If we do get to a desired work position, pregnancy and child-rearing present us with another set of hurdles to jump: either we leave our children to be cared for by others, which can be very difficult; or we climb off the ladder knowing that there is a slim chance of getting back where we were when the children are older. A well-known presenter that I worked for quit a television series because her absences from home had left her child with behavioural problems. I witnessed the process of her decision-making and what it cost her. In the three years since making that decision, this intelligent journalist has done a couple of radio shows and a short day-time cable-television series. This woman is no longer a household name and I know how much she enjoyed her work.

16). If Sarah's son inherited his father's wealth, she too, would be able to maintain her standard of living because under the laws of patriarchy, her son would have been responsible for taking care of her.[70] By attempting to safe-guard her male off-spring's birth-rights, Sarah let on just how concerned she was about her own security.[71] In this light, Sarah the bandit-gypsy matriarch becomes little different in terms of her motivation, from the average upper middle class white woman, driven to protect her own consumerist lifestyle, at the expense of others in the world. Both women can be accused of greedily turning a blind eye, to the needs of those who inhabit the space we all live in.

70. Please see note 170 about widows.

80. This theory would not be substantiated by certain laws in the Pentateuch; one of the primary functions of 'Israelite law is to assure the ... stability and economic viability of the family as the basic unit of society. In this legislation, however, the interests of the family are commonly identified with those of its male head ... Only in rare cases, however, are the laws concerned with the rights of dependents (Exod. 21: 26–27; Deut. 21: 10–14, 15–17 and 22: 13–21). Bird, 'Images of Women', p. 51. Deut. 21: 15–17 concerns the respective inheritance rights of two sons by a man's two wives. It states that the rights of the first-born son of the unloved wife should receive a 'double share of all he has. That son is the first sign of his father's strength. The right of the first-born belongs to him.' (Deut. 21:17) In Sarah's case, Ishmael would reasonably fit into the category of the first-born son of the unloved wife. From a feminist perspective, it is obvious that the said law is 'designed to protect the male and, only secondarily, his mother.' Laffey, *Wives, Harlots and Concubines*, p. 37. This law would however, lend further motivation for Sarah's protection of her son's inheritance rights.

Chapter 6

Huldah's Scroll: A Pagan Reading

Graham Harvey

It is hard to know where a story begins, any story. Huldah's story is entangled with the story of kings, priests, prophets, prostitutes, builders and decorators, city planners, musicians, and many others. It is also entangled with national and international politics and conflicts, religious and cultural upheavals and reformations, coups, exiles, constitutions, genealogies, and more. It is a small part of the story of Josiah, king of Judah, presented in 2 Kgs 22–23 and 2 Chron. 34–35. Not only are these two versions of the story of Josiah and Huldah different in significant respects but, even when read together, they do not tell us what we need to know—let alone what we want to know. Authoritative interpreters of the story seem emboldened not only by these gaps and differences but also by their own commitments and predilections to twist the story to make it suit their own traditions and interests.

My own reading will be a pagan reading. It is informed by having walked the hills and valleys Huldah walked and having participated in an archaeological excavation in tombs of her time (in which a silver scroll containing the earliest extant fragment of what became the Bible, a version of the Priestly Blessing of Num. 6:24–26, was found). In realizing that to do these things is to walk the contours of Mother Earth and encounter the ancestors (not necessarily with proper respect), I have eventually chosen to offer incense to 'other deities'. Even more recently I have realized that the God of Israel (the unspeakable YHWH) is also a pagan God. My reading begins by considering what the texts say and omit to say. Later I will argue that the entwined story of Huldah and Josiah is about the tension between a localizing paganism and an emerging universalism in Israel's religion.

Whose Story, What Story?

Huldah's story almost seems to interrupt the Bible's narrative of an ancient men's movement. Huldah speaks words of condemnation and comfort to a king and his courtiers and then disappears from the text. She does not change the tone of the story by 'feminising' or softening it. The story regains its focus on men and their monumental and fateful deeds. But Huldah's mere presence as a woman is surprising.

She might have disappeared altogether if it was not for the fact that her story is a small part of what became a scripture, every word of which has been endlessly debated and contemplated. However, even in Jewish and Christian commentaries, Huldah's story is rarely elaborated upon in any detail. More often the tangles are smoothed over and attention is diverted elsewhere. Even when the problematic positions, relationships and roles of women within Jewish and Christian communities are debated, Huldah has played only a marginal role in support of one polemic or another. The text itself does not seem to have a problem introducing her in ways that seem unacceptable to those who pretend to be simply reading what's there. She is, for example, a prophetess. This is presented as a fact, equivalent to the naming of Isaiah as a prophet (2 Kgs 19:2). It seems legitimate to suppose that the story-teller means us to understand that Huldah being a prophetess was just like Isaiah being a prophet. But such plain reading is likely to thwart the axe-grinding of many commentators who cannot allow women to be or act like men. Unlike others, I am free to allow the text to assert what it wants about Huldah and her prophecy because it is obvious that the Huldah of the text (the only Huldah there is, maybe the only Huldah that there ever was) would oppose my veneration of the horses of the sun and the flowering pillars of the Goddess. If I cannot co-opt Huldah I can, at least, try to understand her story.

Nearby Women

One indication of how remarkable Huldah is in the Bible (as well as in the religions that build on it) is provided by the poverty of space allocated to the women mentioned before and after her: royal wives and temple weavers.

In the lead up to the events that bring Huldah to centre stage, albeit briefly, we are introduced to King Josiah's mother and grandmother: Jedidah and Adaiah of Bozkath. No more is said about them, here or elsewhere. We can assume, of course, that Jedidah was the wife—or a wife—of Amon, previous King of Judah, recently murdered by his servants for unspecified reasons. Later, when we are told about Josiah's successor, Jehoahaz, we will learn that his mother was Hamutal, daughter of Jeremiah of Libnah. After Pharaoh Neco exiled and imprisoned Jehoahaz, another son of Josiah was enthroned in Jerusalem (by the same Pharaoh). But this son, whose name had been Eliakim until Pharaoh renamed him Jehoiakim, was not the son of Hamutal, but of Zebudah, daughter of Pedaiah of Rumah. After a reign of eleven years, Jehoiakim was succeeded briefly by Jehoiachin whose mother was Nehushta, daughter of Elnathan of Jerusalem. When the Babylonians defeated Judah, they exiled Jehoiachin and placed his uncle, Mattaniah, son of Josiah and Hamutal, on Judah's throne, renaming him Zedekiah. Even these small details of a few women's lives were deemed irrelevant by those who retold the story in 2 Chronicles—which is fairly consistent in its disinterest in women. Another story-teller might have told us, for example, whether Hamutal survived her husband by long, perhaps seeing two sons exiled and grandsons killed. However, it must be significant that while even royal women are marginal or dispensable characters in the story of men, Huldah could not be ignored. Indeed, her importance in Josiah's story is magnified.

The next women mentioned after Huldah in 2 Kings are the women who wove something (banners, hangings or curtains perhaps) for the Asherah in the houses of the male cult prostitutes, *haqdeshim*, within the House of YHWH (2 Kgs 23:7). Like almost everything else in these pages, we are left guessing. How big were these houses? How big were these weavings? How exactly did male cult prostitution proceed while women wove in these houses? How did the weaving proceed while the prostitutes prostituted themselves? If prostitution did take place in the temple precincts, were there any purity rules like those the Bible imposes on priests who wished to serve God? Where were the weavings going to be displayed? What role did prostitution play in the cult? What were the hangings like? Were these communal or individual houses, prostitutes and weavers? Was it really 'the Asherah' or simply 'Asherah' for which or for whom the weaving was being done? And this is not to pretend that we can be completely certain what 'the Asherah' or 'Asherim' meant, or what Asherah's precise relationship to the other deities mentioned (including YHWH, Baal, the sun, and 'all the host of heaven' or 'the skies') was. The version of Chronicles may have been wise not even to hint that any of this was going on. But was this because Chronicles did not want to encourage anyone to contemplate prostitution and weaving for (the) Asherah or because these practices had ceased and would have confused readers even in ancient times? We can never know.

The fact that these texts leave us (if not their ancient hearers and/or readers) with so many questions is precisely my point. On the one hand, the narrative of Josiah does not intend to tell us anything much about women. It does not even include the women condemned by Jeremiah (possibly a relative of Huldah's) for 'baking cakes for the Queen of Heaven'. On the other hand, what it does tell us is that Huldah could not be ignored.

It is true, of course, that these texts do not tell us everything we might want to ask about anything. They do not, for example, tell us why those who assassinated Josiah's father, Amon, did so, nor why they did not kill the entire family, nor how Amon's wife, Jedidah, responded to the murder. Although the biblical authors condemn Amon's wickedness 'in the eyes of YHWH', we might presume that the lynch mob of the mass of the people (i.e. those who killed the murderous servants and seem to have buried Amon with respect) would have assessed him or the situation differently. We may also presume that 'all the people of land' did not place Josiah on the royal throne at the age of eight to be any different from his father. Maybe the populace merely wanted to maintain a royal family from the line of David, no matter how wicked or how young. The texts assure us, somewhat unhelpfully, that everything (else) of importance is recorded in the Records of the Chronicles of the Kings of Judah. We are sorely provoked to fill in the gaps by drawing from the deep wells of our own preconceptions and imaginations.

Prophets, Priests and Scrolls

Huldah's story as told in both Kings and Chronicles hardly belongs to her. It is a brief episode in the story of Josiah and his reign, but one that erupts into it with considerable force. It is Huldah, not Jeremiah or Zephaniah (another contemporary), to whom the king's officials turn when sent to 'enquire of YHWH' about a scroll found by workers repairing God's House. It is she who condemns the people of Judah and comforts their king in the name of the God of Israel. By doing so she joins the company of six other women prophets mentioned in the Bible: Sarah, Miriam, Devorah, Hannah, Abigail and Esther. While these prophetesses are listed by Rabbinic authorities, no ceremony has paid them much attention or awarded them much honour until recently. Now, some Jewish women have been polite enough to invite the seven prophetesses to participate in their Sukkot celebrations along with the seven male 'guests' (*ushpikin*), who are traditionally invited into the *sukkot* (temporary dwellings) for the festival. Along with Abraham, Isaac, Jacob, Moses, Aaron, Joseph and David, the seven prophetesses can also be honoured as guests (*ushpikot*)—and what is offered to them is passed on to the poor. There is something apt about the timing of this more inclusive invitation to multi-generational, trans-epochal festivity: *Sukkot* was when the Jerusalem temple was dedicated and later rededicated, and it includes *Simhat Torah*, the celebration of the gift and receipt of the Torah. If the other six prophetesses contributed to the piety and survival of the people, Huldah had something to do with their response to the Torah.

But what exactly did she do? The plain text of the biblical narrative says that Josiah sent his officials to 'ask of YHWH for me, and for the people, and for all Judah, concerning the words of this scroll that has been found'. According to Chronicles his interest was even wider, including 'all who are left in Israel', i.e. the remnant of the destroyed Northern Kingdom. Some commentators have claimed that Huldah was asked to confirm that this scroll was in fact the Torah or some part of it. This would be an acceptable reading if the story had only told us that the king's secretary, Shaphan said, 'Hilkiah the priest has given me a scroll'. Just a scroll, any old scroll? But Hilkiah, the 'high priest', not just any old priest, had already told Shaphan, 'I have found the scroll of the law in the House of YHWH'. He might even have said 'the Torah scroll'. And Josiah had no hesitation in responding religiously when the scroll was read to him: he tore his clothes in an immediate show of repentance. Clearly, he was not wondering whether this was really divine revelation or whether it might be a forgery. Neither does Josiah ask, 'oops, did someone lose a Torah scroll?' or 'ought we to be obeying these rules too?'. His response demonstrates his agreement with Hilkiah: this is God's Torah. He has no need to ask for confirmation that this scroll can also be called 'the scroll of the covenant' (2 Kgs 23:2). Anyway, if he had entertained such doubts, presumably Hilkiah and the others could have decided that—after all, Josiah was already trusting them to reform and purify the House of God, and they knew he was already 'walking in the ways of David' not of the wicked Manasseh. This case is made even more strongly in Chronicles where the rebuilding of God's House followed rather than initiated Josiah's widespread and aggressive purge of many non-Davidic, non-YHWH-istic practices and locations.

It is hard to guess (even though that is probably all that commentators can do) what part of the Torah had been found—if it was not the whole thing. Once we follow the text's clarity that Josiah already knew this was God's Torah we are freed from speculation about whether the scroll was an artefact produced by conspirators trying to direct Josiah's reform in a particular direction. Huldah gives no support to the claim that Deuteronomy (the interests of which seems close to the conduct of the reform) was newly produced for the occasion. This is not to make a claim for the historical veracity of either the biblical narrative or the historical-critical theory. Rather, it is to assert that once we radically emend or abandon the plain text we can only be left in the extremity of Cartesian doubt, unable to trust anything our senses or our neighbours tell us. I find it more interesting to ponder what the text says and to try to make sense of it as a fascinating piece of propaganda. What intrigues me is to find out what exactly the text's polemic wants me to accept. While I am not promising to be persuaded, I am intrigued.

However, if the text does not require us to think of a newly written scroll, it may still be helpful to think it might have been Deuteronomy as many commentators, including the authoritative medieval Rabbi Rashi, have said. It is possible that Shaphan read Josiah the curses and blessings from the end of Deuteronomy. Perhaps it was Deut. 28:36 and its surrounding verses that particularly upset the king by threatening Israel's kings with being forced to lead the people into the horror and shame of exile and servitude to 'other deities of wood and stone'. These final chapters and these frightening verses might explain Josiah's immediate response, and they fit with Huldah's prophecy that YHWH, God of Israel, will bring 'evil upon this place and its inhabitants, in accordance with the words of the scroll which the King of Judah has read'. However, the focus of what Josiah went on to do, his reforms and his organisation of a massive celebration of Passover, and his statement that 'our fathers have not obeyed the words of this scroll', require him to have heard or read more than the curses. So, although we cannot be sure, it is likely that the scroll, or the part of it read to Josiah, must have included both instructions and warnings.

There is also considerable uncertainty about the actual finding of the scroll. It is, for instance, not really clear that the scroll was lost before it was delivered to the king's messenger or messengers (Kings and Chronicles do not agree on whether Shaphan was accompanied or not). The whole event is mysterious. As part of the king's reform, the repair of the temple had already been initiated. The king's official(s) go to YHWH's House either to tell Hilkiah, the high priest, to gather money previously given to the threshold-guarding Levites and give it to the foremen responsible for workers repairing YHWH's House, or to deliver the money themselves directly to the foremen. Either way, the money is then given to the workers to buy timber and quarried stone to repair the extensive damage and neglect of the House—even roof beams and binders were missing according to Chronicles. Chronicles also provides the information that the Levite foremen or overseers were skilled musicians, but whether this means they entertained the workers or were more cultured than the 'bearers of burdens' is hard to say. Was the job of repairing the temple made pleasant by expert musicians or made irritating by decadent artistes? All this is dealt with at some length before Hilkiah says, 'I have found the Torah scroll in YHWH's House'. Or maybe (as Chronicles says) it was while an unspecified group were bringing out the relevant money that Hilkiah found the scroll and then announced it in a short sentence that does not suggest any accompanying fanfare. The narrative may suggest that the scroll had been lost or that it had simply been stored in the temple.

There is enough confusion here to confound any interpreter and throw them back on their imagination. The confusion is somewhat disguised by the brevity and confidence with which the story is told, but it defies attempts to untangle the threads. However, it seems legitimate to conclude that a scroll that had previously been stored or forgotten in the temple was delivered, somewhat fortuitously but without much fuss, to Josiah. Having listened to a reading of at least parts of the Torah, the reforming king is deeply moved and worried, presumably believing in a God who might view the reforms as too little, too late. A delegation is then sent to Huldah the prophetess to find out what God would do next.

Huldah's Prophecy and Josiah's Death

It seems safest to read Huldah's entry into Josiah's tale as a prophetic announcement of what YHWH's response to Judah's wickedness and Josiah's reform would be. She asserts, quite briefly, that YHWH, God of Israel, feels aggrieved at having been abandoned, vexed at the handiwork of the people in making offerings to other deities, and determined to bring disaster on Jerusalem and its inhabitants in accordance with what the Torah scroll decrees. Israel's God obviously has no intention of being turned from carrying out his threat, no matter how popular or successful the reform movement might be. However, at a little more length (three long verses rather than two short ones), Huldah speaks for God to the king. The Rabbis thought that Huldah began somewhat abruptly, 'Tell the man who sent you to me', and called her proud for not saying 'tell the king'. But the rabbis do not retract their words when Huldah begins the second, personal part of her prophecy 'tell the king'. She tells Josiah that because he had been sorry at what was predicted, and had torn his clothes and wept, God would allow him to die in peace before the disaster struck.

The actual phrase Huldah's prophecy includes is 'I will gather you to your fathers and you will be laid in your tomb in peace'. To be 'gathered to one's fathers' is probably to be interpreted in the light of local burial traditions at the time. A group of tombs just over a valley from the Quarter where Huldah lived provided for a two stage burial process. Soon after death, a body would be lain out on a bed like platform, with the head resting in a cupped hollow. Lines of six or more of these first resting places have been excavated. Later, after the body has decayed, or when all the platforms were full and another corpse needed to be placed there, the dead and their grave goods were collected up and placed in a larger, rock-hewn chamber below the resting platforms. It is possible that the 'fathers' one was 'gathered to' were already in the secondary burial chamber or that in some tombs the chief patriarch remained in an elevated position while his descendants moved via platforms into the more permanent, communal chamber. Being 'gathered to one's fathers' may also refer to the movement of the deceased out of the city or village into dedicated burial areas, mortuary suburbs or ancestor communities. (This is useful to archaeologists who can tell the size of settlements by the position of tombs that ringed them in particular periods.) An exception was made in the case of Jerusalem's kings: they could be buried within the city. It is unlikely that the story suggests anything metaphysical about being 'gathered to one's father'. That is, we should not imagine that after Josiah's death he met any of his ancestors to discuss the relative merits of righteousness or wickedness. The two phrases 'gather you to your fathers' and 'you will be laid to rest' are probably synonymous references to death and burial.

If this seems to belabour the obvious point that Josiah was told he would die, it requires discussion of the words, 'in peace'. Josiah's story includes his death—but it is not at all a peaceful one. The fact that his body was brought back to Jerusalem for burial is the key. That and the fact that his son's succession is narrated before the divine punishment falls. 'In peace' must mean 'before the disaster'. If Josiah had thought that YHWH was telling him that he would die in peace, he might have become somewhat too relaxed about danger in later life. Somewhat foolishly, he decided to take his chariot to battle against Pharaoh Neco at Megiddo. There was no need for this: it is obvious that the Egyptian army was not marching on Judah but had already passed it by on the international highway that led northwards to where the other superpower of the time had its powerbase. The story strongly suggests, in fact, that Neco was trying to gain some ground by attacking the old enemy Assyria before the rising northern power, Babylon, became too powerful. Josiah's skirmish would have been an irritant and a delay. Huldah's prophecy says nothing about this, perhaps the story teller did not imagine this fight as a divinely inspired one but as a bit of folly that hardly affected the larger divine plan: the Babylonian destruction of Judah. Josiah's death and burial were 'in peace' because this conflict was of no interest to God, especially in comparison to what was coming soon.

Josiah was killed and then buried in Jerusalem before the real disasters destroy his city and his state. Huldah's two-part prophecy—to the nation and to the king—are fulfilled in two stages: Josiah is buried 'in peace' and then the Egyptians and the Babylonians destroy Judah. Finally the House of YHWH and Jerusalem's houses are burnt down, the royal line of David and their people are killed, exiled or impoverished and the books of Kings and Chronicles end.

The important thing, however, is not that the prophecy or the words of the Torah scroll are fulfilled—that was never in doubt. The message of the story is that Josiah and the people responded appropriately. Huldah incited Josiah to further his reforms and to vigorously persuade the nation to participate fully. Massive destruction of 'strange' practices and places occurred, and Jerusalem and Judah—and, according to Chronicles, large swathes of what had been the Kingdom of Israel—were turned to practices that were acceptable to YHWH. Unfortunately, previous generations' wickedness meant that the fulfilment of the Torah's curses remained inevitable.

Who was Huldah?

One question remains in this attempt to understand Huldah's story: who was she? Kgs 22:14 tells us that she was a 'prophetess, wife of Shallum son of Tikvah son of Harhas, keeper of the wardrobe, and she lived in Jerusalem in the Mishneh'. That should be clear enough. But none of it is.

Some interpreters don't like the idea that she was a prophetess in her own right, they insist she gained the title because her husband was a prophet. Some insist she must have instructed only the women of Jerusalem, and that the king's men went to her only because Jeremiah (a real/male prophet) was away. Others claim that Huldah was expected to be more compassionate than Jeremiah. The evidence of the book of Jeremiah is that he liked Josiah and would have been compassionate too—if that is really what Huldah's prophesy was! Other interpreters have imagined that Huldah was actually a prophetess of Asherah, wife of YHWH, who would helpfully mediate with her aggrieved husband. But once we make any of these alterations or additions to the story we may as well go all the way and change everything else too. In particular, adding any hint of respect for Asherah at this stage in the story would make a nonsense of everything else that happens. The idea that YHWH could not be compassionate is as sexist as the notion that Goddesses and women are, essentially, 'nice'. The plain reading of Huldah's tale is that she was a prophetess of YHWH and that there was no hesitation in going to her. Just as the Garden of Eden narrative never says that Adam had left Eve alone when the serpent tempted her, so Huldah's story says nothing about the presence or absence of Jeremiah or any other prophet. It simply says that the king's official(s) went to her when the king said, 'inquire of YHWH for me'.

Kings and Chronicles do not agree about the names of Huldah's father-in-law or grandfather-in-law. Whether this makes a difference or has an explanation is now impossible to say—although it might exercise those who do not like the Bible to contradict itself. The career of Shallum or his father or grandfather has also been debated. Given the absence of commas in ancient Hebrew it is hard to know which of them was a 'keeper of the wardrobe'. Perhaps it was an inherited position like royalty and other political offices (a grandson of the messenger Shaphan was appointed Governor of Judah under the Babylonians until he too was assassinated). We should probably not mistake this for a lowly position and place Shallum among the workers while his wife engaged with the elite. Perhaps the 'wardrobe' belonged to the king or the priests, and may have had as little to do with clothing as the Order of the Garter has in contemporary Britain.

Then there's the Mishneh where she dwelt. Or did she just 'sit' there? The most obvious reading is that Huldah and Shallum lived in the new, additional or second quarter of the city, across a valley and up the slopes of a hill west of the temple and northwest of the original city. The remains of large defensive walls have been found on the northwest side of this district—but the suburb itself has been built and rebuilt so many times that we are unlikely to find a wall plaque reading 'Huldah and Shallum lived here'. Some interpreters, however, want 'Mishneh' to refer to a place of study (some rabbis even say that Huldah taught the Mishnah to women). It is not impossible, of course, that Huldah spent her time expounding the words of the Torah—perhaps it was her reputation for doing so that caused the king's men to go to her—but this is never specified in the story given to us. Perhaps the story only tells us where she lived in the same casual way in which it names Josiah's mother as 'the daughter of Adaiah of Bozkath'. Perhaps defining people by their relations and their locations was so common that it was deemed appropriate to locate Huldah as an inhabitant of the city and as a wife. Whether ancient readers would understand any class or caste implications from the reference to the Mishneh is also impossible to guess now. The royal house was still in the older part of the city but the new quarter on the Western Hill must have been a reasonably good address for some kind of palace or temple official and his prophet-wife. If the ancient story-tellers were suggesting anything more by mentioning the Mishneh, they failed to reach beyond their times.

Summing Up

What does all this attempt at close reading amount to? It is hard to summarize the narrative of Huldah without using more words than the Bible does, largely because the existing story does not tell us what we need to know. However, despite the brevity of the texts that mention her, Huldah emerges as a woman of considerable importance. Unlike other women in the text, she speaks as an equal or superior to royal courtiers. She is a prophet not only among women but comparable to other significant biblical characters. While she has been credited with doing more than the texts say, what her narrative does indicate is that Huldah was of inestimable significance to the political and religious life towards the end of the kingdom of Judah. She may not be responsible for the elevation of Deuteronomy to canonical status but she remains important as a woman who challenges interpreters' preconceptions about gender roles and status in ancient Jerusalem. Even if the text eventually marginalizes her and obscures her, it does provide enough light to reveal an individual of considerable authority in her time.

Pagan Reading

What makes this a Pagan reading? So far this close reading of the text has only opened up possibilities by noticing that the text does not tell us all we need or want to know about Huldah and her actions. I have denied myself the right to re-write Huldah's story to justify my own religious and cultural choices. It is obvious that even one change in that direction would necessitate so many other changes that I would end up with an entirely new fiction. For example, Huldah cannot defend the pluralistic and polytheistic cult that Josiah has already begun to attack, and she cannot be a prophetess of Asherah without becoming part of a story that would never have made it into the Bible. The only changes that could be made without doing violence to the trajectory of this story is to allow Huldah to prophesy that God would respond favourably to mass repentance. Jonah was forced to do this in Nineveh, and most of the other prophets offered such a hope to Judah and Israel, but Huldah does not. Things have gone too far, she says, God is initiating evil times and the best anyone can hope for is to die before the punishing desolation begins. So far, it seems, this pagan reading is only able to be clear that Huldah's story is entirely loyal to YHWH and Josiah.

I am not going to claim that Huldah's gender makes this a more pagan tale than those of other religious leaders in the Bible. If Huldah was presented as a male prophet it would make no difference to the story as told in Kings and Chronicles—although it might have gained her a better reception among later generations of Jews and Christians. A pagan reading that refuses to change the story can be quite clear that Huldah's tale challenges her later interpreters. Few of them like the way that the story makes no fuss about her prophesying. They offer increasingly strange solutions to prevent Huldah encouraging other women to think that they might do what she and men did. Even feminist interpreters have wanted Huldah to be different from male prophets, but she steadfastly gets on with acting as if gender did not define how a person mediates between a deity and a king. But there is more to Paganism than being clear about what is in other religions' stories and gender relations.

Some Pagans might find this story interesting as another stage in the rejection of polytheism and female deities from the religion of Israel as the Bible tells it. I, too, am disappointed that all the Israelite priests and prophets who honoured Asherah, Baal, the 'hosts of the skies' and other deities, failed to keep their stories or rituals alive. Of course, they were busy fighting off ethnic-reassignment by YHWH's story-tellers and reformers. When they became 'foreigners' or 'importers of foreign deities' more than half the battle was lost. Perhaps the texts we are reading make a mistake in suggesting that Josiah had little trouble deposing these priests, destroying Asherah's trees and dismantling the ancient high places: mentioning a strong opposition might have justified YHWH's inability to withdraw his punishment. Nonetheless, these changes are part of a reform within a religion that remains pagan in at least some respects.

Just to be clear, I note that Josiah's reform was *not* a revolution and did not mark the moment when YHWH's religion replaced a previously pagan religion. Paganism is not a question of counting divinities: the affirmation of the uniqueness of their God is one any Pagan could make. It is not entirely dissimilar to the affirmation of the uniqueness of one's beloved. A more radical and explicit monotheism took far longer to arise. Josiah and Huldah's God is not the only God in existence, he just wants to be the only God for this people. Nor is Josiah's reform a conflict between immanence and transcendence. Again, this would be to read later concerns back into the story. Only some pillars and altars, priests and actions, are removed. YHWH remains God in Jerusalem, God of a people in a place. He has a house in which the king has a legitimate pillar for a 'standing place', and in which thousands of sheep and bulls are slaughtered. The primary ritual after the reduction of worship sites and foci was a massive seasonal and agrarian feast in which everyone, deity included, participated. In yet another unexplained and strange moment in Josiah's story, during the celebrations Josiah told the sanctified Levites to place the Ark of the Covenant into the Holiest Place of the temple rather than carrying it on their shoulders any longer (2 Chron. 35:3). Earlier chapters seem to have said that the Ark had been placed there as soon as Solomon dedicated the temple. Certainly nothing here suggests a rejection of materiality in YHWH's cult after the reform. At no point in these proceedings did Huldah or any of the other prophets, or Hilkiah or any of the other priests, say anything about the transcendent nature of Israel's deity or religion. Josiah's reform was not a transcendentalising of Israel's previously immanent religion. In fact, that dichotomy is a much later theological nicety that has never worked in actual religious life and has always been dubious in theological thinking.

Almost all of this suggests to me the necessity of opposing dominant Christian and some Jewish readings of Huldah's story with the assertion that this remains a pagan story. What makes my reading pagan is that it recognizes the local within the story. I celebrate the fact that what Huldah and her king sought to clarify was what was local and abiding in the traditions of their place and their people. Their story is about belonging, dwelling, knowing your place, acting in your time. They remove elements of Israel's religion that were widespread and diffuse, common currency among neighbouring West Asian nations, regional rather than local. They concentrated and distilled ancestral practices down to what was unique, rooted, local. It is not that I celebrate their impious rejection of deities who had nurtured Israel's ancestors, but that I recognize a trend in the reform towards rooting people in place and in particularity.

However, that is only part of what happens in the narrative of Huldah and Josiah. I recognize a tension within Josiah's reform (rather than between the reform and the religion of allegedly 'foreign' priests) between tendencies that might be called paganism and universalism. Over against the localization and particularization of YHWH's cult, a universalization and generalization is evident. Like his predecessors and like the authors and editors who produced what we now name the Bible, Josiah was not content to be a Pagan, celebrating the place where he lived. He fooled himself into reaching for a global vision and role for himself, his people and his God. When the Egyptians marched north along the international route down on the coastal plain, miles from the back hills that sheltered Jerusalem and Judah, Josiah took his chariots to challenge them. He was not content to be a small player in global affairs but, like others before and after him, he imagined that Jerusalem was the centre of the cosmos. In fact, all he (and many before and after him) succeeded in doing was provoking the superpowers—Egypt and whatever Empire was dominant in the north—to take a short detour from their quarrel with each other in order to crush the unhelpful irritant from the back hills. The fact that Huldah's prophecy ignores Josiah's military defeat supports the more pagan tendency of the localized reforms. However, Huldah's prophecy also plays a part in imagining international affairs and regional conflict as centred on Jerusalem, as the tools of a God who would use foreigners to punish allegedly foreign practices.

The tension in these last chapters of Kings and Chronicles is between a pagan sense of belonging and a universalizing generalization. The temptation towards universalism resulted in Huldah and Josiah being caught up in a larger story that eventually lost touch with its particular location and imagined itself as binding on all humanity. It is, in the end, universalism which causes interpreters to re-invent Huldah after the image of their own systematized religiosity that fixes roles for women, prophets, deities, locations, and readers. Instead, I have sought to read Huldah's story as defining what a prophet of YHWH might do, what an Israelite woman might do, and how an Israelite religious reform might be torn between eutopian (located) paganism and utopian (place-less) universalism.

Chapter 7

'You Seduced Me, You Overpowered Me, and You Prevailed': Religious Experience and Homoerotic Sadomasochism in Jeremiah

Ken Stone

Toward the end of his book, *The Ethics of Sex*, Mark Jordan emphasizes the need for Christian rhetoric that speaks insightfully about sexual pleasure. While Jordan notes that Christian tradition has often stigmatized sexual pleasure, he also suggests that resources exist for the creation of an alternative Christian discourse that would grant to sexual pleasure a more positive role. Among these resources Jordan includes what he calls 'the highly erotic language of mysticism'[1] Significantly for my purposes, Jordan notes that such mystical traditions find a certain authorization within biblical literature. For a number of biblical texts, including several Hebrew prophets, use the language of sexual relations to talk about human interactions with the divine.

Jordan subsequently attempts to give examples of types of sexual activity that might be reconsidered in relation to religious speech and practice. And here he brings up sadomasochism. For if we compare certain practices associated with prayer and certain 'rituals of sadomasochistic sex,' Jordan suggests, we may 'find ourselves learning that sadomasochism lies closer to many of our "purely religious" experiences than we might have supposed'.[2]

Now Jordan seems to recognize that this point may be controversial. As he notes, even liberal Christian ethicists have difficulty speaking about sadomasochism. And I have little doubt

1. Mark Jordan, The Ethics of Sex (Oxford: Blackwell, 2002), p. 165.
2. Jordan, The Ethics of Sex, p. 168.

that many of Jordan's readers will be horrified by even his, very brief, invocation of it. Nevertheless, Jordan may be on stronger ground than many of his readers will grant. After all, writers on sadomasochism who write from their own experiences have long commented on the spiritual dimensions of S/M. And so as a biblical scholar I would like to reflect on the possible relevance of Jordan's suggestion for the interpretation of a particular biblical text. For if Jordan asks us, on the one hand, to reconsider biblical sexual rhetoric; and if he asks us, on the other hand, to rethink sadomasochism in relation to religious experience; I want to ask here whether biblical sexual rhetoric itself sometimes takes the form of language about God that sounds very much like sadomasochism.

To raise this sort of question may, however, involve us in a risky enterprise. For we have to ask ourselves whether there actually exists a single phenomenon, 'sadomasochism', which reappears across time and space. It seems to me more likely that the various elements which get linked under the sign, 'sadomasochism'—elements such as dominance, submission, pleasure, pain, fantasy, power, ritual, role-playing and physical contact—all of these elements can be articulated in many different combinations, some of which look quite similar to one another but others of which look radically distinct. To ask, in the modern world, about 'sadomasochism' in the Bible may, therefore, run the risk of essentializing and homogenizing phenomena that should instead be historicized, contextualized, and differentiated.

Nevertheless, the greater risk seems to me to be that readers of the Bible will, because of sadomasochism's negative reputation, cordon off the Bible from any association with it. By making such a move, readers imply that sadomasochism is not even a matter on which people of faith may reflect, or over which they may legitimately disagree. It becomes instead a matter about which no discussion need ever take place. The right position, the *only* position, which people of faith could ever adopt on the question of sadomasochism is assumed in advance; and this assumption rules out the possibility that reflection on S/M could have anything to do with reflection on the Bible.

Against this sort of foreclosure, such biblical scholars as Lori Rowlett and Roland Boer have suggested that something which looks very similar to S/M can be found in the Hebrew Bible; indeed, it can seem at times constitutive of the covenant between Israel and

God).[3] We need to assess, then, the possibility that sadomasochism sheds light on other biblical passages, besides those discussed by Rowlett and Boer—so let us turn to the book of Jeremiah.

The Twentieth chapter of Jeremiah opens by introducing Pashhur, the 'chief officer of the house of Yahweh', who clearly represents those authority figures—priests, kings, court prophets and so forth—with whom Jeremiah is often in conflict. Because he has heard how Jeremiah has been speaking in the temple, Pashhur has Jeremiah 'flogged' and 'put in the cell' (20:2), a mysterious place in the temple for which the translations 'dungeon' and 'stocks' have also been offered[4] .The story thus fits into a collection of scenes in Jeremiah which involve, in the words of one commentary, 'the imposition of discipline'.[5] The next day, however, Pashur lets Jeremiah out of the cell; and at that point Jeremiah launches into an oracle against Pashur (20:3b–6), which tells us, in effect, how Pashur and his friends are going to be disciplined by Yahweh in turn.

Immediately following this oracle, however, the literary form changes. We encounter eleven verses of poetry, which are generally divided by scholars into two separate poems, both of which are counted among the laments or confessions of Jeremiah. It is the first poem, comprised of verses 7 through 13, that interests me here. The poem begins, in verse 7, with Jeremiah speaking *to God*. We have, then, the language of prayer, the very type of language that Jordan has suggested might be reconsidered in relation to sadomasochism.

Now in the NRSV, the opening two lines of this prayer are translated as follows: 'O LORD, you have enticed me, and I was enticed; you have overpowered me, and you have prevailed.' The precise meaning of the English word, 'entice', may be a little ambiguous. The Hebrew verb in question can mean 'seduce', in a sexual sense, or 'deceive', depending upon the context. In either case, of course, Jeremiah's prayer is a surprise for conventional piety, since most readers probably do not assume that God seduces *or* deceives God's prophets. The sexual connotations may not seem immediately apparent here, since we recognize them most clearly

3. See Roland Boer, 'Yahweh as Top' in Ken Stone (ed.), *Queer Commentary and the Hebrew Bible* (Sheffield: Sheffield Academic Press, 2000). See also Lori Rowlett, 'Violent Femmes and S/M: Queering Samson and Delilah' in Stone, *Queer Commentary*.

4. Robert Carroll, *Jeremiah: A Commentary* (Philadelphia: WJK, 1986), p. 390.

5. Carroll, *Jeremiah*, p. 395.

in cases where it is otherwise apparent that sexual matters are under discussion. The Torah, for example, uses the same verb to speak of the sexual seduction of a virgin (Exod. 22:25). We know, however, that the book of Jeremiah uses a great deal of sexual imagery, often very graphic, to make its theological points (e.g., 2:20–3:5). And in the verse with which we are here concerned, the meaning of the two occurrences of the verb, 'entice', in the opening line is clarified by the first verb in the second line. For the verb that NRSV translates, 'overpowered', is also a verb used in the Torah to speak about the sexual overpowering of a woman by a man (Deut. 22:25; cf. 2 Sam. 13:11; Judg. 19:25). Most modern scholars argue that the appearance of the two verbs together increases the probability of sexual connotations; and so we can translate the beginning of Jeremiah's prayer as follows:

> You seduced me, Yahweh, and I was seduced.
> You overpowered me, and you prevailed. (20:7a)

Images of sexual seduction and overpowering are used here to speak symbolically about Jeremiah's experience of being a prophet.

But what kind of sexual situation is in view? It is clear that some sort of power dynamic is involved, and many scholars have therefore concluded that the sexual overpowering referred to in the second line is something akin to rape. Abraham Heschel, for example, has argued in an influential discussion that the two terms for seduction and overpowering 'in immediate juxtaposition forcefully convey the complexity of the divine human-relationship: sweetness of enticement as well as violence of rape.'[6]

It is important to note, however, that no word exists, in the Hebrew Bible, which corresponds exactly to our word, 'rape'. The word that I have translated 'overpower' does occur in at least three biblical scenarios that *involve* rape, but the verb in question is not itself a word *meaning* rape. Indeed, in one of those three rape scenarios (specifically, Judges 19), the subject of the verb is not even the subject of the rape. This term for overpowering occurs many times in the Bible, in all sorts of situations where power is involved; and the precise nature of the exercise of power has to be determined by attention to context. When the language is used in a sexual context, then, as it is here, one of the questions we have to ask is

6. Abraham Herschel, *The Prophets: An Introduction* (New York: Harper and Row, 1962), p. 162.

whether sexual overpowering can carry connotations other than those of rape. For it is quite possible that the combination of sex and power is so little analyzed, by those who study and translate biblical texts, that a range of complicated relations between sex, dominance and submission are being reduced by commentators to a single type of sexual overpowering, 'rape.' Perhaps we should remind ourselves, here, of Pat Califia's observation, in an influential article on feminism and sadomasochism, that 'most people do not think there is a great deal of difference between a rapist and a bondage enthusiast.[7] Califia's point, of course, is that there is often a *great* deal of difference, which hostility to S/M obscures; and in that light we might well wonder whether 'rape' is being read into a biblical passage that does express religious experience in terms of sexual seduction and overpowering, but which could more plausibly be construed as something like homoerotic sadomasochism.

We should note that the passage does, in fact, present difficulties for an interpretation in terms of rape. When the specific language of power that occurs here is used elsewhere in connection with rape, the rapist is punished in some way. In Jeremiah 20, however, the rapist would have to be God, the victim, Jeremiah; and yet by verse 11 Jeremiah is asserting his confidence in God, and in verse 13 shouting that his master, the one who seduces and overpowers, should be praised. This combination, in which an individual is both an object of sexualized domination, *and then* a source of praise for the dominating lord, is simply absent from the passages where rape is referred to with language used here.

It is, on the other hand, interesting to note some of the language that is used by scholars to describe the dynamics at work in Jeremiah 20. Thus Walter Brueggemann, after noting the sexual connotations, points out that Jeremiah acknowledges 'Yahweh's power, which is overwhelming and irresistible ...', which 'overwhelms ... the one who seeks to serve him' [8] yet Brueggemann also recognizes that Jeremiah expresses his 'assertion of confidence in Yahweh' with 'a statement of genuine trust'[9] Heschel summarizes

7. Pat Califia, *Public Sex: The Culture of Radical Sex* (San Francisco: Cleis Press, 2000), p. 171.

8. Walter Brueggeman, *A Commentary on Jeremiah: Exile and Homecoming* (Grand Rapids: Eerdmans, 1998), p. 181.

9. Brueggeman, *A Commentary on Jeremiah*, p. 182.

as follows: 'The prophet feels both the attraction and the coercion of God, the appeal and the pressure, the charm and the stress'.[10]

Attraction and coercion. Appeal and pressure. Charm and stress. Overwhelming and irresistible. Power and trust.

These words from the commentaries do seem to capture the complicated religious experience that is elaborated in Jer. 20:7–13, but it is not at all clear that 'rape' is the most appropriate descriptor for a sexual experience that involves not only power but also, for example, trust. We seem to have something closer to sadomasochism; and it is almost as if the commentators on some level sense this. For as they grasp for language to describe Jeremiah's sexualized experience of God, commentators inadvertently replicate terms used to describe S/M.

Indeed, if scholars were to acknowledge this fact, they might find that attention to sadomasochism helps us make sense of certain features of this prayer that otherwise cause commentators to scratch their heads. Consider, for example, Brueggemann's emphasis on Jeremiah's 'assertion of trust in Yahweh'. That this trust is present is, for Brueggemann, obvious. In verses 11 and 12, after all, Jeremiah expresses very clearly his confidence in God. Yet this seems, to Brueggemann, 'almost contradictory'.[11] The assertion of 'genuine trust' in God, toward the *end* of the prayer, is understood to stand in tension with Jeremiah's equally clear experience of being seduced and overpowered by God at the *beginning* of the prayer. Sexual overpowering and trust apparently cannot be made to fit together.

What is for Brueggemann a contradiction, however, fits very well into S/M discourses. For trust is one of the themes most often noted by those writing about S/M. Thus Califia emphasizes the fact that the bottom in an S/M scene must 'completely trust her top'.[12] J.J. Madeson goes even further, calling 'trust' one of her two 'building blocks' of sadomasochism; and asserting that '[t]rust is arguably the most important ingredient to each and every one of us in the SM community'.[13] It would appear, then, that particular features of Jeremiah 20, which seem contradictory to the perplexed biblical scholar, might well be understood better should a

10. Heschel, *The Prophets*, p. 114.

11. Brueggemann, *A Commentary on Jeremiah*, p. 182.

12. Califia, *Public Sex*, p. 172.

13. Charles Moser & J.J. Madeson, *Bound to be Free: The S/M Experience* (New York: Continuum, 1996), p. 68.

hermeneutical lens informed by sadomasochism be adopted. Perhaps, in this scenario, biblical scholarship would do well to surrender its function as authoritative discipline, and submit to the discipline imposed by S/M.

How, then, might we characterize Jer. 20:7–13? The literary context, we should recall, is one of stocks, dungeons and discipline. The prophet who speaks here is represented elsewhere as walking around in a yoke, telling Israel to submit. The vocabulary of power permeates this chapter, as all scholars recognize. We then have a prayer that begins, in verse 7, with language about the seduction and sexualized overpowering of Jeremiah by Yahweh. Jeremiah never says that he finds this experience of overpowering to be, in itself, unpleasant (though scholars normally write as if this is clearly the case). He does, however, complain about the *social* disapproval that accompanies his status as Yahweh's partner. He is aware that he has real human enemies, who do not like the practices in which he engages. He even considers the possibility of refusing, any longer, to engage in those practices, since they do bring about persecution. Yet his prayer moves, in verse 8, to an awareness of acting as if compelled by some will other than his own. In verse 9 we have a description of unusual physical sensations, intense and arguably painful, which are brought on, apparently, by the actions of his master: 'then within me there is something like a burning fire shut up in my bones' (NSRV). Verse 10 acknowledges again the social disapproval that Jeremiah receives from others, as a result of the role that he plays for his lord. Verses 11 and 12 constitute Jeremiah's assertion of trust in Yahweh, who protects Jeremiah 'like a dread warrior' (NRSV). And the prayer reaches its climax in 20:13, where Jeremiah, in ecstasy, sings the praises of his master. It is an emotional poem, and the emotional tone shifts dramatically from the beginning of the prayer to the end. If it is the case, as Califia argues, that a 'major part of the sadist's turn-on consists of deliberately altering the emotional or physical state of the bottom,' then Jeremiah's top must by this point be happy indeed.

The text can therefore be construed, I think, as replicating *dynamics*, at least, associated with an S/M scene.

Now I do not assume that this is the last word on Jer. 20:7–13. And even if it should be granted that the dynamics of S/M shed light on the dynamics of Jeremiah's prayer and relationship to God, we will not have resolved the question of the attitude that we ought to take, today, toward either those dynamics or that relationship. It is important to note, in fact, that many scholars find the sexual language used in Jeremiah to be troubling. Much of this language makes use of images of *female* sexual whoring to symbolize Israel's religious infidelity to Yahweh; and since this tradition of symbolism represents God's punishment of Israel in terms of a husband's physical punishment of his wife, a strong argument can be made that such symbolism contributes to tolerance of the abuse of women and so should be subject to a clear ethical critique. And it will be tempting, I think, to assimilate the presence of something like sadomasochism in Jeremiah 20 to the terms of this critique.

However, I want to suggest that such assimilation should not be accomplished too hastily. For the sexual connotations of Jeremiah 20, such as they are, can be understood in terms of male *homo*eroticism. While Jeremiah may represent Israel as a woman, he does not represent himself as one; and yet he is the figure who is here seduced and sexually overpowered by God. It is interesting, in that light, to recall that Jeremiah is, in chapter 16, explicitly commanded, by his divine master, not to marry or have children. And it is interesting as well that God in chapter 13 commands Jeremiah in the matter of wearing and soiling loincloths. The relationship between God and Jeremiah is an intimate one indeed; and while Jeremiah is by no means an entirely submissive partner, his occasional testiness does not rule out our ability to read his relationship with God in terms of homoerotic sadomasochism. As Califia reminds us, 'masochists are known within the S/M community to be stubborn and aggressive'.[14] Certainly Jeremiah fits easily into this role of the aggressive bottom.

To the extent, then, that the sadomasochism in question, in Jeremiah 20, is a male homoerotic one, I believe it must be evaluated in a different manner than some of the other sexualized passages in Jeremiah. The exchange of power between a male prophet to his male master cannot simply be *equated* with the subordination of women to men that rightly troubles interpreters of the other passages. There is too much difference in the history of these types of power relationship for us to assume that we can reduce the one to the other. And while that does not rule out the possibility of

14. Califia, *Public Sex*, p. 172.

ethical critique of Jer. 20:7–13 or, for that matter, of male homoerotic sadomasochism, it does, I think, make the critical questions distinct.

In conclusion, then, we see that the prayer life and religious experiences attributed to Jeremiah take a form that looks a great deal like homoerotic sadomasochism. Even if the text cannot be reduced to an S/M scene, a hermeneutics informed by sadomasochism seems able to shed more light on this particular biblical text than the now-common hermeneutics of rape. This fact not only lends some support to Jordan's suggestion that parallels sometimes exist, in traditional sources, between the dynamics of S/M and the dynamics of prayer. It also indicates that theologians and ethicists who refuse to engage directly with questions about sadomasochism may be refusing to engage a constituent part of the biblical traditions themselves.

Chapter 8

The Monstrosity of David

Janet Wootton

King David is one of the central figures in the history of Israel, told in the pages of the Bible. Historically, he oversees and consolidates an immense political change in the governance of Israel. Theologically he is a key element in the future hope of the nation, and becomes the type of divine, benign and powerful leadership which Christians see fulfilled in Jesus, the Christ. This brings elements of monarchy and a desire for the omnipotence and submission that go with it, into the heart of the most powerful expressions of the Christian faith and, as such, has shaped the world we live in today. It could be argued that, apart from Jesus, there is no more powerful individual figure in the Bible.

The establishment of a monarchic system in Israel is the outcome of the decline of the former risky but lively political system and developing militarism and national cohesion. The period of gradual coalescence of the tribes and their bloody appropriation of a section of land, by conflict with other local inhabitants, to form a political entity within definable borders, is paralleled in many civilizations.

Naturally enough, Israel, with its emerging identity, looked for models of governance both to the surrounding successful nations and to its own heritage. Very specifically, they wanted a king, 'like the nations' (1 Sam. 16:1–13). Part of becoming a nation (goi) rather than a group of tribes, was the establishment of a hereditary monarchy. The move to monarchy is not sudden—it is foreshadowed in the actions of Gideon,[1] for example—but it is far reaching. It

1. Judges 8–9: Gideon refuses the crown, but acts like a monarch, and his death is followed by a typical succession struggle.

includes changes to religious practices, civil administration, military organization, the distribution of wealth and power, all of which have deep rooted effects on the lives of people at every level of society, not least women.

Two narratives relate the change, both intertwined in the first book of Samuel. One gives an amazingly positive spin. This is history told by the winner—after all, monarchy became not only the political system of the following centuries, but the governing theological symbol for God's ultimate purpose for the people of God, and even the world.

But the other is deeply suspicious. With the ring of bitter experience, this narrator describes the absolute power of a monarchy over the lives of individuals:

> He will take your sons and make them serve with his chariots and horses ... He will take your daughters to be perfumers and cooks and bakers. He will take the best of your vineyards ... When that day comes, you will cry out for relief from the king you have chosen, and Yahweh your God will not answer you in that day. (1 Sam. 8:11-18)

Israel is caught in the moment of change. There is a breathtaking opportunity for someone to harness the power seeking of the southern tribes, and establish an administration that will hold the whole nation together, defeat its enemies and get for the new nation some of the wealth and luxury that they see in the surrounding cultures.

Into this opportunity steps a charismatic leader, called Saul, who is proclaimed king, and begins to fulfil the expectations of nascent monarchy. He wages constant war against the local peoples, coming to focus more and more on the Philistines, and he begins to establish a dynasty, based on the succession of his son, Jonathan, and marriages for his daughters. But Saul's story is hardly told. In these narratives, he is simply the failed forerunner of the one who becomes the archetypal King of Israel—David.

The story of the choosing and early years of David are told with an extremely positive spin, such that his manipulative dexterity and self-promotion are almost universally ignored in the present day. David is very deliberately chosen by God, with his selection emphasized by the rejection of Jesse's entire family until the youngest son, who is not even present, is remembered (1 Sam. 16:1–13). The story of the single combat with Goliath is terribly attractive—the young, unarmed boy going out in all his idealistic courage against the heavily armoured giant, and winning, winning not only the fight, but even the king's daughter (albeit at the second try) in marriage—Oh dear!

This immensely attractive young man gains the loyalty of soldierly men, and has all the women singing about his exploits. Within Saul's own household, he wins the hearts of Saul's daughter and son. His conflict with Saul is initiated and fuelled not by his own ambition—Oh no!—but by Saul's oft repented, insane jealousy. Saul is vilifed, David is lifted up. The reader is carried along, entranced by the magic of his personality. I have heard children's addresses and sermons in plenty, in praise of this wonderful young buck: how wonderful, it seemed, to find stories in the Bible with the same moral values as the fairy tales, in which the wicked die horribly, and the young hero inherits the kingdom and gets the girl—all the girls, in fact. The spin is still working, and I will offer some more examples of it later.

But in the biblical narrative, the spin becomes more cynical when David finally takes power, and the reader witnesses the almost disastrous breakdown of his hold on power and the internecine struggles of his family, in gruesome detail. By the end of his life, the narrative has turned into political record, as the battle for succession ends with the throne occupied by someone who really is a king 'like the nations'.

David's story is very long, and complex. Unusually, his military and political exploits are told alongside his relationships with individual women and men, so that the connection between political and sexual conquest is made very clear.

David Gunn, writing in *A Feminist Companion to Reading the Bible,*[2] describes his own journey in understanding the story of David, from his 1978 book, *The Story of King David,*[3] to the date of writing, 1997: 'I described as a fundamental structure of the story the way men's dealing with women mirrorred what I saw as their "public" or "political" dealings. I did not then understand how politics are written on women's bodies'. He goes on to say that his later understanding engaged his anger and hate. Once the spin is overcome,

2. David Gunn, 'Reflections on David' in Athalya Brenner (ed.), *A Feminist Companion to Reading the Bible* (Sheffield: Sheffield Academic Press, 1997).

3. David Gunn, *The Story of King David* (Sheffield: Journal for the Study of the Old Testament, 1978), pp. 545–62.

what is left is the story of a monster, by no means unique in human history, but a monster nonetheless.

This article will tell his story through the women whose relationships with David, are narrated. This is set against the background of political and religious changes, the movement from local and domestic organization, which empowers women and men, towards elitist and exclusive structures. As David becomes the archetype of the Messiah, seen by Christians as fulfilled in Jesus, the article finishes by examining the interaction between the story of David and the story of Jesus in Christian tradition.

Michal and Abigail

Michal and Abigail's stories mark David's rise to power. In Michal, he claims the prize offered to him (but not given) for defeating Goliath, with the added twist to Saul's misery, that Michal loves David. Abigail's transfer from wife of the boor, Nabal, to wife of David, the charming hero, demonstrates David's ability to move with confidence among the non-Israelite tribes, even while on the run. Both women are depicted as 'worthy' of David's choice. They act independently, and befriend David at risk to their own domestic situations. Each of them chooses him in significant ways. Each relates not only to David, but also to the man and family rejected and left behind.

The rejected person in Michal's case, is, of course, Saul, her father. Her story is that of a daughter as well as a wife. Her loyalty to David, and betrayal of her father works on several levels. It is part of her own development, and part of the ascendancy David gains over Saul. Karla Shargent[4] finds in this a repeated pattern in the first books of the Bible, which gives daughters a position of power. The daughter is technically under the control of her father, but there are other narratives in which the daughter takes control and acts against her father as here.[5]

However, this independence is short-lived. Once the daughter becomes a wife, ironically, the very choice which demonstrated

4. Karla Shargent 'Living on the Edge: the Luminality of Daughters in Genesis to 2 Samuel' in Brenner (ed.), *A Feminist Companion to Samuel and Kings* (Sheffield: Sheffield Academic Press, 1994).

5. For example, Rachel during Jacob's flight from Laban, narrated in Gen. 31:33–35.

her independence from her father in this instance, she essentially disappears from view, or, in the case of Michal, is passed from husband to husband as the story progresses.

There is, of course, another character in this narrative, who also falls for David in a big way: Jonathan, Saul's son and dynastic hope. Jonathan's love for David is described in explicitly sexual terms, and brother and sister connive at David's escape from Saul. In fact, Jonathan can do more, as he is more publicly involved in the household.

In the narrative, something quite remarkable emerges, observed by Adele Berlin:[6] the characteristics normally associated with males are attached to Michal, and those usually perceived as feminine are linked with Jonathan and David ... seems to have related to Michal as to a man and to Jonathan as to a woman, though we shall see that this changes later.

What is evident from this narrative is that David's affections are promiscuous. He is capable of inspiring love and loyalty in men and women, and uses this to further his own ends. His sexual appetite is bound up with his appetite for power, like many ambitious and energetic people. What is implicit is that he is bisexual. The narrative states that Jonathan's love for David was, 'supassing the love of women' (2 Sam. 1:26). What is evident is that both Michal and Jonathan are at first torn and then destroyed by their love for this powerful man.

Once David is on the run, Jonathan and Michal have very different fates. Michal is quickly married off to another man. Jonathan continues to live out his divided loyalties till his death on the battle field with his father. David's reaction to both circumstances is typical.

The death of Saul and Jonathan is extremely convenient for David, the first of a number of convenient deaths, for which David will have no responsibility, and for which he will mourn and even exact vengeance. These two deaths occur during the ongoing war with the Philistines, while David is involved in a quite separate battle to retake people and goods seized by an Amalekite raiding party. David's real ambitions can be discerned from his distribution of booty from the raid to his supporters in Judah and among the friendly tribes (1 Sam. 30:26–31).

6. Adele Berlin, 'Characterization in Biblical Narrative; David's Wives' in David J.A. Clines and Tamara. C. Eskenazi (eds.), Telling Queen Michal's Story: An Experiment in Comparative Interpretation (Sheffield: Sheffield Academic Press, 1991), pp. 91–93.

However, David can take no delight in the slaughter which opens the way for those same ambitions. As on other future occasions, David is carefully separated from the taint of death. When the messenger arrives, ironically, an Amalekite, David has him put to death, as he was 'not afraid to ... destroy the LORD's anointed'—a reference to the doublet, in which David himself has Saul in his power, but refrains from violence on the grounds that he will not harm the LORD's anointed (2 Sam. 1:14, 1 Sam. 24:1–15). The narrator then records a poem of lament (2 Sam. 1:19–27), as on other similar occasions, distancing David not only physically but emotionally from the deaths.

Woven through the rest of the story of David is the fate of Saul's surviving offspring, who are killed or otherwise neutralized. Michal remains a risk, as she may produce pretenders to the throne through her marriage to Paltiel. While David weeps over Jonathan, he simply orders Michal to be returned to him, as part of the political fall-out following the death of Saul and Jonathan. No longer the independent daughter, nor even the wife and partner in adventure, Michal is returned to David. Following her remarks at David's dancing when the Ark of the Covenant is returned to Jerusalem, she bears no children (2 Sam. 6:20–23).

The implication is that she is struck barren, because of her outspoken opposition to the extravagant praise of King David. It may be that she was cloistered from David's presence, as were the violated concubines after Absalom's revolt. Either way the result is that the line of Saul terminates at that point, Michal is utterly humiliated, and David, once again, appears as the righteous man, whose willingness to act the fool in God's praise has been met with a churlish response. However, there is no mourning here, no hint of regret for the passing of love, only the judgement of the king on a wife who has become inconvenient.

Again, the spin still works. David dancing before the Ark has become a symbol of the freedom and exuberance of evangelical praise, and the dynamic between David and Michal at this point has reinforced the male claim to authority over the shrewish woman. The man, like Petrucchio, is bright, exuberant, generous hearted and the woman, mean spirited, a watcher, not a participant, and eventually barren. She has no part in the future.

What is more, Michal's criticism of David is aimed precisely at the characteristic that makes him most attractive. It was his music which first charmed Saul, and his reaction to significant events is typically recorded in the form of song. His association with many of the Psalms suggests an entrenched traditional association with the music and worship of Israel.

The account of his life in the book of Chronicles makes more of this. David is seen as the author of the whole priestly cult. He establishes the central role of the Levites in the ritual. Only they can touch the Ark of the Covenant (1 Chron. 15–16). Before the building of the Temple, which Chronicles regards David as too bloodstained to build, all the tasks of worship, from caring for the ritual objects to responsibility for music and singing, are distributed to the levitical families by him.

This account firmly roots the full exclusive and hierarchical system of worship in the plans and actions of King David. However and whenever the shift from domestic and local ritual to a centralized cult took place, it is associated with the changes that accompanied the development of monarchy and, in particular, with the reign of David, the singer.

This means that Michal represents more than the shrewish woman, pooper of the great party that surrounds David's accession. In that moment of rejection, she turns her back on that whole movement away from domestic worship, focused on the household, towards a male, hierarchical, centralized cult, which only men, and only men of a certain tribe, can administer, and only men are required to attend, by travelling away from the home to the central place of worship (Deut. 16:16).

Still today, we see that centralized hierarchical forms of church are disempowering in general and specifically disempower women, especially where religious power and political power are closely intertwined. The Roman Catholic and Orthodox Churches have not yet consented to the ordination of women, and the Church of England, in its place of establishment (England), moved extremely slowly to admit women to the priesthood, and still (at the time of writing) does not consecrate women bishops. This means that the political and media power, which undoubtedly resides in the Anglican episcopacy in England, is exclusive to male office holders. The legacy of that centralizing move attributed to King David is still disempowering women 3,000 years later.

But it is not only episcopal churches that disempower women in this way. Many fundamentalist or neo-conservative churches and church movements are male dominated. These too are 'hierarchical', in the sense that they vest enormous authority in their religious leaders, and deliberately disempower their congregations. Again, leadership is denied to women, who are supposed to act in a manner that is submissive and passive. Like Michal, they are observers rather than participants, and they are not expected to have a voice, to speak out. Michal's punishment, whether it comes from David's rejection of her as a sexual partner, or from God's power over her womb, would seem perfectly appropriate to many of these followers of the heritage of David the dancing king.

Neither is this group of Christians without political and media power. Robert Jewett[7] describes the American Superhero culture both in *The Captain America Complex*, written in 1973, at the height of the Cold War and *The Myth of the American Superhero*,[8] co-authored with John Shelton Lawrence in 2001, following the terrorist attack on the World Trade Center (commonly referred to as 9/11). He traces American 'zeal' to redeem or conquer the world to its Puritan roots, which saw the new community established in the New World as the inheritors of the titles of Israel: God's Chosen People, and the Light to the Nations.

Following 9/11, Lawrence and Jewett set American response in the context of right wing Christian millennial writing surrounding the year 2000, specifically the apocalyptic, *Left behind* series, which rose to dominate the bestseller market, and American film and music culture of the era. 'Why' they ask, 'do women and people of color, who have made significant strides in civil rights, continue to remain almost wholly subordinate in a mythscape where communities must almost always be rescued by physically powerful white men?'[9] Chillingly, the present Bush Administration is known to draw its inspiration from this same religious right.

While Michal begins her life with David as a fellow adventurer and ends up abandoned and rejected, Abigail first encounters him in a highly dangerous situation, which she immediately controls. Like Michal, she counters the authority of the man to whom her culture dictates that she owes it, in her case, her husband. This

7. Robert Jewett, *The Captain America Complex* (Philadelphia, WJK, 1973).

8. Robert Jewett and John Shelton Lawrence, *The Myth of the American Superhero* (Grand Rapids: Eerdmans, 2001).

9. Jewett & Lawrence, *The Myth*, p. 8.

gives her independence of action and power in decision making at the point where she and David meet. Seizing the initiative, she rides out with a male servant to meet him, and defuse the potential for violence in the stand-off between the two men. She acts with authority and speaks prophetic words about David's future kingship.

Once the situation is resolved, Nabal—like so many others—dies a death which is convenient for David, whose actions now change Abigail's circumstances utterly. Alice Bach comments on the change: 'Abigail seems to have functioned better as the wife of Nabal. While he lived, she demonstrated bravery. She had power of prophecy. After his death, Abigail's voice is absorbed into David's, much as she is absorbed into his household.'[10]

In fact, Abigail becomes David's chattel. He sends his servants to fetch her, and she rides out again, this time with her maids, under the escort of David's servants. Later, she forms part of the plunder taken in the raid by the Amalekites, while David is trying to balance his loyalties by fighting with the Philistines against his own people. It is while David is on the campaign to regain his possessions that Saul and Jonathan are killed in the battle in which he therefore has no part.

So Abigail plays her part in David's rise to power, during the time when he, 'will do almost anything to survive—massacring whole towns to keep his real actions unknown to his overlords ... profiting politically from the chain of violent deaths in the house of Saul while vehemently dissociating himself from each of the killings'.[11] Although she acts and speaks with authority, she yet typifies and is praised for the womanly virtues of good sense and peace-making, and her womanly plight (as a captive) occupies David on a heroic rescue mission, while Saul and Jonathan are killed.

Alice Bach, again, comments on the wives of David: 'Seen through the stereotyping lens of male authority, each of these women typifies a particular aspect of *wife*: Michal is the dissatisfied daughter/wife of divided loyalties; Abigail is consistently the good-sense mother-provider, and Bathsheba the sexual partner. There is no

10. Alice Bach, 'The Pleasure of Her Texts' in Athalya Brenner, A Feminist Companion to Samuel and Kings, pp. 106–28.

11. Robert Alter, The David Story, A Translation with Commentary of 1 and 2 Samuel, (New York: W.W. Norton, 1999), p. xviii.

interdependence of the wives of David, although in their actual lives there might well have been.'[12] Bach speculates whether Abigail might have comforted Bathsheba on the death of her first son. Similarly, one might wonder what was the impact on Abigail of the return of Michal and her subsequent rejection.

In any case, Abigail has become the model of a good woman, as opposed to Michal, the rebellious woman. Abigail is still a popular name in many cultures, where women are credited, or burdened, with the virtue of sound common sense, the ability to hold together family and community, and the function of home-making and the provision of food. Few people call their daughters Michal or Bathsheba. But many daughters are named for this woman, who rises to the occasion, deals with the crisis, and then fades into the background.

Bathsheba, Tamar and the Concubines

It is extraordinary that the story of Bathsheba should have been preserved in the narrative of David's life, and extraordinary that it does nothing to dent his image. It is told in the text of 2 Samuel, as the background to the birth of Solomon, but not in the Chronicles' account, which presents a sanitized version of Solomon's birth and accession. In Chronicles, the polish on the story of David and Solomon is undamaged. Solomon is chosen by God as the king who will reign in peace, following David's bloody rise to power. There is no battle for the succession and no hint of scandal surrounding his birth.

But 2 Samuel contains all the gory details. And I am constantly amazed at the way in which women, as well as men, can still see this incident as the minor slip that adds a touching humanity to the hero. As recently as March 2004, in the otherwise excellent series *Bible Mysteries* (BBC, February–April 2004), the programme on David and Goliath (7th March) included an assessment of the incident with Bathsheba as a rather endearing factor, demonstrating David's 'humanity'. I used to set an essay question about God's choice of David. Most students toed the party line, seeing his rise to power as God's choice, confirmed by David's charm, and the Bathsheba incident as a very natural lapse, a necessary flaw, for which David

12. Bach, *The Pleasure of Her Text*, p. 113.

eloquently repented in Psalm 51. And, of course, 'If God can choose someone like that, then God can choose me.' A few read behind the spin, and saw the adulterous murder as quite in keeping with the self-centred power seeking, characteristic of David's life.

If the incident is given its full weight, Bathsheba tends to be afforded blame equal to, or greater than David, although the text attributes blame to David. I have been the recipient of a full-blown male verbal attack for (as the person in question supposed) suggesting that Bathsheba was in any sense a victim. All loud voice and finger poking: 'There is only one victim in this story—Uriah'. At best, Bathsheba is seen as compliant or conniving, at worst, she is the active temptress. Why, for heaven's sake, was she taking a bath on the roof, where the king could see her, in the first place?

Although the actual narrative does not portray her as a temptress, the broader story of the monarchy sets her in context as the first of a number of spectacular foreign women, who cause the downfall of kings. Solomon himself is drawn into syncretism by his foreign wives, who bring their own religious cults into the harem (1 Kgs 11:1–13). This weakens his power, and the united kingdom only just survives to the end of his reign. Jezebel famously preys on the weak King Ahab, and dies in full make-up at the hands of religious zealots (1 Kgs 16:29 - 2 Kgs 9:37). The ambitious, greedy and unfaithful woman becomes a theological image for faithless Israel, in passages such as the shocking Ezekiel 16 and the abusive Hos. 2:2–13.

Klein suggests that, indeed, Bathsheba may have intended to seduce the king, to escape from her barren marriage to Uriah (no children are mentioned in the text). In this, she sees a correspondence with other foremothers in the Davidic lineage, Tamar (Gen. 38:13–26) and Ruth, both of whom take the initiative in sexual encounters. The thing is, no-one will ever know. The narrator does not give away the secret of Bathsheba's active part in the scene.

However, Bathsheba certainly fulfils and fuels fantasies of the exotic seductive woman. David Gunn explores the portrayal of this story through time. 'Visual depictions of Bathsheba bathing are ubiquitous in Bible illustration in Europe from the Middle Ages until about the middle of the sixteenth century. She is depicted both naked and largely clothed'.[13] The story interacts with modern

13. Gunn, *Reflections on David*, pp. 563–64.

and postmodern story and film, in which the *femme fatale*, the inevitably beautiful and seductive foreign woman, represents otherness, seduction and, in the end, betrayal.

The child of adultery dies—again, for David, a convenient death, and, this time, a repugnant death. At least the others who die so that David can live in peace, are killed in battle or murdered as adults. The death of the infant for David's sin is almost cynically foretold by Nathan as punishment for David's sin (2 Sam. 12:14).

With the maturity of David's earlier children, the battle for the succession begins to rage. Two of his elder sons come into conflict over the intolerable behaviour of one of them to his half-sister. The rape of Tamar works, as do the other narratives, on several levels. The incident leads to Amnon's murder (and removal from the succession) and Absalom's coup. Set immediately after David's adultery with Bathsheba, the story suggests that the moral bankruptcy of David is reflected in his family.

Carol Smith argues that the story of Tamar, like the story of Lot's daughters (Gen. 19:7) is intended to cause shock and repugnance in its readers. 'The wrong done to Tamar cannot be put right, but it is a real wrong and dealt with accordingly'[14] (129) One of Trible's 'texts of terror', this story, following on David's adultery and murder, highlights the chaotic decline in the royal household, with tragic results for members of the household and, eventually, the people over whom they rule.

Tamar is portrayed as totally without blame in the narrative. Amnon first conceives a desire for her, and, egged on by a friend, contrives to get her alone in a vulnerable situation. With sickening accuracy, the narrator describes the revulsion which so often follows violent sexual assault, and the total helplessness of the woman, who, as Smith notes, 'has to suffer the added indignity of being thrown out of her brother's room by a servant'.[15]

Like Michal and the concubines, Tamar's life is virtually ended by the episode. She is cut off from the dignity of marriage and child-bearing and disappears into the household to live out her life in mourning. The outcome for the royal family is a spiral of murder and betrayal, leading through Absalom's estrangement from his

14. Carol Smith, 'Challenged by the Text: Interpreting Two Stories of incest in the Hebrew Bible' in Brenner and Fontaine, A Feminist Companion to Reading the Bible, pp. 114–35

15. Smith, 'Challenged by the Text', p. 129.

father, to his attempt on the throne. This seriously destabilizes the nation. One of Saul's sons, Mephibaal, also makes a bid for power, and the country is plunged into civil war.

As part of his power play, Absalom violates David's concubines—a group of women who, like many in scripture, are nameless, and described only by their function. Possession of a large harem was, of course, a sign of power and wealth. Huge numbers are reported.[16] Violation of the harem was an element in Absalom's coup and was recognized as such, just as Adonijah's request for access to Abishag was recognized by Solomon as a potential attempt to oust him during the battle for the succession after David's death (1 Kgs 2:13–25).

In comparison with the harrowing description of the rape of Tamar, the fate of the concubines is related casually. Following their contamination, and therefore the contamination of the hereditary line, they are cloistered, yet another group of female victims in male power struggles. Again, characteristically, David weeps for the men who die, but expresses anger over Tamar's treatment, and simply cloisters the concubines. His mourning over Amnon's death drives Absalom away. But when Absalom is killed, after his rebellion is put down, despite David's express command to take him alive, David utters his most famous lament of all, 'O Absalom my son, would to God I had died for thee' (2 Sam. 18:33).

Bathsheba Again, and Abishag, the Shunammite Woman

Joseph Heller's novel, *God Knows*, begins with David in old age, in bed with the Shunammite woman, but longing for Bathsheba. Now, at the end of his life, the King is given a young woman, 'to warm his bed'. He no longer has the power to win a woman's heart (like Michal's) or send servants to carry out the orders of his power and lust (as with Abigail and Michal). The reader can only imagine what it was like for this young woman to lie with the old and dying king, and potentially witness the power politics that surrounded his last days.

David had, like so many powerful men, failed to settle the succession. The stage was set for a damaging conflict between rival claimants to the throne. Two of David's sons set up rival courts:

16. Gideon has enough concubines to father seventy sons (Judg. 8:29), and Solomon has 300 wives and 700 concubines (2 Kgs 11:3).

Adonijah, first in succession after the death of Amnon and Absalom, and Solomon. Again, the Chronicles narrative sanitizes the story. There is no battle for succession. David and Solomon work together on the plans for the Temple and its ritual and Solomon succeeds to the throne to reign in peace, as foretold in 1 Chron. 22:9.

However, according to the account in Samuel and Kings, Solomon has a powerful mother. Unlike any of David's other wives, Bathsheba returns to the narrative after the main events surrounding her acquisition by David, now as the advocate for her son. She is supported by the prophet, Nathan, while David's army commanders have sided with Adonijah. Nathan, whose powerful condemnation of David's actions towards Uriah and Bathsheba ended with the death of their first son, now connives with her to claim the succession for their second.

Klein analyses the interaction between Nathan, Bathsheba and David (1 Kgs 1:11–31). Bathsheba clearly takes control of the situation, building on the words Nathan instructs her to speak, and guiding him in what he says in corroboration of her words. Bathsheba is urgent and powerful in defence of her son's claim to the throne. Nathan, who was outspoken in his condemnation of the adultery and murder that led to David's acquisition of Bathsheba, now seeks alliance with her, and is in fact the weaker partner in the exchange.

David's last words are recorded in two versions. The first version (2 Sam. 23:1–7) forms part of a formal assessment of David's reign and is full of pious sentiments. The second version (1 Kgs 2:1–9) is embedded in the narrative and, like the account of the affair with Bathsheba, is startling by its presence in the text. David is speaking to Solomon, whose claim to the throne he has supported against Adonijah. Here are the instructions to carry out further murders, which David has been prevented from for various reasons.

Like his life, David's last instructions are wily and cruel. They set out the conditions for the security of Solomon's reign. Once again, without direct action, David sees to the demise of those who threaten him or his succession. The Chronicles account shows him also ensuring the future establishment of the religious hierarchy, with a rigid structure, centralizing the cult on the Temple and priesthood and removing it from the domestic or local community.

Mary, Martha and Mary

So successful is the establishment of the monarchy under David and his successors, that other patterns of governance are, for the most part, ignored. Despite the arguable anti-monarchic and anti-hieratic tendencies of some traditions embedded in the text, for example, Isa. 66:1–4's polemic against the Temple, no other system of government is considered in visions of the future than a centralized monarchic system. Ezekiel speaks of a 'prince' rather than a king, and Zechariah foresees a joint priestly and kingly reign. Isaiah interprets the messianic tradition in terms of peace and justice. But there is no suggestion of returning to the charismatic but unpredictable leadership of the period of the judges, or the tribal patriarchy of the nomadic years, even though both of these remain in the record.

Instead, post-exilic Israel looks forward to the coming of a Messiah, a king who will fulfill the promise of David's reign and will be from the stock of Jesse (Isa. 11:1). David exists as the benchmark against which all future kings are measured, and fall short.[17] David himself becomes a character of perfection in post-biblical literature.

Shulamit Valler notes this change: 'The Bible presents David, the King of Israel, as a complex character who gradually evolved from a soft, delicate and sensitive boy into (when a grown man) a powerful and lustful king and, finally, into a weak old man.'[18] But according to Talmudic interpretation, David is a spiritual man, whose every action must be seen as glorifying God. This means that the spin which already exists in the biblical narrative is taken to the extreme, also seen in Christian interpretations. In order to preserve intact the moral character of David, the women, especially Bathsheba, must be vilified and blamed.[19]

The New Testament, in its present form, begins with the great roll call of genealogy at the start of Matthew's Gospel, tracing the line of descent, interestingly through gentile female lines as well as Hebrew males, from Abraham and, significantly for this article, David to Jesus.

17. See, for e.g., 1 Kgs 15:3 and 2 Kgs 14:3.

18. Shulamit Valler, 'King David and His Women 'Biblical Stories and Talmudic Discussions' in Brenner (ed.), A Feminist Companion to Samuel and Kings, pp. 129–42.

19. Valler, 'King David and His Women', p. 138.

And there is Mary, the waiting receptacle, the woman through whose submission to the will of an all-powerful male God opens the way for the Messiah, *the* Messiah to be born. Jesus is not portrayed as another king in the line of kings, the restoration of the monarchy as a political system, the king in exile in his own occupied country, waiting to lead his people to victory. Though these expectations exist in the narratives of Jesus' life, they are specifically countered. The canonical literature sees Jesus as far more than this. He is the final and ultimate fulfilment of the ideal of monarchy. As son not only of David but also of God, he represents God's reign, and therefore can never be succeeded. He ends the messianic expectation.

This sets up an interesting interaction between the story of King David and the story of Jesus. On one hand, David becomes simply a type. Heather McKay noted this tendency in the New Testament: 'The powerful male Hebrew Bible characters are no longer afforded the protection 'due' under patriarchy to such venerable figures; in Gospels and letters alike they succumb to being patronized by the New Testament authors'.[20]

On the other hand, tracing the origins of Jesus, theologically as well as genealogically, back to David, creates an expectation of majesty and power, actually at odds with the life of Jesus narrated in the Gospels, at least in the synoptic Gospels. There is an insistence in these Gospels that the 'reign' of Jesus critiques patterns of monarchy established by David and his successors. Whereas the move to monarchy derived from a desire to be 'like the nations', Jesus urges his followers not to behave 'like the nations' in concern for personal glory (Mt. 20: 25-28). He reverses the exclusivity of the Davidic religious and political establishment and operates domestically and locally, empowering all those who have been sidelined by that establishment.

But Christian tradition has relentlessly downplayed the radical nature of Jesus' message, and looked back through the lens of Jesus' descent from King David to the splendour, centralization and exclusivity of Temple worship. The epistles, which had such influence

20. Heather McKay, 'Old Wine in New Wineskin. "The Refashioning" of Male Hebrew Bible Characters in New Testament Texts' in Brenner (ed.), A Feminist Companion to the Hebrew Bible and New Testament (Sheffield: Sheffield Academic Press, 1996), pp. 62-94.

in forming the theology of the early churches, contain hymns to the glory of the risen Christ (Col. 1:15–20, and Phil. 2:6–11). The book of Revelation specifically draws on the imagery of monarchy to describe the heavenly reign of Christ.

The creeds make barely a mention of the life of Jesus, with its uncomfortable focus on inclusivity and challenge to hypocrisy. Instead, they swoop from incarnation to death and resurrection and heavenly glory, spending as little time as possible on the ground. I find this largely unrecognized omission staggering. It is as if Jesus said and did nothing of any importance during his ministry. It is surely no coincidence that the creeds were formulated as the Christian faith made the same move from a local and domestic religion to a centralized and power-based cult. It is a sad fact that the hymn books and worship resources of nearly all Christian traditions have followed the same bias as the ancient creeds.

And the women are there, too. Not Michal, who raises the tricky question of David's sexuality, in his relationship to her brother, Jonathan, nor Abishag, for Jesus never makes it to old age.

But Abigail is recreated in the traditional concentration on Lk. 10:38–42's depiction of Martha. Whereas Jn 11:17–27 gives her a visionary and prophetic role, Luke tells the little story of the sisters' disagreement, resolved by Jesus in words that have put women in a double bind ever since. Abigail's dignity is denied to Martha, and Martha's condemnation reflects back on the honour given to the strong, practical Abigail.

And, of course, tradition furnishes Jesus with a Bathsheba. The sinless Jesus is not going to commit adultery. Far from it. The canonical Gospels portray Jesus as sexless. But the extraordinary treatment by Christian tradition of Mary of Magdala feeds lasciviously off the type of the harlot, whose archetype is Bathsheba, with Jezebel following in her wake.

Whether or not this arises from the real relationship of Jesus with Mary, and the jealousy of the male disciples or the misogyny of the creators of the Christian canon, the perversion of the Gospel narratives to create Mary Magdalene, the redeemed prostitute, is pretty well universal. Even in secular Britain, where the vast majority of people know little of the New Testament, surveys show that they think of Mary Magdalene as a prostitute. Interestingly, the series *Bible Mysteries* showed a programme on Mary Magdalene on the same day (March 7th) as the programme on David. This carefully explored the biblical and apocryphal evidence about Mary and debunked the popular image.

By reading the story of David back into the Christ event, the tradition effectively nullifies any radical outcome of Jesus' life as narrated even in the canonical Gospels. The establishment of centralized and exclusive control over state and religion, with all the trappings of power and wealth, have been transferred from the narratives of the Davidic monarchy to churches—both hierarchical and conservative or neo-conservative evangelical—without making contact with the critique offered by the life of Jesus in the Gospels. Traditional liturgical resources, including the ancient creeds and the powerful hymn tradition, concentrate overwhelmingly on supernatural elements in the birth, death and resurrection of Christ, to the exclusion of his teaching and, in particular, his critique on power and glory.

And the women of the Gospels have been reinterpreted according to norms at least partly set up in the Davidic narrative. Any freedom, power or independent action afforded to them in the Gospels has been written out. Martha has become the complaining housewife, and Mary Magdalene the suppliant fallen woman. Both have been denied their place as speakers and proclaimers.

The legacy of David is a huge influence on religious and cultural life. Long after his actual demise and the collapse of the monarchy in Israel, his establishment of a centralized, exclusive system of religious and political government has been sanctified by identifying him with the central figure of the Christian faith. This continues to give credence to church hierarchies, and to the power and wealth held by churches, often with immense political influence. By tradition's sleight of hand, the message and teaching of Jesus recorded in the narratives of his life magically disappear, outshone by the glory of David. This in turn means that women are specifically and deliberately disempowered not only within the churches but also in cultures influenced by them.

The monstrosity of David lives on, and still wields pervasive oppressive and destructive power.

Chapter 9

Searching for a Queer Sophia-Wisdom: The Post-Colonial Rahab

Marcella María Althaus-Reid

Hermeneutics as a Passion for Cruising

'No luxury in civilization can be equal to the relief from the tyranny of custom'. These words from Stanley, the English nineteenth century explorer, could be used today with reference to the Queer interpretation of the Bible.[1] The 'surplus of meaning' produced by the issue of an imperial explorer interpreting Africa, as the land of the *Other*, while exulting in the transgressive possibilities of his own cultural and probably sexual identity, is intriguing and illuminating for the Queer theologian.[2] Confronted with the 'tyranny of custom' in processes of interpretation, the task of queering the Scriptures has things in common with postcolonial readings. In fact, the explorer and the Queer theologian may have in their reflections the same strategical complexity of imperial journeys, viewed partly as a deep search for freedom from identity constraints. Imperial travellers and even missionaries seem to have the need and desire to establish at times new personal sexual routes in a context of religion and imperial destiny. Imperial journeys, as biblical readings, are not independent of a need for sexual explorations. Missionary enterprises are economic and religious projects not neutral on issues of a sexual understanding of the world.

1. Robert Aldrich, *Colonialism and Homosexuality* (London: Routledge, 2004), p. 53.

2. For this point concerning the implications of homosexuality in a wider political and cultural context, see Aldrich, *Colonialism and Homosexuality*.

The same can be said of biblical hermeneutics. Queering the Bible is an art of cruising.

I am starting this reflection by referring to homosexuality and postcolonialism because the relationship amongst desire, theologies and imperialism is a close one, although not always recognized. At the time that the circle of hermeneutical suspicion was developed in Latin American Liberation Theology, a critique of what today is called postcolonialism was not present. Although issues arising from cultural analysis were considered, what was lacking was the inner suspicion, not just of the redaction of the Scripture in itself, but the suspicion at the core of theology. This suspicion was raised with feminist hermeneutics, but even there, another key element, desire, was found wanting.

Part of the problem has been, as the Brazilian theologian Jung Mo Sung has described, that the introduction of desire as central to the theological critique of current neo-Liberal policies, has been seen in feminist liberationist circles as superficial or a 'subjective shortcut' in the face of serious problems.[3] Any introduction of sexuality and the movement of desire in a materialist theology, such as the liberationist is suspected of individualism and lack of commitment towards social transformation. I have tried to reflect on this attitude before, by considering how to reply to what seems one of the important questions of our time: 'What has sexuality to do with Liberation Theology?' What this question fails to recognize is that we are living in a period of a 'sexual Kairos', or the 'hour of God' in our history. Such sexual Kairos is manifested by a deep understanding of desire, market capitalism and the presence of God in our history. It has profound consequences for our Christian praxis of justice towards the alternative project of God's *Kingdom*.

Liberation Theology in Latin America has always been seen as a hermeneutical theology, breaking with the tyranny of custom. This means that in doing Liberation Theology, there is an implicit ongoing exercise of critical suspicion not only in the re-reading of the Bible, but also in reflection on the corpus of Christian orthodoxy. However, the place of desire, as an 'illusion of power' may be the ultimate idolatry still to be uncovered. According to Ruben Alvez, the prophets in the Hebrew Scriptures denounced desire, revealed as power, and as ultimately transformed as religion. Specifically, 'desire

3. Sung, Jung Mo, *Desejo Mercado e Religiao* (Petropolis: Vozes, 1995), p. 3.

as power' becomes what in Liberation Theology terms is called an 'idolatrous religion'.[4] To this Sung adds the theological dimension arising from the relationship between processes of commodification in our market society and the construction of desires in capitalism.[5] One can see then how reflections on desire, far from diluting the urgency of the struggle in Latin America, helps to unveil the ideological strategies already present in theology which obscure liberationist claims. For instance, one of the early seeds of failure of Liberation Theology in Latin America came precisely by forgetting the role of desire in theology in the Exodus narrative. Our question concerning Liberation Theology and sexuality becomes a crucial one when we observe that the liberation of one people (the Israelites) is structurally linked to the oppression of another (the Canaanites), and that the meaning of imperialism is linked to the (sexual) immorality of the *Other*.

It is interesting that one of the most important criticisms of Queer Theologies relates to the place of desire in theology, as strategically non-viable. It is as if only the domestication of desire can produce actions of solidarity and spirituality conducive of social transformation. Curiously, postcolonial theologies have faced a similar criticism, as if they constituted somehow the return to a highly academic, sophisticated theological discussion, remote from the mythical discourse of 'real people' in theology. The bottom line of these criticisms, is the assumption of a normative discourse on (hetero) sexuality as real, but also one of colonial patronage. By colonial patronage we mean the undervaluation and misrepresentation of the colonial subject in theology and, more importantly, of the existing postcolonial strategies for change and dislocation of power. In other words, desire has no part in any individualist, superficial discourse in theology but on the contrary, is constitutive of postcolonial strategies for dislocation of imperial power.

4. Liberation Theology has an obsession for what I have called 'mono-loving'. Idolatry is a category of loving exclusion, used as a metaphor for something else: the forgetfulness of the project of justice in the religion of the Hebrew Scriptures. Cf Althaus-Reid, *The Queer God* (2003), p. 55. See Ruben Alves, O Poeta, O Guereiro (Petropolis: Vozes, 1992).

5. Sung, *Desejo Mercado*, p. 1.

The Postcolonial Sophia-Wisdom

When Asphodel Long wrote her book, *In a Chariot Drawn by Lions* (1992),[6] she also embarked, in a sense, on a Queer and postcolonial journey of finding the hidden history of the vacation, displacement and re-location of the feminine sacred, the Hochma-Sophia, or the tradition of Wisdom in the Scriptures. That was the pioneering uniqueness of her theological and political project. In reading the Bible, I share with Asphodel a somewhat similar quest, although in a more oblique way. However, we both share the Queerness of this journey, finding the sexual displacement of the sacred in theology, while trying to contextualize it in the lives and struggles of contemporary women. Asphodel's search was for 'the female in deity'. My search is for the deity in the female. This does not represent an opposition, but rather a Queer continuation of Asphodel's theological journey, stemming from a transversal, Queer reading in community, which forms my perspective. This is the community of those who read the Bible to find God not only at the margins of the empire, or amongst its victims, but also as a postcolonial, Queer God. This is a God who disenfranchises Godself from the presence of colonial patronage in theology as well as being active in the Queer, alternative and dis-organized practices of social protest and transformation.

It has been my preoccupation to find how desire functions in the discourse of power in the Scriptures, not in the particular sexual performance of any biblical character, but in the way that sexual epistemologies are confronted. To find 'that of the deity in the female' is not a search for a goddess, in this case, but to find how Queer desires relate to the presence of a Queer God, a stranger at the gates of our churches and theologies, which dislocates sexual ideologies of power in our thinking of transcendence. It is sexual thinking, as in it the 'transcendental signified' of the presence of God is manifested in the sacred discourse. That makes of a Sophia-Wisdom, an alternative intelligence.

6. Asphodel Long, *In a Chariot Drawn by Lions: The Search for the Female in Deity*, (London: Women's Press, 1992).

On Rahab and Sexual Terrorism

In reading the text of Joshua we are confronted with one of the most intriguing texts in the Scriptures in terms of sexual epistemologies of confrontation and struggle. This is a text where sexual terrorism and guerrilla struggles reach their peak. Musa Dube, in her book, *Postcolonial Feminist Interpretation of the Bible*, has linked Rahab's story to the projected desires of the colonizer[7] and shows how this is a text suitable for producing internalized betrayal at more than one level. Dube goes as far as highlighting this text together with the story of the Canaanite woman in Matthew 15 and the Great Commission of Mt. 28:19 as a 'prism' which configures the foundational narratives of imperial ideology. The narrative of Rahab and the spies is a text which colonizes the reader.

Rahab's narrative is centred around an ethos of betrayal and submission to imperial powers, but also of relinquishing the imaginary of female transgression which surrounds the construction of her identity. This is what I have called a bisexual praxis of thinking and living in the frontier, or a territory defined by a wall, or a house which is public (as a business) and yet private (as a family home). Roofs are mentioned (where Rahab hides the spies), thus adding an extra dimension to the construction of the limits (or the lack of them) in the text. A window of her house is described as facing outside the wall (Josh. 1:15), from where a scarlet rope is hung to mark and protect Rahab's house from the massacre. Once again, the physical limits of the house keep expanding and extending between the public and the domestic. These are indications of a sense of the presence of what Gloria Anzaldua called *la frontera*, the frontier space of a *mestizo* ethos pervading the narrative, in more than one sense. Here we have a narrative written on a fence, as if a bisexual epistemology is found struggling against some sacralized imperial ideology which thrusts forward to acquire a definite political, social and sexual identity. Rahab is to be found in the struggle of a Queer-Sophia, a Sophia of a Queer Wisdom standing alone against a process of making her straight: straight in the conversion towards a monotheistic culture and religion, manifested in a process of imperialist expansion. Is then Rahab a bisexual Sophia, trespassing her spaces while negotiating frontiers of sexual and

7. Musa Dube, *Postcolonial Feminist Interpretation of the Bible* (St Louis: Chalice Press, 2000), p. 76.

political identity? Did not Rahab's desires clash with the mimetic desires of the empire which were grounded in a strong heterosexual ideology?

Beyond finding the presence of imperial, heterosexual ideology in the narrative of Rahab (which functions as an inscribed theological interpretation), feminist theologies will ask us to relate this frontier theological narrative to our lives. However, this is easier said than done. The problem we have is the lack of inscription of queer 'real lives' in the Bible, in theology and in the churches. What we have are fragments. Queer interpretation cannot find an exchange with 'real (Queer) lives' in the Bible unless it departs from the naïve idea of interpretation as a process of straightforward translation of meaning. Queer hermeneutics means an engagement with a type of intersemiotic interpretation. To read the Rahab narratives from this perspective is a permutative praxis, where we can recognize that real life experiences are sexually (ideologically) organized, and that includes those of the theologian herself. If we agree that the 'correspondence of relationship' of the liberationists needs more oblique glancing in order to be more honest and creative, it also needs a dislocation of the theologian as a reader.[8] To resolve the problem of simplistic relationships Clodovis Boff produced his 'correspondence of relationships' hermeneutics, in which similar community experiences needed to be put in their corresponding political and economical context. Feminist liberation hermeneutics have worked in a similar way. However, this model has its limitations in that it tends to privilege an ideological and not a critical view of reality, which constructs its own particular (hetero) subject—a hetero-subject theologically organized not according to sexual options, but to sexual ways of acting/reflecting. To this we may add the fact that the theologian as a reader tends to be fused with the hetero-subject of the built narrative.

The need to dislocate the hetero-theologian-reader in the Scripture is crucial for those engaged in the search for an alternative Sophia of the Queer Wisdom. Who is that reader-theologian? Where is she

8. The liberationist style of reading the Scriptures sought to produce an exchange between community experiences in the Bible and, for instance, a slum in Uruguay, but soon it became evident that such relationships needed to be considered carefully. Basically, the different social and cultural milieu produced irreconcilable differences amongst interpretative communities with a considerable chronological and cultural distance.

located when reading the story of Rahab? A Queer permutative process interchanges and re-locates the theologian in a different real life experience which may be obscured by an imperialist interpretation of the Bible. In other words, if we are reading the narrative of Sodom, we may consider locating the theologian as a witness of, for example, Oscar Wilde's trial. We need to read and discover the collapse of Wilde's self-defence and the tragedy which engulfed not only him, but his family and friends. Unless we do that, it will not be possible to uncover the 'real queer lives' in the story of Sodom and Gomorrah, a history of queer desires confronted by the incomprehension of an imperial (hetero) God towards love outside political institutions. The same can be said in relation to Rahab's story. Where is the theologian located here? Can we permute her with a *guerrillera* in Nicaragua during the Contra war? Or with a human right's lawyer in a big city of Latin America during the years of the cold war, when to defend the innocent was an act of disobedience to the values of 'God, Family and Tradition'? Rahab forces the theologian to make political options, which are also sexual, just as guerrilla women were punished not only for their political activities but for having abandoned their gendered place.

The point is that Rahab's narrative asks the reader to take sexual options. As I have said, Rahab's narrative is a deeply, frontier-like bisexual text. The betrayal of Rahab towards her nation corresponds to a heterosexual, mono-loving mentality of only one nation, one God and one faith. To permute this text, or to call another theological witness to this narrative, we need to find the theologian as an insurgent, perhaps scribbling graffiti on the walls of Jericho.

Permutations: Rahab and Sexual Terrorism

> Those who cannot find God here, would not be able to find God anywhere.
>
> Written outside the door of a toilet cubicle.[9]

I intend to read the story of Rahab permuting dreams, facts and fictions from two texts. The first was written by an Argentinian author during the cold war (and the'dirty war' in Argentina). This is a queer, intriguing early novel by (Eduardo) Lázaro Covadlo

9. E. Lázaro Covadlo, *En Este Lugar Sagrado* (Buenos Aires: LH, 1970), p. 76.

entitled *En este Lugar Sagrado* ('In this Sacred Place', 1970). The other text is the poem from Gloria Anzaldúa, 'La Nueva Mestiza.'[10]

Why do I suggest we permute the theological location of the reader of Rahab with the novel from Covadlo and the poem from Anzaldúa? *En este Lugar Sagrado* comes from Argentina during the seventies, the time of the cold war, dictatorial regimes and guerrilla movements. It was also a particular time in the history of imperialist expansion in Latin America, when women joined the guerrilla movements and suffered violent persecution. It was a time when women needed to betray their search for justice and dignity in order to conform to the ideal Christianity of the dictatorial regime, which was based on a 'jealous' (mimetic) God, in the struggle against those who opposed their regimes, and therefore the imperialist forces which put them in place. 'La Nueva Mestiza' is Gloria Anzaldúa's manifesto of trespassing ideological processes of identity formation, which also touch on what Bhaba has called 'the intentional hybrid'[11] or the moment of resistance against imperial discourses of political, sexual , cultural, racial and religious identity.

In Covadlo's *En Este Lugar Sagrado*, the main character is a writer, who intends to write a novel on the walls of all public toilets of Buenos Aires. Written at the time of military censorship and a rigid pre-conciliar Roman Catholicism which constructed the form of patriotism identified with the movement 'God, Fatherhood and family' (*Dios, Patria y Hogar*), Virgilioni, the toilet writer, not only transgresses the censorship of the country, but also produces a bi/ epistemological challenge at more than one level: First, there is a dislocation of public/private spaces in the narrative. The public toilets in the coffee bars of Buenos Aires, represent ambiguous frontiers between the secular and the religious, art and everyday life. They also present spaces of political transgression. Moreover, the pages of the novels are walls, WC table covers and doors which as written texts are complete and fragmentary at the same time. Virgilioni produces a kind of revolutionary, insurgent movement which is defeated when in a context of Capitalism, the author is invited to institutionalize his work.[12] Through rules and new approved laws,

10. Gloria Anzaldúa, Borderlands La Frontera: The New Mestiza (San Francisco: Aunt Lute Books, 1999).

11. Robert J.C. Young, Postcolonialism: A Very Short Introduction (Oxford: Oxford University Press, 2003).

12. Virgilione (a surname with an etymological play with the word 'virgin') is in Covadlo's novel a subversive and virginal writer (in the sense of naïve) which needs to

the revolutionary writing in public toilets is normalized. The queer writer with a queer mystical and political project is incorporated into the system, thus ending the menace of *poiesis* to a dictatorial regime.

The theologian is writing on the walls: the walls of Jericho, and the walls of public toilets in Buenos Aires. Both activities require secrecy and a sense of urgency; the writing is of a subversive nature, and the author needs to make a quick escape. The interesting thing is that the theologian is not only trying to write at the margins of the system, but is also using a form of 'marginal writing' which denies authorship. These, then, are some of the main clues questioning our reading. Should a theologian reading from the margins use the same means of production, the same *escritura teológica,* as one reading from the centre? What would constitute a re-writing of Rahab's narrative from fragments written on the walls of Jericho? Writing on the walls means that the woman theologian reading Rahab has a project, to write a theology about invasions and oppressions, and to do it in these frontier spaces of the intimate and the public, which are the walls of public toilets. She is a guerrilla theologian organizing what seems a fragmentary piece of writing, but if one only could visit all the public toilets of the city, one would see the whole project in place. Yet, writing in toilets, as *señor* Virgilione in Covadlo's story, implies also writing a narrative which changes with the semiotic structure of graffiti. It is erased, modified, or even changed by other graffiti written beside or over it, approving, querying or in contestation with the original text. Such is the fate of the original text on the toilet wall: a graffiti dialogue which is never complete.

Therefore, we need to be able to see the graffiti-like structure of this subversive reading of Rahab. That is, to find what is left of Rahab after the writing on the walls has gone through a process of erasure and re-configuration. In that case we should be able to rescue what was perhaps Rahab's destiny, to be a *good guerrillera,* a woman who could have been a site of transgressive revelations and yet who left only intelligible scribbles on the walls.

be institutionalized. However, Rahab is not interpretatively portrayed as a virgin. In the Hebrew Scriptures wise women are not virgins, nor are virgins necessarily seen as wise. The presence of a Sophia-Wisdom in Rahab comes in any case from promiscuity. A Sophia-Rahab is then a promiscuous wise woman of God, who forgets her wisdom when she opts to convert to the mono-system of Judaism, or her own institutionalization.

The Meaning of Frontiers

> To live in the borderlands means you
> are neither hispana india negra española
> Ni gabacha, eres mestiza. mulata, half-breed
> Caught in the crossfire between camps while carrying all five races on your back
> Not knowing which side to turn to, run from;
> ....
>
> Cuando vives en la frontera
> people walk through you...
> ....
> To survive in the Borderlands
> You must live sin fronteras,
> be a crossroads. (Gloria Anzaldúa).[13]

The idea of the frontier in Rahab is obviously both physical and metaphysical. If in postcolonial criticism the frontier is the borderline that helps in the construction of the imperial self, in a sexual theology the frontier represents trangenderism. In this narrative, it is the mono-God of heterosexuality who calls for an original female act of betraying, as part of the founding narrative of the Promised Land. Rahab's betrayal is not only the betrayal of her nation, the betrayal of her friends and compatriots, her culture and traditional spirituality, it is the betrayal of whatever constitutes Queerness in her life and identity. It is the betrayal of frontier existence. When Jericho was finally burned down by Joshua, he asked Israel to repeat a curse on whoever rebuilt the city. This is a mimetic desire of a God who keeps reproducing Godself in similar affectionate, cultural and economic exchanges. This is the love/logic of imperialism. Rahab leaves the frontier by declaring herself heterosexual. She dis-assembles herself from a Queer identity which transgresses sites of the domestic and the public, and situates her living as oscillating in a border region where she need not fix her identity. That critical bisexuality of Rahab requires conversion and memory of conversion. Rahab is normalized: her fragmentary, subversive graffiti requires some form of archaeological discovery of hidden knowledge or hidden Sophia-Wisdom in the text. Rahab's graffiti is inscribed on the outside wall of the law of the Father. Like the Sodomites, she

13. Gloria Anzaldua, La Frontera/Borderlands. (San Francisco: Aunt Lute Books, 1999).

gives hospitality, but it is the God of Joshua (the same God as the God of the Sodomites) who is inhospitable, who cannot live with the different. It is no coincidence then that in Josh. 6:21, the massacred people of Jericho are declared 'anathema', that is, a sacrifice of idols to the God of Israel. All that is preserved are items of gold, silver and bronze which are kept by the invaders of Jericho in their own sanctuary. Paradoxically, the precious metals stolen from a massacred nation and sacralized, became the real idols, in the sense of becoming an illusion of power. The sanctuary of YHWH ended up as a space defined by the accumulation of commodities.

At the end of this Queer reading of Joshua 2 one gets the feeling that this is a foundational text, which could be called, 'The origin of Queer betrayal'. Queer betrayal becomes a virtue, but did Rahab survive it, and how about God? I have already claimed that ours is a Queer God, a God obscured by theological representations of the re-production of desire in an imperial space. This space already seems to function as a market theology. *Extra agoram nulla salus*: outside the market—of exchanges of affections and the political and religious hegemony of the YHWH project—there is no salvation.

(Eduardo) Lazaro Covadlo left Argentina due to political persecution to live abroad. His parable of the man writing novels on public toilets, exposed and condemned the process by which the writer/interpreter could be bought by the system, the process by which his project of protest became annulled by the forces he tried to oppose. In his novel, Covadlo presented Virgilione as someone who finally succumbed to survival, ending his political and economical persecution. But does Virgilione survive, or does he die somehow in this process? Does Rahab survive? Does she become what Lisa Isherwood has called 'a willing victim of a dominant/submission discourse that does not allow for full flourishing'?[14] Or is Rahab also an anathema sacrifice, a sacrifice of otherness, bi/sexual thinking and frontier-like transgression? Interestingly, the cold war years in Argentina, with the rise of the 'National Security Doctrine' which denounced the presence of internal enemies in the Argentinian nation, has much in common with the destruction of Jericho. In both the narrative of Rahab and the recent history of

14. Lisa Isherwood, 'Fucking Straight and the Gospel of Radical Equality' in Marcella Althaus Reid & Lisa Isherwood (eds.), *The Sexual Theologian* (London: T. & T. Clark, 2005), p. 50.

Argentina, the nation needs to be rescued or saved by a biblical God only through its destruction.[15] The ones who collaborate with the destruction of their nation, in order to uphold imperialist policies are also sacrificed. Meanwhile the Reagan Administration and the Vatican policy of John Paul II declared Liberation Theology to be an internal enemy. Some in the church followed Rahab and were blessed by the gods of the empire; others followed strategies of insurgence and were persecuted and killed. Thirty years have passed and inspired by the ghosts of more than 30,000 disappeared, the protest and the struggle continues.

And was Jericho resurrected, the Jericho which produced wise, sexually and economically independent women such as Rahab? Did the Sophia-Wisdom killed in Rahab's sacrifice of her identity ever come back, or did she perish under the weight of the gold and silver accumulated in the sanctuary of YHWH? There is a continuation, or mimetic reproduction of Rahab mentioned amongst the ancestry of Jesus. That Rahab is of no interest to us. In a way, Asphodel Long has asked also for the continuation of the Rahab of dissent, when she asked about the destiny of the Wisdom goddesses in the Scriptural tradition. To her own question, 'What happens to Wisdom?' she answers '...never totally forgotten.'[16] And I am thinking about the Argentina of Covadlo; the Argentina of the National Security Doctrine which produced one of the most severe gender codes ever devised; the Argentina which deprecated women studying Psychology or Sociology, calling them 'prostitutes'; the Argentina which ordered the burning of Liberation Theology books while at the same time legislating on the length of women's dresses and banning the wearing of trousers by female students; the Argentina where priests asked women to pray to the Virgin Mary and to refrain from politics, forgetting the disappeared and ignoring the crisis of the representability of the dissenters. And I am thinking about Sophia-Wisdom, coming back amongst the transvestites of Buenos Aires, with their blonde hair done up in a bun, publicly identifying themselves with Eva Perón, in a display of political transgression which was also a transgression of the silencing of the right to difference. These are the transvestites of the road which

15. For the use of metaphors of the 'pouring of the blood of Jesus' justifying political repression, see Emilio Mignone, *Iglesia y Dictadura* (Buenos Aires: Ediciones del Pensamiente, 1986), p. 22.

16. Long, *In a Chariot Drawn by Lions*, p. 138.

divides the city from the provinces, a frontier area. Perhaps in some of them, in this reading of Queer permutations in the Bible, Rahab and her Queer Wisdom still survive, in the obstinacy of a Queer transcendence. Their struggle for transgender identity is associated with a political desire to disrupt what Martha Rosenberg has called the 'plan from the God of the Market'[17] which is still demanding a betrayal of life for the sake of a God of death and a forgetfulness of ourselves in order to be remembered in our churches and in theology. And that is what Rahab's graffiti may have left for us, the memory of forgetfulness and the imperial destruction of trangressive women which, paradoxically, is sometimes called salvation.

17. Martha Rosenberg, 'Debate Primer Panel' in J. Fernandez *et al*, *Cuerpos Ineludibles. Un Dialogo a partir de las Sexualidades* (Buenos Aires: Aji de Pollo, 2004), p. 68.

Chapter 10

Taste and See; A Midrash on Genesis 3:6 and 3:12

Daniel E. Cohen

Abstract

The story of the Garden of Eden is one of the foundation stories of Christian and Jewish cultures, which is often used as a justification for the oppression of women. In my version of this story I look at what *might have happened* if Adam had accepted responsibility for his actions. It is one of a series of re-tellings and re-visons of myths and traditional tales from a male pro-feminist viewpoint. A commentary indicates sources for some of the less familiar points in my story.

Oh taste, taste and see
How good is the fruit that falls from the tree
Oh taste, taste and see
How good is the fruit of the garden.

(Betsy Rose)[1]

Eve was not made from Adam's head to reign over him,
nor from his feet, to be trampled by him,
but from his side, to be his equal,
under his arm, to be protected,
and next to his heart, to be loved.

(Traditional)[2]

Let me tell you how it happened. It's not the way He told Himself it must have happened, the way He persuaded everyone to tell the

1. Betsy Rose, 'Taste and See', A Song on in My Hands (Berkeley: Parallax Music, 1988).

2. Mathew Henry, Commentary on the Whole Bible, http//www.ccel/henry/mhcl.html.

story. But so far I can still remember the truth, even despite His pressure to tell it His way.

Of course, He blamed Eve.

'You were always the best of My creations,' He assured me. 'The one most like Me. You always listened to what I said.'

'The woman must have tempted you,' He decided.

In those days He spoke to me often, and it is true that I listened, perhaps paying too much attention. Then, and later, some of His edicts seemed arbitrary or cruel, but I always assumed He had a good reason for them. Yet somehow He did not bother to talk to Eve.

That led to problems, but it also had advantages for Eve. It made her much freer, more capable of making decisions for herself.

I had named the animals, as He had told me to do. But it was Eve who decided that the plants also needed naming. 'Oak,' she said, and 'rhododendron.' Ordinary everyday names, those were, much like animal names such as 'cat' and 'rhinoceros'. But then she got more fanciful. 'Forget-me-not,' she mused, and 'old man's beard.'

'I don't understand. What do these names mean?' I asked her. 'They seem the right names somehow. They came to me, and I don't know who suggested them' was all she would answer.

And then she came to *that* tree. 'Fig,' she declared confidently.

I quickly pulled her away from the tree. 'You know what He said about that tree,' I reminded her.

But she kept going back to that tree, whose smell and appearance delighted her. I could sense her making up her mind.

At last she reached out and touched the fruit. Urgently I called out once more, 'You know what He said about that tree'.

'He never spoke to me about it. If He wants to ignore me, then I can ignore Him. I know He told you not to eat. But I don't know if He also wanted me not to eat' she added.

As she plucked the fruit, she said 'Good? Evil? I don't know what they mean, but they must mean change of some sort. And we need a change in this unchanging place', as she bit into the ripe fruit.

I knew it would mean trouble, He had warned me often enough, but what was I to do? If she was going to be troubled, then I had to share it. Above even that, I trusted her judgment and admired her courage in choosing change and the unknown rather than staying with what was familiar. So I reached out, took the fruit from her hand, and took a bite myself. And we each ate half of the fruit she had taken.

Well, you know what happened after that. How He asked if we had eaten the fruit He had forbidden. I could have placed the blame on Eve, insisting that it was her fault that I had also eaten the fruit, that she had persuaded me. But I had made the choice to eat it when she offered. If there was a fault, it was mine as much as hers. And so we answered together that we had, that we had felt the need for change. He drove us out of the Garden and pronounced a fate on us.

It's been a hard life since then, with much toil and grief. But there has also been joy.

Eve was right. In the Garden there was no change and so there were no stories. But now there are many stories, and there will be stories until the end of time.

But there is one thing that worries me. He continues to talk to me. And He keeps telling me that I should not have listened to Eve, that I was the head of the household and it was her duty to obey me.

I have always been used to listening to Him, accepting what He says as the truth. So far He has not convinced me when He says this, as I can remember what really happened. But if He keeps on telling me this, sooner or later I will come to believe him. And then the story will take a sadder turn, lasting for many generations, until people stop listening to His voice and seek the truth for themselves.

Commentary

The first quote, and the title, are taken, with permission, from the song *Taste and See* on Betsy Rose's cassette of songs, *In My Two Hands,* based on the teachings of Thich Nhat Hanh and Creation Spirituality. Ps. 34:8 says 'Taste and see that the Lord is good'.

I do not know the origin of the second quote, which I have known for many years, but I think it is thirteenth or fourteenth century English. It seems to be a version of a remark by the twelfth century theologian and bishop Peter Lombard (quoted in several articles on the Internet, in particular one by Yolande Barber.[3] Thomas Aquinas[4] says 'It was right for the woman to be made from a rib of man. First, to signify the social union of man and woman, for the woman should neither use authority over man, and so she was not made from his head; nor was it right for her to be subject to man's contempt as his slave, and so she was not made from his feet.' Note that Aquinas did not include Lombard's comment that Eve was taken from Adam's side that she should be his partner. There are also many other Jewish and Christian discussions as to why Eve was made from Adam's rib rather than from another part; I do not cite these as they are mostly extremely misogynist.

In its strictest sense, 'midrash' refers to rabbinic biblical interpretations of the first five centuries C.E. Nowadays, it is commonly used 'as a name for all "creative" interpretations of the Bible that seek to move beyond the historical, "original" sense of the biblical text.'[5] The spirit of midrash has '[an] imperative to connect to the biblical text, [an] irrepressible playfulness, and [a] delight in multiple, polyvalent traditions of interpretation'.[6]

Who is the 'villain' of the story? In the conventional telling it is Eve (more so than the serpent, even when identified with Satan). A feminist emphasis might cast Adam as the villain, because of the way he refuses to take responsibility for his actions. I am particularly interested in creating new images for men, so I change the story so that Adam accepts responsibility. The 'villain' in my telling is Yahweh, who seems to have fixed views on the status of women.

Gen. 3.12 (in the translation by Mary Phil Korsak, which is a particularly accurate rendition of the Hebrew[7] for the use of 'groundling' rather than 'man') states 'The groundling said "The woman you gave to be with me, she, she gave me of the tree and I ate." 'This seems to be denying responsibility and putting it onto the woman, or even ('the woman *you gave*') onto Yahweh, but it

3. Yolande Barber, at http://ourworld.compuserve.com/homepages/CCFHUB/ORDWOMEN.HTM.

4. Thomas Aquinas, (Summa Theologica, question 92, cited at http://www.ccel.org/a/aquinas/summa/FP/FP092.html).

5. Stern, 'Midrash and Midrastic Interpretation' in Adele Berlin and Marc Zvi Brettler, *The Jewish Study Bible* (Oxford: Oxford University Press, 2004).

6. Stern, 'Midrash'.

7. Mary Phil Korsak, *At the Start: Genesis Made New* (Louvain: Leuvense Scrijversaktie, 1992).

says nothing about temptation. That comes in verse 13, where the woman said 'The serpent enticed me, and I ate.' However the concept that Adam was tempted by Eve is common, both in Judaism and Christianity. Interestingly, the Koran simply records that both ate the fruit of the tree, and that Satan tempted Adam, with no specific mention of Eve (Suras 2.36, 7.22, and 20.120–121).

We are told (Gen. 2.20) that Adam named the animals. Someone must have named the plants, but no details are given, so my story suggests that Eve named them.

Genesis does not say what fruit the Tree of Knowledge produced. It is commonly regarded as being an apple, but this may simply be because the Latin word for apple is *malus* and that for evil is *malum.* Some rabbinical writings suggest that the fruit was a fig. (In *The Story of Eve,* Pamela Norris mentions several different suggestions. This book is an account of the many different stories and beliefs that have made up the composite picture of Eve).[8]

The tree is named as the Tree of Knowledge of Good and Evil. This is commonly taken to mean an understanding of morality, of what behaviour is to be called good and what is to be called evil. But it may also mean knowledge of what is helpful and what is harmful—'weal and woe' is suggested in the notes of the *Jewish Study Bible.* That Bible uses the same words in the related phrase of Isa. 45.7, which it translates as 'I make weal and create woe', whereas the Authorised Version says 'I make peace and create evil.'

The *Jewish Study Bible* makes two other suggestions about this. The words may, like 'heaven and earth', imply all things by referring to two polar opposites. And knowledge itself may be both good and bad, or pleasant and painful. Rabbi Yossi New[9] said that the Hebrew does not contain the word 'of', so that the phrase should read 'Tree of Knowledge—good and evil', with the same implication.

Gen. 2.8 refers to two trees, the Tree of Life and the Tree of Knowledge of Good and Evil, of which only the latter is forbidden (Gen. 2.16–17). The prohibition on the Tree of Life, and the related banishment from the Garden of Eden, only come after Adam and Eve have eaten from the Tree of Knowledge (Gen. 3.22). I have often wondered what would have happened had they first eaten of the fruit of the Tree of Life, which was not forbidden, and then gone on to eat of the forbidden fruit—but that is another story. It

8. Pamela Norris, *The Story of Eve,* (London: Picader, 1998), p. 338.

9. In a talk at the *Mythic Journeys* conference, Atlanta 2004.

would be too much of a digression to discuss the interesting Jewish and Christian traditions regarding the Tree of Life, as well as its connection with the goddess Asherah.[10]

Gen. 3.4–5 tells of the serpent tempting Eve. But it says nothing about whether Eve was interested in the serpent's claim that eating the fruit would make her like gods. Instead, 3:6 just says that the fruit was good to eat and pleasing to the eye, and gives no more reason than that. Perhaps all that interested Eve in the serpent's speech was that touching the fruit would not lead to death.

Was Eve told by Yahweh not to eat the fruit of the tree, or did she only hear of it from Adam? The prohibition was given to Adam before Eve was created (Gen. 2.17). If we take the common interpretation of Gen. 2.21, that Eve was created from Adam's rib, then she plainly was not told directly. However, the Hebrew word actually means 'side' and not 'rib', and there is a suggestion that an originally androgynous being was split into two.[11] That possibility would mean that Eve also heard the prohibition. Note also that the prohibition was against eating the fruit, but (Gen. 3.3) Eve states it as a prohibition against eating or touching. This enables the serpent to reply that touching it does not lead to death. It is not said in Genesis whether it was Eve who added the prohibition against touching or if Adam added it when he told her. Jewish legends state that it was Adam who added it, intending to add extra force to the prohibition (this is discussed by Shira Halevi,[12] which gives as a reference *Bereshith Rabbah* XIX.3). Steinsaltz refers to Eve as 'arch-temptress'. He also remarks that it was Eve who tempted Adam, not the other way round, because 'Adam had been commanded directly by God, while Eve received the commandment only through Adam. Obedience to the divine imperative, whether negative or positive, must be based on a direct personal relationship.' This, at least, does not present Eve as a person inherently more liable to be tempted than Adam.

Shira Halevi's book: *The Life Story of Adam and Havah* is a re-telling and re-interpretation, with a commentary based on a variety of

10. Asphodel Long, *Asherah, The Tree of Life and the Menorah* (Neath: BISFT, 1998).

11. Adin Steinsaltz, *Biblical Images* (New York: Basic Books, 1984), p. 5. See also the Talmudic references Berachoth 61a, Erubin 18a and Genesis Rabba 7.)

12. Shira Halevi, *The Life Story of Adam and Havah* (Northvale: Jason Aronsen Inc, 1997), p. 174.

ancient to medieval Jewish sources, which is a fascinating approach to the difficulties of translation and interpretation. She suggests that the prohibition may not have applied to Eve, and gives a reason why this might be so.[13]

Both Milton and St. Augustine indicate that it was love for Eve that caused Adam to eat the fruit[14] puts it positively ('Bone of my bone thou art, and from thy state Mine never shall be parted, bliss or woe'), whereas Augustine[15] considers that Adam should not have let love and desire influence Adam's judgment. I suggest that he made a positive judgment based on love for her and realization of her strengths.

The Jewish and Christian interpretations of the story are significantly different. Christianity, following St. Augustine, claims that we are all born sinful as a result of Adam's sin. 'In Adam's fall We sinned all' is a commonly used phrase which, according to the Web site http://www.answers.com/topic/new-england-primer, originated in the seventeenth century schoolbook, *The New England Primer*. Judaism only states that as a result we are born with the likelihood that we will sin, but the newborn child is not sinful.[16]

Readers may wonder why there is no serpent in my telling. One reason is that I am telling the story from Adam's viewpoint, and he does not know of the serpent until very late on. Another reason is that the serpent's role and motivations are so important that they could take over any story. But the primary reason is that the serpent chose not to be in my story.

There are many modern retellings of the story, in both poetry and prose.[17]

A version of the story that particularly appeals to me as a story-teller has been told by Jean Houston. In my words to her version, it runs as follows:

God looked down at the Garden of Eden, and sighed deeply. His best friend, known to us as Satan, asked what was the matter.

13. Halevi, *The Life Story*, p. 191.

14. Milton cited in Norris, *The Story of Eve*, p. 192.

15. Norris, *The Story of Eve*, p. 192.

16. For Jewish understandings of sin, see Abraham Heschel, *God in Search of Man* (New York: Farrar Strauss and Giroux, 1955), pp. 361–66 and Adin Steinsaltz, *The Strife of the Spirit* (Northvale, Janson Aronson, 1988), pp. 110–15, although these references do not address this specific point.

17. Penelope Farmer, *Eve: Her Story* (London: Victor Gall Ancz, 1985).

'I can't understand it,' said God. 'I've told them and told them not to eat of that tree, and what happens.'

'What does happen?'

'Nothing, that's the problem.'

'Let me see what I can do,' replied Satan. And he went off to the Garden in the form of a serpent, with the results that we all know.

God was happy. '*Now* the story can begin.'

Chapter 11

'Eat, Friends, Drink. Be Drunk With Love' [Song of Songs 5:2] – A Reflection

Lisa Isherwood

In the Song of Songs the patriarchs are given a run for their money and the prophetic tradition may be challenged while the villainous interpretations of this text have led to centuries of body-denying repression and even witch hunting. It is then a text that sits well in this book since it offers much by way of a challenge to the patriarchs and prophets and can illuminate how interpretations can be treacherous villains.

The biblical base for the celibate life is traditionally, and ironically, understood as the Song of Songs. The Bride of Christ is encouraged to seek total union with him in a mystical marriage such as that spoken of by Bernard of Clairvaux. For Bernard, the Song of Songs is the greatest biblical revelation of divine love but not one of mutual love. Here he claims we see the soul [viewed as the female voice] having been loved first by God responding through gratitude for this love. In his sermons on the Song of Songs[1] he stresses that one must love and not study as it is the contact between the soul and God that makes the commitment real and enduring and the transformation of the soul complete. This transformation comes with obedience as a necessary prerequisite to holy repose of the soul. Focussing on the humanity of Jesus rather than the divinity of Christ, Bernard points out the exceptional grace that the spouse seeks when asking for the kiss of the Word made flesh. Bernard is radical when he suggests that the Word may not come from without as he is closer to the self than the self is to humans but this all fades away

1. Bernard of Clairvaux, on the Song of Songs, Books 1–4 (Michigan: Cistercian Publications, 1979).

when he talks of the carnal affections being quieted by the contact with the Word.[2] Bernard believes that fear accompanies love when a soul seeks God, in addition there is a purgatory of love, that is having known the loved one he moves away and leaves one desolate and always longing for his return. For Bernard, then, the Song of Songs, speaks of the love between the soul and God, it lays before us the spiritual marriage in which the spouse is consumed in love and transformed in the presence of the beloved. The soul is passively consumed and transformed, here is the stuff of Mills and Boon on the spiritual must read list, the passion is in the inequality. It means, of course, for Bernard, that a celibate life devoted to the pursuit of this spiritual marriage, one repressing sexuality and desire for all except Jesus, is the path best travelled. He was not alone in reading this text as a manual for the celibate life.

That celibacy should be based on one of, if not the most, erotic pieces of biblical literature is worth pondering, particularly for women. Women have, under the guise of desire, been encouraged to deny the physical nature of that desire and become domesticated through chaste reflections on the object of their love. A reversal has taken place, whereas the Song of Songs clearly shows the body as a medium of divine/human expression and creativity, celibacy has, as defined over the centuries since Origen tended to close people down. It has moved them from a healthy relationship with their bodies and other people into an unnatural world of divine marriage and relationship. A place, where at its worst, any other relationship could appear adulterous. Of course, human sexuality does not just give up and go away and we have a wealth of mystical writing by women that is highly erotic and at times sexually explicit, with Christ as the object of desire. Catherine of Sienna rolled on the ground moaning as she received the foreskin of Jesus as her profession ring, while Margery Kempe married God and declared that sex with him was more satisfying than with her husband. We read of women being penetrated by love until they are on fire with passion for Christ and others who persecute their bodies out of love for Christ. The whole range of human sexuality can be seen despite the fact that it takes place within a celibate framework. It would be too easy to dismiss these sexual manifestations as outbursts of frustration clothed in acceptable garments, that is piety and spiritual enlightenment. It seems that they are much more than this,

2. Bernard of Clairvaux, Sermon 74, Book iv, pp. 90–91.

the body is part of the human/divine process and it makes itself available even when held in close check. I would rather see these outbursts as the glorious celebration of embodiment then neurotic symptoms of repressed women.

If we get away from the fanciful readings of the Fathers what is it we are faced with? I say fanciful because after all there is no mention of marriage in this text let alone a mystical one and in fact there is also no mention of God, one of only two biblical texts that in fact has no mention of God at all. What we hear is an unmediated female voice, the only unmediated female voice is all the biblical literature, which comes through love poetry not the usual biblical songs. Indeed these love poems are more after the style of the Near Eastern love poems than the biblical models of songs. That is to say they are frank, open, tenderly longing and erotically bold and on the lips of a woman they act as an exploration of female sexuality in a wholly positive way. These texts are quite unlike those of many of the prophets where female sexuality is conceived of in negative terms with the sexually aware women being imaged as adulterous and unfaithful to the ever patient and long suffering husband, the almighty patriarch. This woman is empowered and this picture of her lends itself to questioning some of the more engrained assumptions of the world in which the poems were written as well as calling into question many of the body denying interpretations it has suffered at the hands of Christian exegetes. I think it would be a mistake to see this as a purely celebratory text since there are hints of danger and ill treatment of the woman [5:7] but more than any other biblical text this is not a text of terror for women it is a text of empowerment, if it is allowed to be.

The villains in relation to this text have been those who have taken it away from women through a very dualistic interpretation of what is clearly a celebration of the sensual pleasure of bodies in relation with each other's passions. These villains need to be challenged and their co-conspirators, patriarchs and prophets need to take heed too! Here we have a truly rare and wonderful text, a text that prioritizes female sexual pleasure and gives agency to the woman, who in claiming it challenges the power of patriarchy in many of its forms. It is not a romantic text precisely because the pleasure so beautifully spoken of is never far away from the danger— any woman indulging in the body based sensual challenge to patriarchy that this woman is immersed in will always run the risk of backlash, of danger to herself and her pleasures. In this sense then it is a real text, not the stuff of romantic myth cut off from the perilous reality that lurks not too far beneath the surface of that 'appealing' rhetoric.

What we actually read is of two lovers of different races meeting with disapproval from people in both communities and families. She is black, 'I am very black'[1:5] and this offends the daughters of Jerusalem who would have this man for themselves. Her brothers are offended because she gives herself freely to her lover beyond the legal contract, the 'knowing' of marriage.[3] In this way she diminishes her worth as a family asset, she will not actually be able to make a good marriage after such an affair. And the lovers' passion for one another further challenges the patriarchal system as it is not linked at all to procreation, simply to attraction, beauty beyond the normal bounds of the acceptable face of attraction and pleasure. The text abounds with references to the non-penetrative nature of much of their love making and the pure delight that they both experience in this. From the beginning of the text the woman is asserting that his love is better than wine and his fruit is sweet in her mouth [2:3]. His joy is also evident in the text when he declares her genitals are 'an orchard of pomegranates with excellent fruit.'[4:13] The orality of these passages and the constant emphasis on fruit are both significant when we look to this text for a challenge to the dualistic patriarchal interpretations of old.

The Christian tradition has used this text to underpin its dualistic and hierarchical rhetoric about the sustaining power of the mystical marriage as opposed to the fleeting and shallow pleasures of sexual love. Here with an emphasis on sexual love as food, indeed fruit, we find a real challenge to that rhetoric. Food is life sustaining and fruit a wonderful riot of juicy taste and texture, a delightful addition to any diet but nonetheless a life sustaining and preserving addition. [Five a day we are told!] By coupling sex and fruit in this text the author is celebrating the life sustaining aspect of sexuality beyond that of the merely procreative and introducing us to the idea that the more tastes, textures and smells we encounter the richer life is. So the more immersed in sensuality we become the more our lives are enriched and indeed the more we challenge the patriarchal order of bland procreative sex. The Near East certainly used agricultural

3. To know was a phase to do with the legal part of a marriage rather than the sexual part.

images when referring to sex but they were highly patriarchal, the seed was planted in the field and the valuable issue came forth. There is none of that in this text, the seed and field are replaced with the ripening, taste and engorgement of fruit and phallic procreative images are not to be seen.[4] This is an important starting point for any challenge to heteropatriarchy as practised today. I have argued elsewhere[5] that women learn their submissive role in society through their skins and an important component in that lesson is heterosexuality as practised under patriarchy. This is evident in the more conservative religious groups where missionary position sex for the bearing of children still remains the expected norm. Such groups would claim that their practice is biblically justified and they would challenge others to find a biblical alternative that they consider valid. Well, here is the alternative, but will they see it as valid beyond the centuries of body denying interpretation? My own view is that the Pauline texts and a certain reading of Genesis is not the place to begin when considering Christian views of sexuality—here seems as biblical as any!

Indeed, this text challenges Genesis in many ways through some interesting parallels and overturning of the Genesis viewpoint. We can hardly fail to notice that Christian tradition situates the supposed tragedy of the human condition in a garden. We have however failed to notice that the garden mentioned in the Song of Songs is that belonging to the woman, it is her sexuality, her body and it is the place where worlds are overturned through the way in which she claims it as her own and expresses its desires beyond the narrow confines of heteropatriarchal 'normality'. There is no lurking serpent and the tension between humans and creation disappears as the lovers use the language and imagery of creation to express their desire for one another. The whole of creation embraces them as they play with and explore each other through their bodies. Much more than that, as they challenge the world in which they live through the ways in which they, such diverse people, embrace and pleasure one another outside the frameworks of their world. The garden of the Fall is replaced with the garden of erotic power in connection. In this garden many of the points of power over and

4. Ken Stone, *Practicing Safer Texts: Food, Sex and the Bible in Queer Perspective* (London: T. & T. Clark, 2005), p. 100.

5. Lisa Isherwood, *The Power of Erotic Celibacy: Queering Heteropatriarchy* (London: T. & T. Clark, 2006).

[s]uspicion of the 'other' are overcome in the expression of love [b]etween the two. The woman desires her lover but unlike the woman in Genesis this does not lead to him 'lording it over her', he responds wishing to give her pleasure and to embrace her world.[6] This can be seen by her wish to take him into her mother's house where they may continue their intimacy, an intimacy that goes far beyond their physical touching and pleasuring. It is an inclusive intimacy, one that not only includes the whole of creation but other people too. There is no hint here of a man having to leave his family and cleave to his mate, this kind of isolating arrangement that neatly builds hierarchies based on individualism, is entirely lacking in this text. The Song of Songs places eros in community, community of human and non-human alike. In claiming that, 'My lover is mine and I am his' [2:16; 6:3], a phrase that appears only twice, the woman is affirming their bond as the core of their engagement with a set of relationships beyond them. They challenge in these relationships as they refuse to fit the norm.

The interesting use of fruit in this text places the lovers within a larger circle of creation but also makes it difficult to identify the giver and receiver of pleasure, the mouth being an active receptor in eating. This is an important point as it lifts these texts from the worst excesses of male pornographic fantasy into a more empowering position for the woman and the man. The man is ecstatic in his claims that he has 'come to my garden… I have eaten my honeycomb with my honey, I have drunk my wine with my milk.'[5:1] The eating images disrupt phallic notions with 'their frequent demarcation of subjects and objects, known to us from many ancient representations of sexuality.'[7] The clear desire of the woman for oral stimulation is not the epitome of patriarchal phallic sexuality. The woman here is no simple object she is also a subject of her own desire. Indeed, she is also able to make the man the object of her vision, he comes under her desiring gaze [5:10–16] and this reversal of the gendered gaze is very important as it further emphasizes that she has sexual agency. This agency is textually supported by the fact that the woman has 53% of the voice while the man only 34%. Clearly it would be wrong to suggest that men should remain this silent for all time but given the systems under

6. Phyllis Trible, *God and the Rhetoric of Sexuality* (Philadelphia: Fortress Press, 1978), p. 160.

7. Stone, *Practicing Safer Texts*, p. 101.

which we, and the woman of the Song lived, it is refreshing to l the silence of the one and the voice of the other.

The woman in this text challenges views about her body expressed by those who would oppose her or control her, she is a very body positive woman. She affirms her black comeliness against the comments of the daughters of Jerusalem and pushes back her brothers comments that she has no breast with an emphatic celebration of their magnificence [8:10]. Further she asserts clearly that she keeps her own vineyard, that is to say that her sexuality is her own and not theirs to control. She tells her lover that her body is a bountiful feast which she will give to him, no question here that he takes it, but rather that she bestows her great beauty and bounty upon him. This is a self-confident and body celebratory woman, we could do with more like her in the present day when women spend much of their time and resources attempting to reshape and repackage their comeliness. Her celebration of her ethnic origin is also an inspiration in a world where the signifiers of beauty have become largely European or American. Many women of colour are reshaping eyes, mouths, noses to conform to the European model, it would be a revolution of some proportions if they declared their pride in the beauty of their embodied selves as this woman does.

There is no mention that these lovers are thinking of marriage as they are engulfed in the moment and absorbed in each other's pleasure. These two are then clearly unmarried but the text gets a little 'queer' since the woman wishes that her lover was her brother and if he was she would lead him into the house of their mother where she would give him 'the juice of my pomegranates' [8:2]. There are echoes here of the Christian mystic Margery Kempe who in the heat of her physical passion with Christ queers all family relationships, human as well as divine. She becomes the mother of Christ as well as the bride of God the father in a strange and challenging familial arrangement that goes beyond the rigid boundaries of patriarchal social and theological expectation. In the text of the Song of Songs the woman is longing, much as Margery did centuries later, for a space in which the lovers can be outside the censure of the society in which they live, as her brother she could kiss him and no one would notice but clearly in the house of their mother she would go further. Within her context what is obviously being challenged is the father's household since in the house of their mother [mention of the mother's house is exceptionally rare in biblical literature, it occurs twice in this text and only twice elsewhere Gen 24:28 and Ruth 1:8] even incest seems not to be beyond limits. This, of course, draws us to examine the strict relations between the patriarch and his family, he would own her and his son would be guilty of trespass and theft if he slept with her. The patriarch may, of course, sleep with his daughter but the young male may not—in their passion the woman of this Song is transgressing the boundaries even of the patriarchal household. By returning to the mother's house the woman envisions a turning on its head of the patriarchal order. She further queers this sexual arrangement by declaring, 'this is my beloved and this is my friend' [5:16] not a relationship that would have been evident in patriarchal marriage of the day.

The woman in this Song will not be owned, her actions even place her beyond being desired for ownership in the future, she is free to love her friend and to take delight in her own body as a source of her undoubted revolution. She is no passive creature waiting to be consumed by love as Bernard would have us believe, no shrinking, shaking violet fearful in the presence of her beloved. She is not to be moulded and transformed but rather will engage with her desire and find empowerment in it. All the way through this celebration of sensuality the woman is challenging patriarchy, in the shape of patriarchs, her brothers, and in the shape of patriarchal attitudes, such as those towards the way she looks and how she may conduct herself. She places herself outside the system of economic exchange that has for so long rested on the bodies of women through labour and marital exchange and the production of the next generation of workers. In addition she is also challenging the prophetic representation of woman whose sexuality had been stigmatized and held before us as a way in which the holy fall from grace, the adulterous and ultimately untrustworthy sensuality of woman. All this challenge appears to rest on her finding of a voice and the ability to express her sexuality and her desire beyond what is expected. She offers back to women the pleasure and beauty of their own bodies as a real and embodied enactment of agency through desire. Ever aware of the dangers that she faced and that we today face, we should nevertheless see in this woman an inspiration for our own embodied revolutions. She is nameless even though she has a voice—is she then every woman? Are we to name her in our own desire and erotic becoming? 'Eat, friends, drink. Be drunk with love'!

Chapter 12

Sexual Hospitality in the Hebrew Bible: Patriarchal Lineage or Matriarchal Rebellion?

Thalia Gur-Klein

Little discussed and little known, the custom of sexual hospitality sounds obscure and outlandish. However, since the early Middle Ages throughout nineteenth and twentieth centuries, travellers' reports on the Middle East, North Africa and Asia have recorded a kind of tribal hospitality that includes sexual gratification as part of the hospice. This social world is divided between affiliated brothers and foes; and if a stranger is accepted he will share the privileges of brotherhood. Moreover the stranger could embody a god in disguise who would bestow blessing and fertility on the tribe. Fear of virginal hemorrhage forms another motivation for handing daughters into the strangers' arms. Frequency of occurrences of sexual hospitality show the custom to be a consistent template and not a series of isolated events. In such societies the host's honour depends on the satisfaction of the male guest, and likewise his neglect would be the host's liability.[1] The question to be raised cautiously is whether our anthropological evidence of tribal life can be set up as a model for ancient times, the biblical time or the Hebrew people.

In his book, *Sex and Family in the Bible and the Middle East,* Raphael Patai offers a survey of customs and traditions regarding family values and sexuality in the Ancient Middle East and biblical time.[2] Patai first presents the conventional viewpoint that patriarchal

1. Robert Briffault, The Mothers: A Study of Origins and Institutions of Marriage (London: Allen and Unwin, 1927), I, pp. 635–40.

2. Raphael Patai, *Sex and Family in the Bible and the Middle East* (New York: Dolphin Books, 1959), pp. 139–45.

hospitality was so highly regarded that it might override the strict considerations of women's chastity. The host would thus sacrifice the chastity of his wife, mistress or unmarried virginal daughters to safeguard his guest's honour and protection. Genesis 19 and Judges 19 present two cases in which virginal daughters and one's wife are offered to outsiders when the protection and honour of a guest are at stake. Patai, however, proposes an additional hypothesis namely that other cultural templates may have survived in these stories, materializing as their socio-cultural pre-texts.[3] To support his hypothesis Patai provides extra-literary information from travellers' reports dating from the twelfth to the nineteenth centuries.[4] Templates of alternative sexual codes would demean the dichotomy of patriarchal hospitality versus female chastity competing and culminating in irreconcilable conflict. He thus claims that the custom of sexual hospitality allows us to view biblical stories from a different angle: 'this custom which has been reported from various Arabian tribes, throws additional light on the mores and the relative evaluation of hospitality versus female chastity which constitutes the background to the sexual incidents described in Genesis 19 and Judges 19.'[5]

In order to classify a behavioural pattern as a template, signifying characteristics ought to apply to its occurrences. The following characteristics would sum up to a coherent template. The custom has been practised among tribal, nomadic and decentralized societies and has been practised from Yemen through Central and North Arabia, North Africa and Australia and from Egypt to Afghanistan. The origin of the custom seems to be rooted in ancient times, surviving into and often tolerated by the Islamic era. Commonly, the man concerned is an outsider and not a tribesman. The outsider and/or guest would be led by a family member who thus plays the procurer. The template may vary from one community to another. In some tribes sexual hospitality concerns unmarried daughters,

3. Pre-text, resonating socio-reality; arche-text—the generic type underlining a text, ante-text—defines a prior text; post-text, a later one relating to the former; all covering inter-textual relations, Mieke Bal, *Death and Dissymmetry: The Politics of Coherence in the Book of Judges* (Chicago: University of Chicago Press, 1988), p. 254.

4. Patai mentions the following sources: Kitab al-Aghani 817–967; Ibn el-Mojawir fourteenth century; John Lewis Buckhardt, notes on the Bedouins and Wahabys from the beginning of nineteenth century and the reports of Count Carlo von Landberg, 1848–1924.

5. Patai, *Sex and Family*, pp. 139–45.

while in other tribes only married women will practise it. In some tribes, the woman would be led to the guest by a family member: a brother, a husband, a mother or even an in-law. In other tribes of Arabia, the woman would look for a guest herself outside patriarchal hospitality altogether.[6] In some tribes sexual hospitality endorses complete consummation while in other tribes any sexual pleasure will be tolerated except penetration, in which case a death penalty would be due. Sexual hospitality may vary from one tribe to another and still be classified as a template according to generic signifiers.[7] A religious conviction impends on the custom. The tribes that practised it believed that if they failed to perform the rite, nature would show its displeasure by way of a catastrophe. This belief connects sexual hospitality to cultic mysteries that propagate magical correspondence between fecundity cults, nature and divinity. One could categorise sexual hospitality among customs of sacred or cultic sexuality.

Highlights from Part I

Genesis 19

In Genesis 19, Lot is a patriarchal host and insider. The function of the outsider is divided over two roles. The first protagonists who play the role of the outsider/guest are the 'strangers/angels'. They fully answer to the requirements of the role. The second type of outsiders are the Sodomites. They are outsiders in space in relation to Lot's house, which embodies the inside. As townsmen, they are disqualified as guests and outsiders proper. They demand to be satisfied by the host's male guests but the host offers his virgin daughters instead. Their demand represents a permutated residual of the custom in which the outsider and guest expects to be satisfied by the host's female family member. We find the constituents of

6. Yaqut Al-Rumi, 1179–1229, shows relational similarities to customs conducted in ancient as well as medieval Middle East. Yaqut Al-Rumi relates the following: 'The customs there are those of Ancient Arabs. Though good people, they have rough and repulsive customs, which explain their freedom from jealousy. At night, their women go outside the town and entertain such men, who are not forbidden to them, sporting with them for the greater part of the night. A man pays no heed when he sees his wife, his sister, mother or father's sister in a neighbour's arms; but himself seeks some other mate and is entertained by her as though she were his wife' as quoted in Patai, *Sex and Family*, p. 140.

7. Patai, *Sex and Family*, p. 143.

the cultural template: outsiders and insiders and a sexual offer in which a family member waives female chastity. Lot the insider/ host offers his female family members, his daughters, to the outsiders. This move could contain a transposition of sexual hospitality.

The angels function as metaphysical outsiders in relation to both groups, which lends them their supernatural power exercised on both the townspeople and Lot's family. The angels save lot's family twice: they strike the inhabitants with light and save Lot's family from the mob, and they save Lot's family from the catastrophe brought upon the city by God. The angels/guests, represent the divine blessing brought upon the host by the outsider/guest who is sheltered and provided for by the hosting family.

Genesis 39

With this analysis in mind, I review the story of Joseph and Potiphar anew. Ignoring the roles of slave and master, we could highlight some recurrent formula of sexual hospitality. Potiphar, the insider, offers lavish privileges and supervision to Joseph, while Joseph the outsider brings divine blessing on Potiphar's house. The motive of compromised female chastity then surfaces. In the deep structure this motive may shed some light on the implausible treatment of a Hebrew slave by his Egyptian master. The relationship of insider/ outsider—host/guest is camouflaged by the social and ethnic dichotomy of Egyptian master and Hebrew slave. The master/slave relationship is modified by ethnicity. Joseph the Israelite is the outsider and the insider is an Egyptian. In its Hebrew representation, the ethnic aspect allows the motive of divine blessing brought forth by the guest to surface. Joseph the outsider endows the insider's household with divine blessing. This sets off the dichotomy of the insider's supervision and protection against the divine blessing embodied in the outsider sheltered by the host. Relaxing her chastity, the host's wife exposes the structure, if we consider sexual hospitality in the story's pre-text. Sexuality however remains unconsummated, and no continuity is secured. The affiliated element of catastrophe appears indirectly. Ignoring chronology in Joseph's narrative cycle, seven years of plenty befall; however seven years of draught follow bringing hunger over the land (Gen. 41:54-57).

Judges 19 and Genesis 19

Judges 19 exhibits elements similar to those found in Gen. 19. The outsiders are divided into functions of outsiders who are welcomed as guests and outsiders who, being the local people, are disqualified as guests but demand to be sexually gratified. An additional dichotomy is provided by two kinds of locals; those who faithfully fulfil patriarchal hospitality, Lot in Gen. 19 and the old man in Judges 19 and those who show alienation and disrespect to rules of hospitality, the Sodomites and the mob of Gibeah respectively.

In Judges 19 both insiders and outsiders are Israelites. The dichotomy of ethnicity is exemplified by tribal distinction. The recurrent structure emerges. The guest shifts position with the townspeople. While the guest does not demand his 'rights', the locals perceiving uninvited outsiders, demand to be sexually gratified. Like the Sodomites, the Gibeah people demand to be sexually satisfied as if they were patriarchal guests from outside town. Their demand reverses the custom too as they claim the male guest for homosexual gratification. The female family members are offered not to the outsider and guest, but to soothe the outsiders who are neither proper outsiders nor guests.

The respective plots enunciate a subliminal pattern. The insider offers his daughter(s) and his guest's wife to outsiders. The motive of homosexuality hints to a secondary layer of marginalization, aimed to increase the effect of abomination towards all forms of cultic sexuality. This however suggests that the customs were still practised.[8] One can reflect on Patai's hypothesis. On the surface presentation, the *inside* functions as a place of patriarchal protection, supervision and hospitality for the male guest by the male host, indicates patriarchal bonding. Male bonding overrides the safety and chastity of the female insiders: a daughter, mistress or wife. Patriarchal protection of the female insider(s) is waived for the sake of patriarchal protection of the male outsider. On the other hand, beyond the narrative variant, the pattern of sexual hospitality re-emerges in the recurrent motive of the host offering his female family members to outsiders. This recurrence may denote a marginalized form, embedding the cultural template.

8. Deut. 23:17-18 forbids sacred sexuality of both genders; A. Keefe, 'The Female Body, the Politic and the Land: A Sociological Reading of Hosea 1-2' in Athalya Brenner (ed.), Feminist Companion to the Latter Prophets (Sheffield: Sheffield Academic Press, 1995), p. 82.

If the assumption of marginalization is accepted, there is an ideology behind it. Could the abominable story of rape be read as propaganda? I would suggest that odd elements expose the ideology behind the story of the unfortunate Levite's mistress. Consider the following: The plot moves smoothly from one event to the next; so smoothly that one fails to notice the contradictions it entails. In the first place, a man goes to great lengths to avenge his mistress' life and honour, whom he had so lightly jeopardized without the slightest resistance or effort to protect. Then an entire nation is mobilized by means of a motive that seems too lean. Consider the odd detail of severing the woman's body. Hebrew culture forbids the Israelites, let alone a Levite, to commit desecration, or touch a dead body or even the belongings of a deceased (Num. 19:11–22). Even accidental touching would involve a series of purifying rites under threat of excommunication. Here, not only does the Levite desecrate a dead body, but he also sends its parts by Israelite messengers to other Israelites all over the land. The Levite cuts his mistress' body into twelve parts sending it to all the Israeli tribes. However, two tribes should have been discarded; one being the Levites who are spread among the other tribes and do not own land; and the other being the tribe of Benjamin who are the perpetrators. The mutilated feminine body corresponds to the symbolic number of the Israelite tribes for whom the message of the story is meant. The woman's body embodies the divided nation; it sends a message that unfaithfulness to God and partition would bring disaster. The underlying message strengthens the moralizing plot; the sinners suffer a terrible predicament. The partners of the sexualized event meet with catastrophe, i.e. the woman who had exercised alternative sexuality and the Gibeah people who craved after homosexual rape. The condemnation, however, attests to its social existence. The morally deductive message reinforces the extra-literary purpose of the story, which is allegorically bound. The allegorical structure is reinforced by the feature that all characters remain nameless and thus function as types: a good priestly Levite who is an outsider and guest, a sinful mistress, an old man who observes customs of hospitality and the locals who disregard them and play the role of villains. As an allegorical story, it serves an extra literary purpose, which is ideological rather than narrative. To support this thesis I quote from Ezekiel who deploys the domestic relationship between an unfaithful wife and a good man to delineate Israel craving for foreign gods. In this paradigm God is put on a par with the good husband.[9]

> Behold, therefore I will gather all thy lovers, with whom thou hast taken pleasure, and all them that thou hast loved, with all them that thou hast hated; I will even gather them round about against thee, and will discover thy nakedness unto them, that they may see all thy nakedness. And I will judge thee, as women that break wedlock; and I will give thee blood in fury and jealousy. And I will also give thee into their hands, and they shall throw down thine eminent place, and shall break down thy high places; and shall strip thee also of thy clothes, and shall take thy fair jewels, and leave thee naked and bare. They shall also bring up a company against thee, and they shall stone you, and thrust you with their swords. And they shall burn thy houses with fire, and execute judgement upon thee in the sight of many women. And I will cause thee to cease from playing the harlot…(Ezek. 16:37–41).

The pertinent elements recurring in both Genesis 19 and in Ezekiel 16 can be read as follows. There is a righteous man of God embodying the locus of morality and a woman who chooses multiple sexual partners over him. The righteous man exercises a punishment on the woman like an almighty god. He hands the woman over to the lethal mob to be sexually abused; her nakedness is exposed in public and she is shamed, raped, degraded and tortured, her body desecrated and penetrated by a sword. The prophetic text also legitimizes the victim's fate morally, which is only implicit in Judges 19. The prophetic text, moreover, links us to the target audience. It answers the question to whom the ominous message is directed with the explicit purpose of repelling and frightening them away from alternative sexuality. The answer is, the women folk. 'And they shall burn thy houses with fire, and execute judgement upon thee in the sight of many women. And I will cause thee to cease from playing the harlot…(Ezek. 16:41).

I conclude the following. In Genesis 19, angels who strike the mob blind with divine light save the chastity of Lot's virgin daughters. In Judges 19, the function of female chastity at odds

9. Brenner, *Feminist Companion*, pp. 256–74; van Dijk-Hemmes, 'The Metaphorization of Woman in Prophetic Speech: An Analysis of Ezekiel 23' in Brenner, *Feminist Companion*, pp. 244–56; Graetz, 'God is to Israel as Husband is to Wife: The Metaphoric Battering of Hosea's Wife', in Brenner, *Feminist Companion*, pp. 126–45; Sherwood, 'Boxing Gomer: Controlling the Deviant Woman in Hosea 1–3' in Brenner, *Feminist Companion*, pp. 101–25.

with patriarchal protection is embodied by one virgin daughter and one sinful mistress said to have committed prostitution (Judg. 19:2). No angels appear here in contrast to Genesis 19. However in Judges 19, the virgin daughter disappears from the narrative without an explanation, her honour and life saved. The story culminates with the Levite, the guest, exposing his mistress to the lethal outsiders, and still no angels in view. The ideological message of the story must have been clearly read by the ancient audience.

Gen. 12:10–20, 20 and 26:1–14

My thesis claims that the theme of sexual hospitality has survived in permuting structures. From this point, I will expand Patai's paradigm related to Genesis 19 and Judges 19, and apply it to Gen. 12:10–20, 20 and 26:1–14. For the sake of isolating paradigmatic isotopes, unity and chronology of narrative will become secondary. Considering the cumulative character of biblical narrative, one should also bear in mind that Aristotelian principles of narrative unities and chronology would show their influence in post-biblical periods a few centuries later (Noy, 1968).[10]

Roles and functions shift and intersect in various combinations and induce dichotomy in the selected biblical texts.[11] The stories presented in Gen. 12:10–20, 20 and 26:1–14 bring to the surface recurrent functions of outsider and insider juxtaposed with relaxing the notion of a woman's chastity. The synchronic structure can be perceived in Abraham-Sarah-Pharaoh, Abraham–Sarah-Abimelech and Isaac-Rebecca-Abimelech constellations. The roles of outsider/ guest, husband/brother collapse into one figure, respectively seen in Abraham and in Isaac. Synchronically, Sarah and Rebecca also merge into the relational figure of a wife and/or sister. This shows that these narratives are permutated variations.

These stories exhibit a tension between the level of presentation and the level of generation. The level of presentation contains narrative elements like chronology, characterization, plot, recurrent motives and aspects of time and place. The level of generation represents paradigmatic structures, like themes, ideas or types

10. Dov Noy, *Folklore in Talmudic and Midrash* (Jerusalem: Universita ha-ivrit birusalyaim, 1968).

11. On function and roles as formal components, see Vladimir Propp, *Morphology of Folktales* (Austin, Tx: University of Texas Press, 1968).

drawn from subliminal concentration.[12] On the level of presentation, Gen. 12:10–20, 20 and 26:1–14 present a story involving the relaxation of restrictions concerning a woman's chastity. This motive interlinks these stories with Genesis 19 and Judges 19. The hosts, Lot and the old man of Gibeah both offer their virgin daughters' sexuality (and that of the guest's wife) to the outsiders to protect the guest. However, the Levite offers his mistress for self-protection out of fear of the male outsiders. This motive associates the story of the Levite with the Genesis stories. In Gen. 12:10–20, 20 and 26:1–14, the male guest fears the male host, and suspecting that the latter's patriarchal hospitality might be wanting he offers his wife and/or sister to the insider for self-protection. Genesis 26 seems a fragmented mutation of the two former narratives filling the triangle with Isaac-Rebecca-Abimelech (or his men). Isaac, like his father Abraham finding himself under distressing circumstances of hunger, moves down to Gerar, the land of the Philistines ruled by the recurrent figure of Abimelech; and like his father before him he presents Rebecca as his sister and makes her sexually eligible to other men.

In the Genesis stories and Judges 19, the theme of patriarchal protection is transposed to ironic transpositions as the woman's chastity is waived by the guest/outsider for his own self-protection, though motivation may vary.

On the generating level, these stories show a series of transformations of one cultural pattern; their subliminal templates generate various representations on the level of presentation. Paradigmatically, these texts cross and hybridize patriarchal hospitality with relaxation of female sexual restrictions in guest/host–outsider/insider situations. The synchronic structure determines the recurrent triangle of Abraham-Sarah-Pharaoh and Abraham–Sarah-Abimelech and Isaac-Rebecca-Abimelech (or potentially his men). The roles of outsider/guest, husband/brother collapse into a pertinent function complementing one role. Twice Abraham and once Isaac fill the role of outsider, stranger and/or guest. Both men function as procurers to their female family member, wife and/or sister. Synchronically, Sarah and Rebecca also merge into a relational role of a wife and/or sister whose sexuality

12. Susan Witting, 'Theories of Formulaic Narrative' in Semeia 5 (Philadelphia: Fortress Press, 1976), pp. 82–84.

is offered to a man outside the patriarchal marital codes. Twice Abimelech and once Pharaoh fill the role of the insider/host; however, in relation to the marital structure they embody outsiders.

Most interesting, illicit sexuality surfaces in Gen. 12:10–20, Gen. 20 and Gen. 26:1–14 in diminishing degrees of representation. In Gen. 12, sexuality is consummated between Sarah and Pharaoh. In Gen. 20, Sarah is brought into the host's house for a nocturnal visit but an angel interrupts the consummation at the last moment. In Gen. 26 Rebecca's chastity is made publicly available under the same false pretences. Yet the woman remains with her husband though her chastity is nearly broached. This can be read in two ways. It could expose a diminishing mutation of the template on the level of narrative presentation. On the other hand it could connote the sexual hospitality, which endorses all degrees of sexuality, from mere foreplay to consummation and penetration. Synchronically in all three cases, the male family-member still functions as a procurer to his female family member, while female sexuality is made available outside marital exclusiveness.

Other elements of presentation could relate to the subliminal structure of sexual hospitality. On approaching Egypt, Abraham does not consider offering Sarah's chastity as a mere necessary evil, but foresees himself as the beneficent of the situation (Gen. 12:13) *yetav li bavorehk*, (I will better myself on your account). Pharaoh showers Abraham with slaves, maids and livestock. This element could enunciate the custom of bride price, 'And he (Pharaoh) entreated Abraham well for her sake...' (Gen. 12:16). However, if Abraham's reward was a bride price for a sister on wrong assumptions, why would Pharaoh not retrieve it when he restores Sarah to Abraham? Having been forced by draught to come to Egypt as a hard-pressed man, Abraham emerges a rich man returning home (Gen. 12:20, 13:1–2). What he did for toil was cheating a mighty ruler whom he had feared in the first place. The reward and provision could denote a pertinent reward offered to the woman's procurer. Though Abraham offers his female family member to the Pharaoh and not the other way round, it could denote the custom in an inverted representation, for a husband offers his wife to an outside man.

Gen. 20:14, Abimelech bequeaths Abraham with a reward nearly identical to that of Pharaoh in Gen. 12:16. Like the former it amounts to men-slaves, women-slaves and livestock surfacing a synchronic pattern: 'And Abimelech took sheep, and oxen and men-servants, and women-servants, and gave them unto Abraham, and restored him Sarah, his wife,' (Gen. 20:14). However, Abraham's reward in Genesis 20 is not paid when Sarah is offered, as seen in Gen. 12: 16, but after Sarah is retrieved. In addition, Abimelech tells Sarah, not Abraham, that he will reward Abraham one thousand silver pieces on her account (Gen. 20:16). This could reinforce the role of Sarah as a sexual agent, and Abraham as her procurer duly rewarded for his role.

Fertility and Infertility

The thesis I am offering is a structural and anthropological one. For this reason narrative chronology is overlooked. On this line of analysis, I will connect the motive of infertility and fertility to the template of sexual hospitality. I will therefore relate the event of Sarah's barrenness and pregnancy to the context of sexual hospitality.

Lack of offspring constitutes a determining function in the aforementioned narratives.[13] An underlying motive of barrenness appears in the stories of Abraham and Sarah, which is counter-balanced by conception in Gen. 16:1-4, and 21:1. Barrenness might provide the missing link in the puzzle. Barrenness is addressed once by a wife offering her husband to another woman, and analogously twice by a husband offering his wife to another man. This structure concerns the thesis offered here. The barren Sarah is offered once to Pharaoh (Gen. 12) and once to Abimelech (Gen. 20). Genesis 12 and 20 show pertinent elements within a consistent pattern. The pattern corresponds to anthropological templates of alternative rules of sexual conduct other than the strict patriarchal matrimony. Deconstructed from this cycle, the relevant pattern emerges as follows: barrenness (Gen. 16:1)—female chastity is waived for sexual hospitality (Genesis 20 and 12)—barrenness is removed (Gen. 21:1-2). Barrenness is modified by the waiving of female chastity to an outside man—outside in relation to the matrimonial structure, which symbolizes a closed space. The outside man is a man other than the husband, who appears as a permutation of the tribal outsider and guest. On the level of presentation, the

13. 'Lack', one of preparatory functions, Propp, *Morphology of Folktales*, 1968, pp. 1-30.

woman is sexually objectified. On the level of generation, the template involves an outside man, who equally functions as a sexual object to the woman resulting in a blessed fertility.

Abimelech – Abimelech's Wife & Maids – Abraham

Once the pattern is established, it can be further refined and re-defined. The subliminal structure shows the following isotopes: barrenness—an outsider—hospitality—a woman's chastity waived—barrenness removed. The argument so far has remained on the level of inverted transformation, which leaves some space for doubts. I will now expose sexual hospitality as a subtext, which could directly represent it.

The main pattern in Gen. 20 was seen in the narrative of Abraham—Sara—Abimelech. Concomitant to the main construction, the parallel structure is furnished by Abimelech being an insider/ host—Abimelech's wife & maids being the insider's female members—and Abraham functioning as an outsider/guest. The pattern of: barrenness—an outside man—barrenness removed resurfaces as the recurrent template in the secondary narrative, too. If we ignore the narrative's chronology for the sake of deconstruction, we see that corresponding to Abraham's household struck by barrenness, Abimelech's wife and maids are inflicted by barrenness too. Thus one can deconstruct the marginalized pattern outside the matrix structure. This would be formulated as follows. Abimelech's household is struck by barrenness. Abraham as an outsider and/or guest functions as a sexual agent endowing fertility onto the female family members of the insider and host, transposed into the blessing of a God-called man (Gen. 20:7,17). The insider's wife and maids conceive (Gen. 20:17). The guest is then rewarded with privileges and supervision (Gen. 20:14–16). The pertinent elements construe the recurrent template of sexual hospitality proper with clear-cut roles: an insider/ host, a host's female family members and an outsider/guest. Abraham comes to Gerar as an outsider and/or guest. As a blessed stranger and guest, he is endowed with the power to inflict infertility and to re-instigate fertility upon the insider's female family members, namely Abimelech's wife and maids (Gen. 20:17). Having fulfilled his destination, he is rewarded with supervision, the right to settle, property and money by the host.

The Divine Stranger, Guest and/or Outsider

Called a prophet (Gen. 20:7), Abraham functions as a catalyst of fertility for the insider's family. Anthropologically, Abraham as a God-called man can be seen as a biblical transposition of the outsider, stranger and/or guest who brings a misfortune upon the hosting clan if the custom is ignored and removes a catastrophe when the custom is observed. Paradigmatically, Abraham embodies the divine fertile outsider, who could incarnate a god in flesh for the host.

This fragmentary story sheds some new light on the story of the great lady and the prophet Elisha in 2 Kgs 4.[14] Married to an old man, a woman of means is said to have no children. She invites the prophet to enter their house and eat at their place. Eventually she prepares a room for him in the attic and provides for his needs whenever he visits the town. Blessing of fertility comes unto the woman, the child himself is metaphysically blessed, when he dies and is restored to life by the prophet. The story brings to the surface a few significant details. Elisha is epitomized as a holy man (*kaddosh)* not only as a prophet, like Abraham (2 Kgs 4). The husband's old age implicitly alludes to the cause of his wife's barrenness. Most significant is the active role the woman takes playing the host. She entreats the man to come into her house to share bread and lodge with them, like Lot and the man from Gibeah. However, the great lady of Shunem is not the only active hostess in the Bible; Jael also plays the host for Sisera (Judges 4,5). On another note, we can subtract a recurrent template in this text, i.e. the encounter between the holy man and the barren woman, concluding with the holy man endowing tidings of fecundity on the woman, and her conceiving in consequence thereof. This template takes me back to 1 Sam. 1–2. In these texts, the holy man is juxtaposed twice with fecundity, seen once in Eli and once in his sons. We see Eli, the priest endowing a blessing of fecundity on a woman, Hannah, resulting in pregnancies (1 Sam. 1:17, 2:20). Most significantly, Eli's second blessing (1 Sam. 2:20) is juxtaposed to the practice of his sons lying with the women who are described to crowd at the tabernacle (1 Sam. 2:22). Since the Hebrew scripture is not shy of denoting a rape if there is one, I suggest that the text describes a voluntary practice carried out by both sides.

14. I am indebted to Prof. Silvia Schroer, from the University of Bern, for drawing my attention to this story and its relevance to my discussion on sexual hospitality.

Anthropological data valorize such customs. Reports of Mediterranean cults of saints attest to pre-Islamic customs in which sacred or alternative sexuality of various forms survived. By transformations from ancient periods, such holy men are believed to possess the *Baraka*, the divine blessing that descendants of the Prophet Mohamed inherit. It is told that women who dream of sexual intercourse with holy men conceive as a result. It is sometimes condoned to have intercourse with holy men themselves in such communities. Sacred festivities may endorse the practise of blessed sexuality with God-called men themselves or undiscriminating sexuality among the pilgrims at sacred vicinities and saints' tombs during seasonal saints' cults such as the *ziyara*.[15]

Popular religion thus sheds an additional light on the outsider who instigates fertility in women. The messenger of tidings of fecundity is subject to recurrent 'framing'[16] perceiving the divine outsider within the cultural template. We could revisit the appearance of God's messenger before Hagar (Gen. 15:7–15), Sarah and Abraham (Gen, 18:1–18) and before Manoah's wife with tidings of fecundity Judg 13:1–11).[17] An underlying arche-text[18] runs through these texts. In various degrees of representation, intermediaries represent the fecundity of God in the deification of the outsider and stranger. The biblical fecund outsider and/or stranger transposes intermediaries into God: the metaphysical messenger, *malach*, an angel and the prophet. It is indicative that the divine outsider appears before Hagar and Manoah's wife alone and communicates directly with the latter twice before he forms a discourse with the husband. Deification of the fertile outsider applies to the three angels who visit Abraham with a divine message of divinely blessed fertility (Gen. 18:1–17). Sarah's laugh may underline a transposition of sexuality as the biblical word laugh *zahak* carries

15. Issachar Ben-Ami, Saint Veneration Among the Jews in Morocco, (Jerusalem: The Magnes Press, 1984), p. 188; Christopher Taylor, *In the Vicinity of the Righteous: Ziyara and the Veneration of Muslim Saints in Late Medieval Egypt* (London: Brill, 1999), p. 64.

16. Jonathan Culler, Framing the Sign: Criticism and its Institutions, (Oxford: Oxford University Press, 1988), as quoted in Bal, 'Death and Dissymmetry', p. 134.

17. On the sexual aspects of Manuah's wife and the angel, see Bal, 'Death and Dissymmetry', p. 74.

18. A generic type underlying texts in Intertextual relation, Bal, 'Death and Dissymmetry', p. 254, see note 1 above.

sexual connotations.[19] The stories of Abraham and Abimelch's wife and maids and Elisha and the great lady of Shunem present the prophet as their fertile agent and metaphysical intermediary.

These stories concern women who have some involvement with outsiders leading to sanctification of offspring in various degrees of transposition. Sanctification of offspring can be traced in the angel's blessing bestowed on Hagar's son, Ishmael, (Gen. 21:13), in God's blessing over Sarah's son, Isaac, (Gen. 26:3–6), and in Rebecca's son, Jacob, perceived in his father's blessing, Isaac (Gen. 27:28–29; 28:3–4). On leaving for Haran, Jacob is endowed with a dream revelation of angels going up and down a heavenly ladder at the top of which God reinforces his father' blessing with His own, with a heavenly promise of protection (28:13–15). On returning, Jacob goes through recurrent encounters with metaphysical intermediaries on the border between Haran and Canaan, which forms an area of limbo. Such encounters consist of a company of angels (32:2–3) followed by a wrestling contest with God in flesh (32:26–31). In Samson's supernatural powers, we could recognise residuals of the offspring deified by an outside intervention. After the appearance of the angles, Samson is promised by his mother to be a *nazir* already before birth, a man dedicated to God from birth. She herself must refrain from touching anything but pure food and drink no wine. Samson's 'deification' is reinforced by the magical interdiction, which endows him with supernatural power unless his hair is cut.

Part II – Sanctification and Coexistence

Robert Briffault describes the ideology underlying fertility rituals as follows:

> Human marriage cannot achieve its object and be fruitful unless it is preceded by a divine marriage of the woman with the powers whence her fertility truly derives. That union is, we saw, effected by various means, by unrestricted promiscuity, prostitution with strangers, ritual defloration by priest or prince, hierodulic prostitution in temples,

19. The biblical idiom 'to laugh with', or 'to make laugh' *sihek*, *le-sahek* (pattern *kitel*) has a sexual connotation meaning to make love to, a foreplay, to fool around with, as in Gen. 26:8: 'Abimelech king of the Philistines looked at a window, and saw, and behold, Isaac was laughing with (me*sahek*) Rebecca his wife.'

> mechanical defloration by the image of the god. Those measures achieve more than one purpose; the Holy Matrimony not only secures the fertility of the woman, and that of the field and the cattle, but also protects the husband against the perils of defloration. Those perils are minimised or abolished by the ritual character of the Holy Matrimony; the participants in rites of promiscuity, the stranger, the priest do not incur the dangers attaching to defloration for they are representatives of the god.[20]

Sexual hospitality and sacred sexuality in general challenge two major objectives of patriarchal dominance as presented in the Hebrew Bible, which are pre-nuptial intercourse and adultery. Confluent customs of fertility like sexual hospitality and sacred sexuality render pre-nuptial intercourse and adultery imperative. Reversibly, the Mosaic constitution outlaws them. The Mosaic constitution targeted the abolition of these rites, and the Hebrew God alone claimed the objectives of fertility of women and land. Though theologically this policy made the Hebrew God the richer in metaphors and character, the transition has never been absolute nor complete, if we consider that as late as the mysteries of the *Kabbalah* the Hebrew God still retained His female divine partners, the Matronite, the Shekhina and Lilieth.[21] This is beside the present analysis, but I find it important to bring it up, in view of anti-Judaic voices among Christian feminist theologians blaming the Hebrews for killing the female goddess, as if one alleged *deicide* was not enough for us Jews.

The stories discussed here were created in the midst of social and cultural clashes of beliefs and customs laying equal claims for sanctification. This tension spanned over periods of intercultural transition; and in this ideological limbo sentiments could have culminated in struggles for life or death but could also have peacefully prolonged in coexistence, compromise and relaxation of rules.

Virgin Daughters

The first pattern presented stories in which a father offers to hand over his daughter(s) to outsiders (Gen.19, Judges 19). These events surprise modern readers generally led to believe that virginity was highly valued in ancient cultures, if not sanctified. Relying initially

20. Robert Briffault, *The Mothers*, III, pp. 222, 316.
21. Patai, *Sex and Family in the Bible*.

on Patai's assumption, I tried to prove that another custom might have intersected the narrative, in this case sexual hospitality. This point alludes that virginity could have been overshadowed, made redundant and/or discarded by other templates. In his book, *The Mothers*, Robert Briffault attests to the fact that virginity consists of a permuting value bound to time and place.[22] Deducing from reports of old tribal cultures, some communities, regarded virginity as a trifle, a burden and a fearful dread to be rid of before the woman is wed. In these cultures virginal haemorrhage has been associated with the taboo around menstrual blood and was thus equally dreaded.[23] The stranger and the outsider, the priest, the ruler and/or landlord were believed to be divinely protected, and being elevated above the common man were asked to take the duty of relieving maidens of their virginity. We could newly review a detail in the story of Esther relating how maidens *en masse* were brought to the King's palace to be deflowered (Est. 2:2–3,12–15). The custom of prenuptial defloration by another man has been practised as close as the Sahara and as far as Ireland and India. These data may shed an additional light on the tribal custom of offering virgin daughters to outsiders surviving in biblical stories. In addition, this custom highlights the motive of deification of offspring endowed by outside intervention.

A Wife Offered to an Outsider

The second related pattern shows a situation where a wife is sexually offered to an outsider in a (possible) situation of hospitality, linked to the motive of fertility and continuity. Narratives of barrenness are known to solve the problem by a wife offering a secondary woman to a man. Sarah (Gen. 16:1–4), Rachel (Gen. 30:3), and Lea (Gen. 30:9) transform their maids to surrogate mothers. The template of sexual hospitality may indicate a compensatory structure applied to the opposite sex. Perhaps the custom purports to solve the problem of a barren husband and a fertile male outside strict matrimony is called in like a surrogate woman to secure offspring. Gen. 20 indicates that all the wombs in Abimelech's clan were closed. However, with Abraham's blessing not only the wife and maids

22. Robert Briffault, *The Mothers*, p. 227.

23. On the psychological aspects of fear of virginity and defloration, and defloration by someone other than the bridegroom, see Mieke Bal's interpretation and Freudian approach (Bal, 'Death and Dissymmetry').

were cured—the text implies that Abraham's prayer also cured Abimelech. This may elucidate that Abimelech had been struck by barrenness (20:17). 2 Kgs 4, also interlinks the husband's old age with woman's barrenness which leads to the masculine addition to the family represented by the holy prophet, endowing the family with fertility.

The belief that the gods bestow fertility mutually impends on the theology that a woman's sacred union with the divine is its accessory to human marriage. This ideology underlines the concept of sacred union with the divine bridegroom. The fertility god intersects the divine bridegroom and may be incarnated in the stranger and/or outsider as well as a sacred personage, a priest, a high lord or ruler.[24] A woman may form a carnal union perceived as *hieros gamus*, a divine marriage prior or along side her earthly marriage. In carnal appearance, the divine bestows the blessing of fertility that is a prerequisite to the human marriage and its purpose, which is continuity.[25] This ideology explains the fact that sacred hierodules, unmarried and married women participating in sacred festivities would join with strangers without reservations. Also on other occasions the fecund outsider interchanges with the blessed guest, mighty ruler or stranger who may conceive of a god in disguise.[26]

In the narrative cycle of Abraham and Sarah the fertile agent shifts positions. The male characters, Abraham, Abimelech and the three angels embody the fertile outsider. As a guest, Abraham plays the role of a holy person functioning as a fecund agent towards Abimelech's female family members. This is enhanced in the verse in which God Himself announces to Abimelech in his dream at night that Abraham is a prophet (Gen. 20:6). Abimelech on his part plays the role of a host and landlord thus functioning as the extra-marital outside-man towards Sarah. Abraham and Abimelech, whose names both contain 'father' (*av* in Hebrew) and a high position above the common man, can be perceived as mutations of the divinised outsider before whom female chastity is waived, resulting in a blessed fertility. The three angels in Gen. 18 embody the recurrent metaphysical outsider announcing the blessed tidings of pregnancy. This metaphysical figure has previously appeared before Hagar to

24. Briffault, *The Mothers*, pp. 203, 220, 221.
25. Briffault, *The Mothers*, pp. 218, 219, 225-26, 228-29.
26. Briffault, *The Mothers*, p. 221.

comfort her with the news of her pregnancy in the form of an angel, *malach*, which means both a messenger and an angel in Hebrew (Gen. 16:7); and the angel resurfaced again to save her son Ishmael, calling her this time from the distance of heaven to see the brook (Gen. 21: 17). The angels reappear to lead Lot and his daughters away from the catastrophe; they also indirectly precede the birth of Lot's daughter's sons. The angel in Judges 13 proclaims the event of Manoah's wife's forthcoming pregnancy, which recalls the pattern seen in Genesis 16 and 18.

A Wife or Bride Offered to a Landlord

The following motif highlights events in which a landlord is juxtaposed with the relaxation of chastity of another man's wife. Genesis offers a number of stories in which one's bride, newly wed bride or wife is offered to the lord of the land. In all these stories the husband is a stranger, guest, or a landless wanderer. Anthropological data valorize that notion that once the wife is lent to the mightier man, the landlord's offspring legitimizes the right of that family to settle on the landlord's land and/or share the rights of the privileged offspring of the mightier man (Briffault 1927: II, 237).[27]

Perceived in space, the stories of Sarah and Rebecca show female chastity offered from the direction of the *unsafe outside* entailing wandering and hunger in the direction of the *safe inside* of settlement and plenty. Coming back from Egypt Abraham's clan has grown from a hungry wanderer to a man rich with servants and live stock (Gen. 12). This denotes an independent narrative structure. In Genesis 21, coming to Gerar, Abraham's family is eventually subjected to the same insecure and dire conditions. Only after Sarah's nocturnal visit to Abimelech's bedroom, does Abraham receive the privilege of settling on Abimelech's land, and (re)gains the similar riches, this time by another lord to whom he had offered his wife. From that point onwards, Abraham's status changes from the position of a landless wanderer fearing for his life, to that of a legitimate settler on the land of the same man he had dreaded. With the birth of Isaac that follows, the claim of the Abrahamic family on the land seems irrefutable. This pattern is reapplied to

27. Briffault, *The Mothers*, p. 237. According to Briffault, this ancient template could be the origin of the *jus primae noctis* first night right surviving through the Middle Ages.

Isaac's family. In the cycle of Isaac and Rebecca, the same recurring elements synchronize and complement one another, which supports the thesis of one and the same subliminal structure.

In various forms and degrees of representations, the stories involve two wives, Sarah and Rebecca, who are offered to outsiders, juxtaposed with events in which their chastity is waived within the context of a guest, host, outsider and/or a mighty ruler of the land. From the sexualized event with the landlord, significantly recurring twice in the figure of Abimelech, both Abraham and Isaac respectively are allowed to settle on the land of the Philistines. Both Abraham and his son Isaac establish the same settlement named Beer Sheba twice in different times. The city is first established by Abraham, and then all over again by Isaac. In both cases, the settlement was initiated by the mercy of the same Abimelech and the same Pikhol his aid (Gen. 21 and Gen. 26). The subliminal structure seems nearly identical in these fragments, though there are forty or sixty years lapsing between them.

On suggesting a subliminal template, I return to the story of Dinah. The story mentions Shechem's high status twice: 'prince of the country' and 'more honourable than all the house of his father' (Gen. 34:2 and 20). We revisit here the recurring template of a sexualized event juxtaposed with privileges offered by a high lord of the land. Shechem offers Jacob's clan a permission to settle on their land like Abimelech before him: 'and ye shall dwell with us; and the land shall be before ye' (Gen. 34:10). Jacob like Isaac and Abraham, his father and grandfather, wishes to cooperate with the custom that demands the waiving of female chastity of his family member, his daughter, for a mighty ruler and thereby secure his position. His sons reject it. The violent conclusion of the negotiation results in the Hebrew clan resuming wandering, exposed to danger of genocide, unlike their predecessors who establish a city for themselves on the landlord's land Jacob expresses his disappointment before his sons: 'I being few in number, they shall gather themselves together against me, and slay me; and I shall be destroyed, I and my house' (Gen. 34:30b). Remarkably, after the turmoil period of Dinah, the Hebrew clan enters a new period. Building a new altar for the Hebrew God proper they revert into puritan cleansing of all foreign customs: 'And Jacob said unto his household and to all that were with him, Put away the strange gods that are among you, and be clean, and change your garments' (Gen. 35:2).[28]

The Blessed Son

The motif of a woman's chastity erased before a landlord may yet deconstruct another recurring theme, namely the tension between heirs. Genesis brings twice a pertinent structure in which first-born rights are overruled in favour of another son, while the first-born is sent away from the tribal land. If we consider the custom that legitimizes only the rights of the landlord's son on the land, this socio-economic custom favours the offspring of the extra-marital union with the landlord over the offspring of the biological father.[29] We could reread the stories of Isaac and Ishmael and Jacob and Esau as a paradigmatic mutation of the custom. Eventually, only one of the offspring inherits the rights over the land. God's protection and blessing conceive as a transposition of the landlord's protection and blessing endowed to his privileged son by the weaker man's wife. The other son is denied inheritance, protection and blessing and is destined to leave the tribal territory for a life of wandering and insecure existence like his natural father in his days (Ishmael—Gen. 21:10-21 and Esau—Gen. 27:39-40).

This leads me to reflect on Abraham's origin. Abraham is mentioned first among Terah's three sons, which hints at his being first-born. However, Abraham leaves the clan's dwelling to wander off to another land (12:1-9). Like the story of Ishmael's expulsion, the decree is perceived as God's plan and is conveyed as a divine command. The pattern is repeated in the next generation. A paternal decree merges with God's promised protection as Abraham sends away Ishmael, the first-born (21:12-13). It is repeated in another variation in Isaac's blessing of Jacob, his second-born offspring, eventually resulting in Esau moving away from the clan territory (27:28-29). Returning to Abraham's genealogy, we find that when he sends his servant to find a bride for his son Isaac he calls Haran, 'my country and my homeland' (Gen. 24:4). The son that had remained at the original clan's dwelling resurfaced as Abraham's brother Nahor. A paradigm offered in Genesis 25 supplies me with conclusive evidence. Lean in literary elaboration the text delineates

28. One should be reminded that Rachel stole her father's idols and was never so far mentioned to have gotten rid of them (Gen. 32:19).

29. Briffault, *The Mothers*, pp. 230-31, 237.

a harsh reality of only one son holding his place within the clan and inheriting all, while all other sons are sent away, similar to the paradigm of Ishmael's expulsion. Neither female rivalry nor divine voice explains this policy of inheritance in this seemingly unimportant text. Abraham bluntly gives all that he has to Isaac and for his sake and interest sends all other sons away with mere presents: 'And Abraham gave all that he had unto Isaac. But unto the sons of the concubines which Abraham had, Abraham gave gifts, and sent them away from[30] Isaac his son, while he yet lived, eastward, unto the east country,' (Gen. 25:5). Who the mistresses' sons referred to here are, remains ambiguous. Ketura was his second wife after Sarah and not a mistress, and Hagar who is not mentioned here had only one son who had been sent away before.

This enigmatic text however makes a clear division between one legitimate son who inherits all and other sons who are sent away. The expulsion of all but one son runs counter to egalitarian division between heirs. The latter is demonstrated in Numbers 36, which establishes inheritance laws according to members of patrilocal houses, and even considers daughter's rights to inherit under the restriction that if there are no brothers to inherit their father's land, they should marry within their clan. Job reaffirms the rule of egalitarian inheritance; as not only his sons indiscriminately receive an equal share of land but also his daughters along with them (Job 42:15). The expulsion of offspring runs counter to the paradigm of an inheritance shared among legitimate heirs. These texts may show that in ancient times, a legitimate heir was chosen according to other customs than we expect.

Multiple Male Partners

Within cultural templates of alternative sexuality, we find pertinent customs impending on pre-nuptial sex as a prerequisite to marriage. Abiding by the custom, a bride-to-be or a newly-wed woman forcefully or voluntarily joins with another man, or other men, prior to or even after her marriage, before her husband is allowed to join her. The latter denotes a custom restricted by a fixed period of continence.

Herodotus, Pomponius and Diodorus recounted of a custom known as the Nasamonian custom practised in the Arabian peninsula

30. Hebrew text, *al penei*, which would mean here 'in preference of'.

and still found among the Aboriginals until recent time.[31] The Nasamonian wedding custom forces a bride to lie with the wedding guests, before her husband comes to her. It can be thus seen as a variation of sexual hospitality. A period of sexual continence may be integrated in the custom, which traditionally may take a fixed time, days or weeks.

This leads me to review some odd details in Samson's story. The wedding feast that Samson gives requires seven days as accustomed among the Israelites. However, Samson's wedding feast is juxtaposed with a Philistine custom to recruit thirty wedding guests of their men to play as the bridegroom's companions. These guests are obviously neither Samson's friends nor acquaintances: 'And it came to pass that when they (the Philistines) saw him, that they brought thirty companions to be with him' (Judg. 14:11). The phrase, 'thirty companions to be with him,' should alert us. This odd addition pertains to a custom the purpose of which remains enigmatic. The Nasamonian custom mentioned above might shed some light on the odd detail of thirty wedding companions, who are strangers to the bridegroom but are assigned to accompany him. It seems that the Philistine custom pertains to a fixed number of consummating wedding guests who are recruited whenever a wedding takes place. This detail remains obscure unless we refer to customs of sacred sexuality. Here, the context of the fecund stranger and the deflowering guest resurfaces again in a sexualized event juxtaposed with an entangling framework of a host and outsider/guest.

The text may underline the cultural tension between the two ethnic groups, of which one may have regarded sacred sexuality as an abomination. The Israelite Samson meets his 'guests' with hostility and aggravation, which are deeper than mere ethnic dislike or economic considerations of having to provide for them for seven days. Surrounded by his Philistine wedding 'guests', he tries to evade the sacred obligation by imposing an impossible bet. At this point, I would turn the tables and claim that the riddle does not lead to but embeds the core of the tension. The opening line enfolds Samson's sexual accusation. Samson says, 'If ye had not plowed with my heifer', (Judg. 14:18). The preposition the Hebrew text employs is *b* meaning into, *inside, in* as well as *with*. The Hebrew

31. Briffault, *The Mothers*, III, pp. 223–26.

word *egla* heifer, a female calf, may also read as *agala*, a wagon, in this text. Both words are female nouns, denoting servitude, submission, and objectification, while a heifer also denotes female virginity as well. The connotations of ploughing juxtapose the field with a woman's body opened up by masculine force to be sown by his seed. Samson is thus accusing the Philistine companions of having sexually used his bride; which reflects the Nasamonian custom. It is thus a cultural tension that clarifies Samson's extremely violent assault on the Philistine 'wedding companions'.

Samson's departure to his father's house after the wedding seems another odd detail in the story, and so does his belated claim to his rights as a husband.[32] Philistine customs of sacred sexuality might shed a new light on this odd detail in Samson's history: 'And his anger was kindled, and he went up to his father's house. But Samson's wife was given to his companion, whom he used as his friend. But it came to pass that a while after, in the time of the wheat-harvest, that Samson visited his wife with a kid...' (Judg. 13:19–20; 14:1). According to the Nasamonian custom a husband may consummate the union only after the bride has lain with the wedding guests. Both the Nasamonian custom and sexual continence are closely affiliated and may have been practised side by side. Both relate to rites of sacred sexuality purporting that a union with the divine bridegroom is an accessory to earthly marriage and fertility. Robert Briffault asserts that marital continence springs from the same pertinent customs expecting the bride to consummate a union with a representative of the gods represented by the holy man, priest, prince, guest and/or stranger, before she joins with her earthly husband.[33] The Nasamonian custom might also protect the husband from the 'perils' of virginal haemorrhage at defloration. Through a collective defloration, the wedding guests protect the bridegroom, and as a group each other as individuals.

The story of Samson's wedding and his thirty guests may elucidate another enigmatic verse found in the Song of Songs:

> Behold his bed, which is Salomon's; three scores valiant men are about it, of the valiant of Israel. They all hold swords; being expert in war; every man hath his sword upon his thigh because of fear of the night' (Song 3:7–8).

32. On Samson's unconsumed wedding, see, Mieke Bal, *Death and Dissymmetry*, p. 78.

33. Briffault, *The Mothers*, pp. 232–39.

Why should sixty valiant men surround Salomon's bed? What perils are they protecting him from? Significantly, this verse is juxtaposed with Salomon's wedding day:

> Go forth, O ye daughters of Zion, and behold King Solomon with crown where with his mother crowned him in the day of his espousals, and the day of the gladness of his heart,'(Song of Songs 3:11).

Thus both texts are concerned with wedding and male companions surrounding the bridegroom.

The customs described above objectify women in a way that is certain to disturb modern women. However, anthropological data also valorize the custom of multiple male partners voluntarily chosen by women. Morocco and Egypt are the closest contexts to the Hebrews to provide such pertinent templates. Until the recent century, tribes in these areas believed that the prosperity of the tribe and its crop depended on the tribal women practising sacred promiscuity. In the Maghreb area of Morocco, the women of a sacred tribe entitled Walad Abdi claimed to descend from saints. They divorced 'husbands' in succession and in between practised sacred promiscuity.[34] An Egyptian paradigm pertains to a similar class of noble prostitutes who belonged to a sacred tribe called Barmaky.[35] Known by the name of ghazye, they led a life of sacred prostitutes and were organized around a female *sheikha* of their own. When they settled down they would marry a *sheikh* and were considered holy. Bearing these data in mind I read the opening line of 2 Kgs 4:1 with a new mind; it epitomizes a woman as one of the female members or wives of the sons of prophets. As the story relates to a widow the holy title valorizes her own status belonging to a holy group.

A pertinent template can be seen in the custom in which a woman chooses herself as many sexual partners as possible before her marriage to prove her desirability, or may be eligible for marriage only after having been impregnated proving her fertility to her future husband.[36] These customs allow additional insights to the biblical stories discussed here. It is possible that these stories echo such fertility customs, or surface the tension between communities

34. *La soiete musulmance du Maghreb et Religion dans Láfrique du Nord,* Adolphe Jourdan, as quoted in Briffault, *The Mothers*, pp. 200, 217.

35. Briffault, *The Mothers*, pp. 200, 217.

36. Briffault, *The Mothers*, pp. 200, 217.

of which one group observes the customs while the other considers it an abomination. Both Genesis 19 and Judges 19 juxtapose the issue of virgins, a mistress or wife with multiple sexual partners. Judges 19 opens with a mistress or wife who practises sexuality with multiple partners on her own accord in the first place. Her husband then fetches her from her father's house without much ado, which may suggest tolerance towards the custom. Eventually, he hands her over to the mob, which sardonically mirrors her initial choice to choose multiple sexual partners herself.

Conclusion

Alternative rules of sexual conduct attest to the biological fact that sexuality practised by women outside an exclusive partnership increases the prospect of conception, offering the highest chance of pregnancy to every woman. Such practices of sacred sexuality may even ensure better breeding by seed imported from outside the clan.

Has sexual hospitality served the patriarchal structure, or has it served the matriarchal interest? Could sexual hospitality be seen within the patriarchal society, or did it function within matriarchal society? Evidence of alternative sexuality in general speaks for the fact that sacred sexuality may not necessarily have undermined the patriarchal rules proper. I tend to believe that cultural templates of alternative sexuality, outside or side by side with patriarchal rules, may have complemented the coarse conditions of continuity unconditionally bound to survival, both on the communal or individual levels. Templates of that nature may have coexisted alongside, condoned and even blessed by the community when they enhanced the same goal safeguarding the interest of both genders. These assumptions may bear witness to a richer, more pragmatic and perhaps even more tolerant communal life than we perhaps can imagine.

Chapter 13

Culture Clash in Sodom: Patriarchal Tales of Heroes, Villains, and Manipulation

K. Renato Lings

Certain patriarchal procedures in the Hebrew Bible (HB)[1] are deeply disturbing to modern commentators. Nowhere is this more poignantly illustrated than in the texts that describe the dramatic destruction of two cities, namely Sodom (Genesis 18–19) and Gibeah (Judges 19–20). While the biblical story-tellers present their patriarchal protagonists as suffering heroes as opposed to the groups, cities, tribes or peoples depicted as villains, modern scholars tend to bring a different focus to the text, often including the patriarchal heroes among the villains. This is so much the case that one might well speak of the encounter between the biblical narrators and their modern interpreters as an authentic culture clash. The collision of these two interpretative cultures seems to have gone unnoticed in many quarters. However, its critical importance has become very clear to me during my ongoing doctoral research, which focuses on the original Hebrew texts of the narratives in Genesis 18–19 and Judges 19–20.

This paper[2] aims to give a brief overview of some of the striking contrasts between the biblical approach to the hero/villain issue and representative modern approaches. Given the limited amount of space, I am aware that some of the generalizations that follow may give an incomplete picture of the variety of opinions and views to be found among Bible interpreters today. Nonetheless, the evidence that has emerged so far is significant enough to merit a

1. Throughout this essay, 'Bible' and 'biblical' refer to the Hebrew Bible.

2. I wish to express my gratitude to Sue Glover, James Haines, and Mary E. Mills for many helpful comments and suggestions.

discussion. Finally, I shall briefly explore some of the questions that I have wrestled with after becoming aware of the culture clash, particularly how the decoding of manipulative agendas behind biblical narratives can become a tool of liberation, notably for lesbigay people and, I would suggest, for other oppressed groups and communities.

The City of Sodom

To take the villains first, Sodom is the first noteworthy example in HB of a city being described as 'evil'. In 10:19 the name of Sodom is introduced alongside Gomorrah; both cities being founded by the early Canaanites. The latter have just been listed as descendants of Ham (9:6, 20), a fact that inextricably places them under the curse pronounced by Noah (9:25–27). The Canaanite connection is reaffirmed in 13:7, and very soon the impending destruction of the city is announced (13:10) because the inhabitants are 'wicked' (13:13). The exact nature of the evil in this city is not specified. The King of Sodom is mentioned (14:2, 22–23). The narrator reintroduces the theme of Sodom in chapter 18, where Abraham's visitors look towards the city (18:16), and Yahweh reveals his plans to Abraham (18:20–21).

The Sin of Sodom: Genesis

Some room is left for doubt as to the extent of the wickedness prevalent in the city, as Abraham intercedes for those citizens who are 'righteous' (18:23–32). The only factual evidence of Sodomite wickedness provided by the text is finally presented in 19:1–14. Three facts emerge. First, the people of Sodom are perhaps not seen to compete with Lot, who is a resident alien, as he offers hospitality to the visiting angels. Lot distinguishes himself by promptly inviting them to stay at his house (19:1–3). Second, all the men of Sodom behave disrespectfully toward Lot.[3] Instead of offering him their assistance, they arrogantly tell him not only to interrupt and relinquish his responsibilities as host but even to bring the visitors outside, which would imply handing them over to the townsmen's control (19:5). Lot instinctively opposes the idea. Within

3. The text twice underlines the fact that *all* the men of Sodom are there, which naturally includes the rulers (19:4, 11).

the parameters of ancient patriarchal culture such a proposal is totally unacceptable.

The Sodomites then respond by resorting to threats accompanied by physical violence, thus confirming their evil ways (19:9). On these grounds the villains of the story are punished in two ways: (a) they are effectively barred from achieving their stated aim, namely, to become acquainted with the divine visitors (19:5), and (b) their violent procedure triggers not only their temporary 'blindness', but also an even greater punishment in the form of their total destruction. From a biblical perspective, perhaps the transgressions of Sodom can be viewed as religious. The Sodomites fail to show the visiting angels due respect, and they maltreat Lot, the resident alien. Their selfish, violent behaviour causes offence to the divine.

The Sin of Sodom: HB

All biblical interpreters quoting Sodom see the men of the city as villains. The terms describing the sin or crime committed cover a wide spectrum, which cannot be reduced to a simple formula. By and large, however, these different terms can be subsumed under the following categories: idolatry,[4] rebellion against God,[5] false prophets,[6] pride and arrogance,[7] adultery and promiscuity,[8] iniquity, corruption,[9] social injustice,[10] violence and murder.[11] A frequently used term in Ezekiel is 'abominations', which applies to most categories of sins, particularly idolatry.[12] Outside the book of Genesis, the issue of inhospitality to strangers is not singled out by HB interpreters. In all probability, inhospitality or, more accurately,

4. Deut. 29:16–27; 32:5, 15–18, 21, 37–38; Isa. 2:8, 18, 20; Jer. 23:13; 50:2, 38; Ezek. 16:16–21, 35; Amos 2:4, 8; 5:26; Zeph. 1:4–6; 2:11.

5. Isa. 1:2–5, 23; 3:8–9; Jer. 50:14, 24; Lam. 1:18, 20; 3:39, 42; Ezek. 16:59; Amos 2:4; Zeph. 1:13, 17; 3:11.

6. Jer. 23:11, 15–17, 21–27, 30–39; Lam. 2:14; 4:13; Zeph. 3:4.

7. Isa. 2:11–12, 17; 3:9, 16; 13:11; Jer. 49:12, 16; 50:31–32; Ezek. 16:49; Amos 6:8, 13; Zeph. 2:8, 10; 3:11.

8. Jer. 23:10, 14; Ezek. 16:15–17, 20, 22, 25–29, 31–38, 41, 43, 58; Amos 2:7. Typically these sexual terms allude to polytheism.

9. Isa. 1:4, 16, 18, 21–23; 13:11; Jer. 23:2, 10–11, 14–15, 22; Lam. 2:14; Ezek. 16:47; Amos 2:12; 5:12; Zeph. 3:7.

10. Isa. 1:15–17, 21, 23; 3:14–15; Amos 2:7; 4:1; 5:7, 11–12; 6:12; 8:4; Zeph. 3:1, 3–4.

11. Isa. 1:21; Lam. 4:13–14; Ezek. 16:38; Zeph. 1:9.

12. Ezek. 16:2, 22, 36, 43, 47, 50–52, 58.

breach of hospitality, is covered by one or several wider categories such as rebellion against God, pride and arrogance, iniquity, social injustice, and violence. However, within Genesis itself, the theme of patriarchal hospitality is strongly emphasized by juxtaposing the generosity displayed by Abraham (18:2–8, 16) and Lot (19:1–3, 6–8) with the uncharitable, aggressive behaviour displayed by the Sodomites (19:4–5, 9).

The Sin of Sodom: Modern Interpreters

Modern interpreters agree with the biblical text insofar as the men of Sodom are seen as villains. The importance of the hospitality/inhospitality issue is widely accepted and discussed,[13] although several commentators are uncomfortable with it or even dismiss it.[14] When it comes to defining other aspects of the exact nature of the sin of Sodom, a wider gap emerges. Whereas no part of HB describes the sins of Sodom in homosexual terms, most interpreters today do just that. Contemporary readers take it for granted that the phrase 'so that we may know them' (19:5) is a euphemism that contains sexual innuendo. This approach is also reflected in a large

13. Thomas Brodie, *Genesis as Dialogue* (Oxford: Oxford University Press, 2001), pp. 250, 253; Michael Carden, *Sodomy* (London: Equinox Publishing, 2004), pp. 26, 37; Gary David Comstock, *Gay Theology without Apology* (Cleveland, Ohio: The Pilgrim Press, 1993), p. 38; Robert Gagnon, *The Bible and Homosexual Practice* (Nashville: Abingdon Press, 2001), pp. 74, 76; Robert Goss, *Queering Christ* (Cleveland, Ohio: The Pilgrim Press, 2002) pp. 193, 195–96; Steven Greenberg, *Wrestling with God & Men* (Madison: The University of Wisconsin Press, 2004), pp. 71–72; Thomas Hanks, *The Subversive Gospel* (Cleveland, Ohio: The Pilgrim Press, 2000), pp. 220, 243; Daniel Helminiak, *What the Bible Really Says about Homosexuality* (Tajique, New Mexico: Alamo Square Press, 2000), p. 46; Rose Sallberg Kam, *Their Stories. Our Stories* (New York: Continuum, 1995) pp. 44, 46; Gareth Moore, *A Question of Truth* (London & New York: Continuum, 2003), pp. 71–72; Martti Nissinen, *Homoeroticism in the Biblical World* (Minneapolis: Fortress Press, 1998), pp. 44, 48; Miriam Winter, *Woman Wisdom: A Feminist Lectionary and Psalter* (Melbourne: Collins Dove, 1992), p. 216.

14. For instance, Cheryl Exum, *Fragmented Women* (Valley Forge: Trinity Press International, 1983), p. 182, criticizes 'the amount of attention commentators devote to the issue of hospitality', the point being that traditional biblical hospitality has applied to men only while women have been excluded. Mieke Bal, *Death and Dissymmetry: The Politics of Coherence in the Book of Judges* (Chicago: The University of Chicago Press, 1988), p. 122 coincides. Acknowledging the validity of this point, I have used the term 'patriarchal hospitality'.

number of current English Bible versions,[15] and the same is true for a majority of commentators.[16] What is more, recent scholarship tends to make a clear distinction between consensual male–male sex on the one hand, and forced intercourse on the other.[17] As regards the latter category, there is broad agreement on the concept with a number of variations in the terminology. This stretches from abuse, abuse of strangers, and abuse and assault at one end of the spectrum, going via attempted sexual assault and attempted gang rape all the way to rape, male–male rape, gang rape, homosexual gang rape and violent gang rape at the other extreme. Common to them all is the idea of sexual aggression, often depicted as anal rape.[18] In other

15. Cf. Contemporary English Version (CEV), Jerusalem Bible (JB), JPS Hebrew-English Tanakh (JP99), New American Bible (NAB), New English Bible (NEB), New International Version (NIV), New Jerusalem Bible (NJB), New World Translation (NWT), Revised English Bible (REB). Other Bible versions quoted in this article: Christian Community Bible (CCB), Good News Bible (GNB), New King James Version (NKJV) and New Revised Standard Version (NRSV).

16. Representative examples are Tammi Schneider, *Judges* (Collegeville: The Liturgical Press, 2000), p. 260: 'the male residents of the town wanted to know the male visitors sexually'; Alice Bach, 'Rereading the Body Politic', in Alice Bach (ed.), *Women in the Hebrew Bible* (New York and London: Routledge, 1999), p. 396; 'homosexual intercourse'; Gagnon, *The Bible and Homosexual Practice*, p. 75: 'same-sex eroticism'; Moore, *A Question of Truth*: 'a demand that Lot deliver them up that they might use them sexually' (p.71), 'a certain kind of sexual act' and 'to use them for sexual pleasure' (p. 72). Likewise, Nissinen, *Homoeroticism in the Biblical World*, p. 46 mentions 'same-sex interaction' and 'the sexual nature of the sin of Sodom'.

17. Carden, *Sodomy*, p. 35: 'the evil is not homosexuality but the abuse of strangers'; Goss, *Queering Christ*, p. 193: 'the story ... has nothing to do with same-sex sexuality; it has to do, rather, with male rape'; Hanks, *The Subversive Gospel*, p. 223: 'the sin of violence, not of "homosexuality"'; Helminiak, *What the Bible Really Says*, p. 45: 'what is at stake is male–male rape, not simply male–male sex'; Moore, *A Question of Truth*, p. 83: 'not a homosexual act but an act which will humiliate the visitors'; Nissinen, *Homoeroticism in the Biblical World*, p. 49: 'the men were motivated not to satisfy their sexual lust but to show their supremacy and power over the guests'; Dan Via, in Dan Via & Robert Gagnon, *Homosexuality and the Bible* (Minneapolis: Fortress Press, 2003), p. 5: 'these ... stories have no direct bearing on the validity of contemporary consensual homosexual relationships but rather ... condemn homosexual gang rape'.

18. See Bach, 'Rereading the Body Politic', pp. 391, 396; Brodie, *Genesis as Dialogue*, pp. 243, 245, 251, 253; Carden, *Sodomy*, pp. 6, 9, 13, 14, 21, 26–29, 35, 37, 38; Comstock, *Gay Theology without Apology*, pp. 38, 40; Brian Doyle, 'The Sin of Sodom: yada, yada, yada', in *Theology & Sexuality* No. 9, 1998, p. 89; Goss, *Queering Christ*, pp. 193, 194, 195, 196, 197; Greenberg, *Wrestling with God & Men*, pp. 67, 72, 73, 192; Hanks, *The Subversive Gospel*, pp. 220, 223, 237, 244, 245, 248; Helminiak, *What the Bible Really Says about Homosexuality*, pp. 45, 46, 47; Moore, *A Question of Truth*, pp. 71, 72, 73, 82, 83, 84, 85; Nissinen, *Homoeroticism in the Biblical World*, pp. 46, 47, 48, 49, 91, 93; Letha

words, with its emphasis on sexual violence, the interpretative lens used by modern scholars differs radically from that of HB.

Heroes of Sodom: HB

The first individual to be cast in the role of hero is Abraham. For his nephew's sake, Abraham undertakes the perilous military operation by which he succeeds in liberating all the people of Sodom, including Lot (14:14–17). Likewise, Abraham intercedes before Yahweh in order to secure the survival of the righteous of Sodom, a group that Abraham is convinced would include Lot (18:23–32). The second hero is a combination of Yahweh and his angels. First, Yahweh listens to Abraham's concerns and respects them (18:26–32). Secondly, the angels visiting Lot rescue him from physical assault (19:9–11) and lead his entire family to safety (19:15–23).

From a biblical perspective, the only 'righteous' man living in Sodom is Lot. Up until this point, virtually nothing has been said of Lot's personal qualities. Indeed, these are not really revealed until Genesis 19. Here Lot acts in accordance with patriarchal values as he practises traditional hospitality. He insists on bringing the visiting angels to his house (19:2–3), takes responsibility for the preparation of the meal (19:3), and, when subsequently challenged by the men of Sodom, defends the inviolability of the patriarchal hospitality concept (19:7–8). From his perspective, the only possible way out of the sudden emergency is the idea of protecting his male guests by offering his two unmarried daughters to the mob as a pledge of his loyalty. He literally asks them to do 'what is good in their eyes' with the girls. Unthinkable as this may seem in the twenty-first century, this is in keeping with ancient patriarchal procedures.[19]

Thanks to his commitment to the virtues of patriarchal hospitality, HB unquestionably regards Lot as belonging to the minuscule group of righteous citizens of Sodom whose cause Abraham pleaded

Scanzoni & Virginia Mollenkott, *Is the Homosexual My Neighbor?* (San Francisco: HarperSanFrancisco, 1994), pp. 58, 59, 60, 72; Michael Vasey, *Strangers and Friends* (London: Hodder & Stoughton, 1995), pp. 87, 125.

19. In the book of Genesis, Abraham on two occasions hands over his wife Sarah to a local king, passing her off as his sister, in order to avert danger to his own life (Gen. 12:11–16; 20:1–7). For similar reasons Isaac makes his wife Rebekah pose as his sister, exposing her to potential sexual harassment and the risk of involuntary adultery (26:6–11).

before Yahweh. This becomes clear as the visiting angels tell Lot and his family to leave the city immediately (19:12–13, 15–17) and then grant him the favour of seeking refuge in the nearby town of Zoar (19:20–23). Finally, as soon as the survival of Lot and his daughters is ensured, the text makes the point that their escape is the result of Yahweh's agreement with Abraham (19:29).

Lot's name occurs in three biblical passages outside Genesis. Deuteronomy speaks of the land that God has given to Lot's descendants (Deut. 2:9, 19), and the book of Psalms describes Assyria as 'the strong arm of the children of Lot' (Ps. 83:8). From this, it would certainly seem that HB in Genesis considers Lot 'righteous'. Likewise, Deuteronomy clearly considers the descendants of Lot as worthy of occupying the territory in which they live. Only Psalms portrays the Assyrian 'children of Lot' in a negative light—and evidently for political reasons, given that Assyria is listed among the enemies of Israel.

Heroes of Sodom: Modern Interpreters

Today's scholars have little to say on the subject of Sodom's heroes. Carden (*Sodomy*, p. 15) sees the deity taking the hero's role as he describes Genesis 19 as 'an account of one of YHWH's liberative, mighty deeds'. In the view of Mark Sturge, Lot is another hero.[20] Indeed, Sturge offers what is probably the most positive view of Lot: 'I want to encourage the acceptance of Lot as a fellow saint who had to overcome extreme difficulties in his life and who also experienced the grace of God' (p. 63); 'he recognized that his adopted city needed to be transformed ... he persevered to become the judge of the city ... he was the one who cried out to God against the inhabitants' (p. 75). More complex, but still basically positive, is the interpretation of Lot's behaviour offered by Lyn Bechtel.[21] She explains: 'Lot's incongruent, offensive and seemingly 'evil' offer of his daughters ... is actually 'good' because it diffuses a potentially hostile situation' (p. 126).

20. Mark Sturge, 'Don't Dis Me if You Don't Know Me!', in *Black Theology in Britain*, 4.1 (November 2001), pp. 62–77.

21. Lyn Bechtel, 'A Feminist Reading of Genesis 19:1-11', in Athalya Brenner (ed.), *Genesis: A Feminist Companion to the Bible, Second Series*, (Sheffield: Sheffield Academic Press, 1998), pp. 108–28.

Villains of Sodom: HB

From a biblical perspective, it would seem that the villains of Sodom are well identified. First of all, the male inhabitants are mentioned. Secondly, the city is a kingdom. An event of the magnitude reported in Genesis 19:4–11 would have to be orchestrated by the rulers, who indeed are present at Lot's house. The narrator provides this information by emphasizing that everyone is there, 'all the people, from boy to old man' (19:4, 11). Thirdly, it may well be argued that Sodom represents the early Canaanites, whom HB consistently depicts as villains.

Villains of Sodom: Modern Interpreters

If non-sexual versus sexual interpretations of the crime of Sodom have caused the first major divergence between HB on the one hand and modern commentators and translators on the other, Lot's role in the plot of the Sodom story registers the second significant discrepancy. As noted, the Bible presents Lot as a suffering hero standing up for what he believes in, and he is rewarded with a guided escape and subsequent survival amid cataclysmic destruction.

Modern interpreters, for their part, are shocked by the way in which Lot exposes his daughters to physical degradation, humiliation and danger.[22] Along similar lines, Brodie (*Genesis as Dialogue*) judges Lot's character in unflattering terms: 'the limited hospitality of Lot', his 'limitedness in communicating', 'Lot is not an authority on hospitality', 'his actions, including his offering of his daughters, are suspect', 'a narrowness of vision', 'there is uncertainty ... about his accuracy and truthfulness' (p. 250); 'Lot's limited awareness' (p. 251), and 'Lot's limitedness, his closeness to Sodom' (p. 252). A similar critical view is held by Doyle ('The Sin of Sodom'). He speaks of 'Lot's ambiguous behaviour' (p. 87); 'the ambiguity of his character' (p. 96); the 'impenetrability' and 'complexity of the character' (p. 97); 'a high degree of ignorance on the part of Lot', 'his lack of knowledge' (p. 97); 'Lot ... is in the

22. For instance, Goss, *Queering Christ*, p. 193: 'Lot's offer of his daughters to the mob is shocking to readers'; Nissinen, *Homoeroticism in the Biblical World*, p. 46: 'this violent trade of women makes a contemporary reader shiver', and Greenberg, *Wrestling with God & Men*, p. 64: 'a horrific suggestion to contemporary sensibilities'.

dark, does not understand' (p. 87); 'a divine presence which is ... sometimes misunderstood' (p. 91); 'he does not know God' (p. 92).

Greenberg (*Wrestling with God & Men*) takes the critique one step further: 'Lot revealed in the offer of his daughters to the crowd how much he had learned from his neighbours', 'for Lot the rule of no predation between men (all men are brothers) did not exclude male predation of women', and 'Lot translated Abraham's ethic of brotherhood in bluntly patriarchal ways' (p. 73). Likewise, Carden (*Sodomy*) feels that 'questions gather around the character of Lot' to such an extent that Lot cannot be seen as 'a positive character in the story' (p. 21). In short, Carden takes 'a negative view of Lot's character' (p. 39). Thus Lot is 'rescued on the basis of his kinship with Abraham and not for any intrinsic merit on his part' (p.21). This negative view is fuelled by the fact that Lot's daughters 'were offered up for rape by their father' (p. 22). Moreover, Lot is presented unfavourably because he 'appears weak, prevaricating and distrustful of the angels' guarantees' (p. 27). This leads Carden to conclude that 'Lot is revealed as subscribing to the same ideology as the men of Sodom' (p. 35), and that Lot 'shares their ideology' (p. 39). Likewise, Winter (*Woman Wisdom*, p. 215) strongly disapproves of Lot's behaviour, blaming it on his character: 'he callously offered a local mob the opportunity to rape them'. She is joined by Bal (*Death and Dissymmetry*, p. 92): 'Lot [may seem] commendable—that is, if we ignore the nature of the gift and the subsequent fate of the daughters'.

Carden (*Sodomy*) provides a surprise as he identifies two additional villains, the first being none other than the deity himself. Indeed, through his annihilation of an entire city Yahweh is accused of the crime of genocide: 'the genocide at the heart of YHWH's mighty deed' and 'the genocide wrought by the deity' (p. 14), 'YHWH's program of genocide', and 'we, too, should stand beside Lot's wife and condemn YHWH's crime' (p. 41).[23] The other surprise villain happens to be us, the readers: 'mass death by fire and brimstone is swift, leaving no rotting corpses to accuse YHWH and ourselves of murder' (p. 40).

23. Curiously this contrasts with Carden's other listing of YHWH under 'Heroes of Sodom' (*Sodomy*, p. 15).

The City of Gibeah

Although Gibeah is not as well-known as Sodom, the name occurs frequently in HB. Nearly all the contexts are narratives; primarily the books of Joshua, Judges and 1 Samuel. Often it is just 'Gibeah', with no epithet.[24] At other times it is referred to as 'Gibeah of Benjamin', or similar,[25] while a third variant is 'Gibeah of Saul'.[26] The first and second terms may be described as technically neutral given that Benjamin is one of the twelve tribes of Israel. Nonetheless, in the dramatic story that unfolds in Judges 19–20, it acquires sinister overtones because of Benjamin's crucial involvement in the horrific events described.

The Gibeah of Judges 19–20 provides a scenario not unlike Sodom. The narrative includes two scenes that depict ancient patriarchal hospitality (19:3–9; 17–21). On both occasions, the male visitor is not an angel but a Levite; in other words a man connected to the religious sphere by his priestly functions. He is travelling with his young *pilegesh*,[27] his young male servant and a pair of donkeys. After his arrival at Gibeah, the Levite is offered hospitality by an old man—a resident alien originally from Ephraim like the Levite himself. The local population belongs to the tribe of Benjamin (19:14, 16).

The Sin of Gibeah: Judges

Later the same evening, certain local men surround the house and pound on the door. They ask the old man to bring the visiting Levite outside so that they may 'know' him. The old man resists the proposition and makes a counteroffer consisting of handing the mob his own unmarried daughter together with the Levite's *pilegesh*. But the townsmen are undeterred (19:25). This prompts the Levite

24. Josh. 15:57; 18:28; 24:33; Judg. 19:12–13, 15; 20:5–6, 9, 13–15, 19–21, 25, 29–31, 33–34, 36–37, 43; 1 Sam. 10:10, 26; 14:2, 5.

25. Judg. 19:14, 16; 20:4, 10; 1 Sam. 13:2–3, 15–16; 14:16; 2 Sam. 23:29; 1 Chron. 11:31.

26. 1 Sam. 11:4; 15:34; Isa. 10:29.

27. The Hebrew word *pîlegeš* translates as 'concubine' or, perhaps more accurately, as 'wife of secondary rank'. Given the disagreement among scholars as to the exact English rendering, I will use the simple transcription *pilegesh*. For a more detailed discussion of the term, see Bal, *Death and Dissymmetry*, pp. 81–84, 89; Schneider, *Judges*, pp. 128–29, 247–49, 254.

to act quickly. He makes use of his *pilegesh*, the only woman over whom he has right of possession, by pushing her outside. Regarded as a diversionary tactic, the move is successful in the sense that it keeps the Levite safe. In addition, it saves the host from putting the honour of his young daughter in jeopardy (19:25). Yet the move has a fatal price. The *pilegesh* does not survive the abuse to which she is subjected all night long (19:27–28; 20:4–5). Subsequently, the Levite instigates a civil war to avenge the crime (19:29–20:11).

The first sin of Gibeah to be pointed out by this text is the fact that the citizens are clearly not keen on hosting travellers. They uncharitably leave the visitors to wait in the open square (19:15, 18). The townsmen who come to the old man's house at night are described in no uncertain terms as scoundrels or 'sons of worthlessness' (19:22; 20:13). Thus, the second sin of Gibeah is the fact that these men behave disrespectfully toward the old man as they arrogantly tell him to interrupt and relinquish his hosting duties. Thirdly, their demand that the Levite be brought outside and handed over to their control is extraordinary (19:22). The old man finds the proposition 'wicked' and 'foolish' (19:23–24). The narrator specifies the crime of Gibeah in further detail. In addition to the serious breach of hospitality, there is a threat to kill the Levite (20:5), not to mention the actual abuse and murder of the *pilegesh* (20:4–5). In sum, the outrage is characterized as 'evil' (20:13), 'folly' (20:12), and 'lewdness' or 'depravity' (20:6).

The Sin of Gibeah: HB

Outside the above-mentioned narrative contexts, the name of Gibeah occurs very little in HB. Two such rare cases may give a hint as to the manner in which the prophets interpreted the story. Isaiah mentions how many Israelites, including 'Gibeah of Saul', flee before the advancing Assyrian army. What is described here in poetic language seems to be a situation of widespread panic. The other prophet is Hosea. He alone utilizes Gibeah as a metaphor as he speaks of the sins that Israel has committed 'since the days of Gibeah'.[28] The transgressions that Hosea seems to lambaste in the same chapter are primarily what he describes as idolatry, injustice and a false sense of security based on military resources.[29]

28. Hos. 10:9.
29. Hos.10:1–2, 5–6, 8, 13.

The Sin of Gibeah: Modern Interpreters

Similar to the case of Sodom, the culture clash between HB and modern interpreters emerges when it comes to defining the sin of Gibeah. While HB appears to be unconcerned about possible threats of sexual assault aimed at the Levite, twentieth and twenty-first century commentators are in no doubt: they see the problem as being primarily sexual, based on the assumption that 'so that we may know him' (19:22) is a euphemism for proposed sexual intercourse.[30] The commentators are followed by a large number of modern English Bible versions.[31] What is more, today's interpreters tend to define the perceived sexual scenario for the Levite as one of abuse and rape. It might be argued that only a relatively small number of translators are that specific,[32] but the commentators taking this view are clearly in the majority.[33] This perceived scenario is visualized as a prelude to the actual *hetero*sexual gang rape that takes place; namely of the *pilegesh*.

Heroes of Gibeah: Judges

When it comes to portraying the male patriarchal characters in the Gibeah story, that is, the Levite and his host, the narrative is

30. Some representative examples are Bach, 'Rereading the Body Politic', p. 396: 'have intercourse with him'; Bal, *Death and Dissymmetry*, p. 159: 'homosexuality'; Mieke Bal, 'A Body of Writing: Judges 19', in Athalya Brenner (ed.), *A Feminist Companion to Judges* (Sheffield: Sheffield Academic Press, 1993), p. 228: 'to know and to possess are both expressions for the sexual encounter'; Gagnon, *The Bible and Homosexual Practice*: 'so that we may know (= have intercourse with) him' (p. 93), 'homosexual intercourse' (p. 95), 'the original demand to have sex with the Levite' (p. 97); Henriette Howarth, *The Breaking of Her Dawn* (Hyderabad: YWCA, 2000), p.47: 'the men of Gibeah ... wanted to have intercourse with him'; Schneider, *Judges*, p. 260: 'so that they could be intimate with him', 'what they wanted to do with the man is "to know", a clearly sexual term', and 'knowing the man sexually'.

31. Cf. CEV, JP99, NEB, NIV, NJB, NKJV, NRSV, NWT, REB.

32. Thus BBE, CCB, JB, NAB.

33. See Schneider (*Judges*): 'they wanted to use him sexually' (p. 267), and 'he had been threatened sexually' (p. 268); Bach, 'Rereading the Body Politic': 'homosexual attack', 'the horror of homosexual rape' (p. 395), 'homosexual rape', 'the Benjaminites' threat to sodomize him', 'the shame and horror of sodomy' (p. 397); Bal, *Death and Dissymmetry*: 'the threat to rape the husband' (p. 158), 'they had threatened to rape him' (p. 218), 'the threat of homosexual rape' (pp. 92, 119, 157); Exum, *Fragmented Women*: 'the rape of the Levite himself. This is what the men of Gibeah are portrayed as having in mind' (p. 183), 'the threat to rape the man' (p. 182), 'homosexual rape' (p. 183), 'the humiliating threat of homosexual rape' (p. 186), 'the men of Gibeah want to humiliate the Levite in the most degrading way' (p. 183).

restrained. Little is said about and by each one. If anyone is a hero, the host perhaps comes relatively close to playing this role. The old man from Ephraim appears in a positive light in the sense that he possesses at least two virtues. Firstly, he is in solidarity with his fellow countryman the travelling Levite. Secondly, he is hospitable in the patriarchal sense to the extent of defending the safety of his male guest at all costs. However, the narrative contains the irony that this old man's efforts possibly go unrewarded. Perhaps his only gain is the certainty of having fulfilled his traditional patriarchal obligations and having been spared the potential disgrace of losing his daughter's honour. Other than that, nothing is said of either him or of his family during Gibeah's destruction (20:37-38, 40-41, 48), which may imply that they have become undeserving victims of the ensuing civil war.

Concerning the Levite himself, it would seem that he is not portrayed as a hero but rather as a victim. At first he is the victim of his *pilegesh*'s deserting him (19:2). Soon after retrieving her in Bethlehem he loses her on that fateful night in Gibeah in a move that, within the patriarchal universe of HB, is perhaps best described as self-protection.[34] At the subsequent people's assembly convened at Mizpah, the narrator seems to be in sympathy with the Levite given that the latter is referred to respectfully as 'the husband of the woman who was murdered' (20:4). An additional hero is perhaps important to include, namely the tribe of Judah, to which the *pilegesh* belongs. Judah is chosen to initiate the battle against Benjamin (20:18).

Heroes of Gibeah: Modern Interpreters

The virtual consensus among contemporary scholars is that none of the main characters intervening in this biblical narrative deserves to be portrayed in positive terms. It becomes obvious that to the modern mind, Gibeah produces only villains and victims, and the category of heroes does not apply.

Villains of Gibeah: HB

The text does not hesitate when it comes to identifying the villains. Indeed, they can be divided into four groups. The first group

34. See note 18.

comprises the townspeople who saw the visitors in the square but failed to invite them in. The second group is the gang who started the riot outside the old man's house. The third group of villains are 'the lords of Gibeah', a concept that either includes the city's leadership who did nothing to stop the outrage, or all male citizens. In this manner, the whole city by implication stands accused by the Levite of playing a part in the crime (20:5). The fourth group of villains is the entire tribe of Benjamin as they close ranks and refuse to hand over the primary suspects of Gibeah for execution (20:12-13).[35]

Villains of Gibeah: Modern Interpreters

Contemporary scholars pay little attention to the hell-raisers of Gibeah. It would seem that, for this group, the role of villain is taken for granted. In other words, on this score there is a fundamental convergence with the attitude of HB. In other cases, however, the discrepancies are noticeable. For instance, this applies to the old host who at times is regarded as a man of dubious character. This view is held by Carden and Schneider, among others, while Exum finds him culpable of contributing to the outrage, together with the Levite.[36] As regards the latter, few would agree with HB in seeing him as a victim. Indeed, modern opinions about the Levite are so overwhelmingly negative that the only slot available to him is among the villains. The descriptions of him range all the way from impersonal, irresolute, half-hearted and blind to callous, dishonourable and disreputable.

Thus, Schneider sees the Levite as a man 'of questionable character' (*Judges,* p. 260) and draws attention to the man's 'insensitivity' (p. 263), given that he 'did not express any remorse' (p. 264). Exum calls him 'the true culprit' (*Fragmented Women,* p. 183) while pointing out the Levite's 'baseness' (p. 186), and his behaviour is labelled as 'scandalous' (p. 196). Likewise, Peggy

35. A possible fifth group would include the house of Saul, with whom the house of David was embroiled in a long, bitter feud that is played out outside the framework of the book of Judges, cf. 1 Sam. 16–24; 25:43; 26–28:2; 2 Sam. 2–4.

36. Carden, *Sodomy,* p. 40: 'the old man resembles Lot and I have a similarly negative view of his character'; Schneider, *Judges,* p. 261: 'he even offered them ideas, telling them to have their pleasure with them and do what they liked with them'; Exum, *Fragmented Women,* p. 183: 'the guilt of both men'.

Kamuf[37] entertains the possibility that 'the Levite may have been ... the original criminal' all along (p. 194). She elaborates: 'the mutilation he performs repeats in a calculated fashion the brutal, frenzied mutilation of the same body by the Benjaminites' (p. 201). Thus, the Levite's 'gruesome act' is 'the mutilation and dispersion of a woman's dead body' and, finally, 'the guilty one will also be the avenger' (p. 205). Bal ('A Body of Writing') is equally scathing: 'the man is lying' (p. 219), 'his perverted speech' (p. 230), 'the unambiguous guilt of this unnamed individual', 'this man is beyond redemption' (p. 218). In another work Bal adds:[38] 'the husband ... displays the cowardice that we know' (p. 329), and 'her hand on the threshold, points in accusation to her murderer' (p. 330). Gagnon (*The Bible and Homosexual Practice*, p. 96) agrees: 'the Levite sought to exaggerate the danger to his own person in order to rationalize his own complicity in the atrocity'.

On a similar note, the narrator's character may be seen as dubious, or perhaps impenetrable. Thus, Bach observes 'the absence of anger or moral outrage on the part of the narrator' ('Rereading the Body Politic', p. 397). Some scholars indirectly view the tribes of Israel as villains. This particularly applies to the moment in which the latter proceed to exterminate the citizens of Jabesh-Gilead, only sparing the lives of four hundred unmarried girls who are handed over immediately to the remaining men of Benjamin (21:10–14). The same is true for the abduction and forced marriage of the dancing girls of Shiloh.[39]

The Culture Clash: Few Heroes and Many Villains

Clearly the number of heroes identified in this essay has been negligible for both narratives. The only obvious candidates to be cast in this role, namely, Lot and the old resident alien of Gibeah, may meet with the approval of the biblical narrators, but modern commentators tend to reject them and often vehemently so. As noted, many scholars seem to distance themselves emphatically from

37. Peggy Kamuf, 'Author of a Crime', in Brenner (ed.) *A Feminist Companion to Judges*, pp. 187–207.

38. Mieke Bal, 'Dealing With Women: Daughters in the Book of Judges', in Alice Bach (ed.) *Women in the Hebrew Bible*, pp. 317–33.

39. See Bal, *Death and Dissymmetry*, p. 127; Exum, *Fragmented Women*, pp. 193–94; Schneider, *Judges*, p. 272.

the general approach of HB, and the question of heroes certainly seems to highlight the gap. This is despite the fact that many interpreters claim to have the narrator on their side.[40]

While reflecting on the culture clash between ancient narrators and modern interpreters, I have been struck by the large number of real and potential villains that contemporary scholars have so far identified. The following tables illustrate the few similarities and the many differences between biblical and modern approaches when it comes to identifying the villains of Sodom and Gibeah.

Table 1: Villains of Sodom

Hebrew Bible	*Modern Interpreters*
The men of Sodom	The men of Sodom
The Canaanites	Lot
	Abraham
	Yahweh
	We the readers

The discrepancies between the two columns of Table One are striking. The only point of convergence is 'the men of Sodom'. Yet this convergence is imperfect. Under HB the narrator has discreetly subsumed the rulers of Sodom under the categories 'from boy to old man' (19:4) and 'from the small to the great' (19:11), while modern interpreters ignore the role and presence of the king. Contemporary scholars focus primarily on Lot, viewing him as no better than the townsmen. Intriguingly Mark Sturge ('Don't Dis Me...'), places the Yahweh-favoured patriarch Abraham among the villains,[41] while Carden (*Sodomy*), as noted, suggests two additional kinds of villains: the deity himself and the readers of the narrative.[42]

40. See, for instance, Schneider, *Judges*, p. 268: 'the narrator casts doubt on the trustworthiness of the man'; Nissinen, *Homoeroticism in the Biblical World*, p. 51: 'the narrator depicts the dishonoured Levite not as an innocent victim but as a coward'; Gagnon, *The Bible and Homosexual Practice*, p. 100: 'the narrator ... appears to treat the Levite's callous and cowardly behaviour towards his concubine as deplorable'; Exum, *Fragmented Women*, p. 197: 'the narrator of Judges 19 allows us to feel moral outrage at their behaviour—and this, I think, is his goal'.

41. See, Sturge, 'Don't Dis Me if You Don't Know Me', pp. 63, 66-67, 73, who mentions this patriarch's 'personal character flaws' (p. 63), 'the real villain, Abraham', and 'Abraham's cheating, lying, deceiving and selfish ways' (p. 66), presumably in allusion to those situations in which the patriarch put Sarah in an untenable position.

Table 2: Sins of Sodom

Hebrew Bible	*Modern Interpreters*
Breach of patriarchal hospitality	Breach of patriarchal hospitality
Idolatry	'To know' sexually
Pride, arrogance	Attempted gang rape
Selfishness	Cruelty
Adultery and promiscuity	Sadism
Corruption	
Injustice	
Violence	
Murder	

In short, the direct emphasis of HB is on a Canaanite city (Sodom), while the modern approach overwhelmingly puts the spotlight on individuals.

Again in Table Two, the two columns can only be said to have one obvious item in common, namely 'breach of patriarchal hospitality'. Yet even this commonality is partial. Modern scholars tend to be less interested in the hospitality issue because the safety concept involved does not cover women.[43] HB is concerned with a long series of transgressions which, as noted, are only vaguely reflected on the opposite side. Conversely, HB ignores the main concerns of modern commentators, which primarily hinge on sexual matters and occasionally include the perceived cruelty and suspected sadism of Lot. Stated differently, HB seems to present the Sodom story as a theological, political and ethical treatise, whereas most contemporary scholars focus on sexual concerns, particularly the perceived issue of gang rape.

Table Three moves the focus to Gibeah:

Table 3: Villains of Gibeah

Hebrew Bible	*Modern Interpreters*
The citizens of Gibeah	The men of Gibeah
Certain men of Gibeah	The Levite
The rulers of Gibeah	The old sojourner (host)
The tribe of Benjamin	The narrator

42. See the section 'Villains of Sodom: Modern Interpreters'.
43. See note 14.

An important distinction may be appreciated in Table Three. The Hebrew narrative lists four groups of villains, all of which belong to or represent a city, a clan or the whole tribe of Benjamin. This contrasts with the contemporary approach, where only one such group is represented, namely, the men of Gibeah. All other villains on this side of the table are individuals who are pilloried or criticized to varying degrees. I have chosen not to include the divine here, even if several commentators have noted that no deity or angel comes to the rescue of the innocent *pilegesh* as she is thrown to the wolves.[44]

Finally, Table Four compares the two approaches to the sins of Gibeah:

Table 4: Sins of Gibeah

Hebrew Bible	*Modern Interpreters*
Inhospitality	Breach of patriarchal hospitality
Breach of patriarchal hospitality	'To know' sexually
Death threat	Attempted male-male gang rape
Heterosexual gang rape	Heterosexual gang rape
Adultery	Treachery
Murder	Cruelty
Tribal complicity	Sadism
Desecration	
Cover-up/dishonesty/lies	

In Table Four, two items are found in both columns, namely 'breach of patriarchal hospitality' and 'heterosexual gang rape'. All other items have no opposite number. HB is clearly patriarchal given its focus on the violation of ancient social and legal norms. As for the right-hand column, it can be divided into two parts. The first four items reflect two of the undisputed crimes committed by the men of Gibeah, plus two perceived sexual offences. The other five items deal primarily with the Levite. Because of the insistence of many scholars on his alleged character flaws, the Levite's behaviour is alluded to under 'treachery', 'cruelty', etc.

44. See Bal, *Death and Dissymmetry*, p. 125; Mark Jordan, *The Invention of Sodomy in Christian Theology* (Chicago & London: University of Chicago Press, 1997), pp. 30-31; Bach, 'Rereading the Body Politic', p. 397; Schneider, *Judges*, p. 262.

Patriarchal Villains or the Villainy of Patriarchy?

A few modern scholars reflect on literary and cultural factors that have a bearing on the interpretation of the two narratives under discussion. Bal (*Death and Dissymmetry*) seeks to explain the underlying causes of the outrage of Gibeah and the subsequent civil war in Judges 19–21 in terms of conflicting marriage institutions. She posits that the central issue at stake is 'patrilocal' versus 'virilocal' marriage. By this, Bal refers to two opposed systems in which a young woman either continues to live at her father's house after marriage or goes to live with her husband.[45] Where I find Bal's observations useful is in highlighting the fact that the Gibeah narrative unfolds within a specific cultural framework. This very concept is approached, but from a different angle, by Bechtel ('A Feminist Reading of Genesis 19:1–11'). She has noticed the discrepancies between HB and most modern interpreters (pp. 108, 126) and explains it by locating HB within a group-oriented or communal culture, whereas modern western approaches tend to hinge on the individual (pp. 109–12). This insight is helpful for the discussion of my subject. As we have repeatedly seen—and particularly on the subject of villains—HB does indeed focus primarily on communities (groups, cities, tribes), while today's scholars are much more likely to engage with individuals (Lot, the Levite).[46]

Given the venom expended on some of the patriarchal figures intervening in the Sodom and Gibeah narratives, one occasionally gets the impression that modern interpreters attack the individuals concerned for representing—and being faithful to—their patriarchal culture. It seems timely to recall an observation by Carole Fontaine: 'The Bible is the *heir* of patriarchy, not its originator'.[47] Indeed, the biblical books were written by people who were steeped in the ancient patriarchal mindset of the Near East, as both narratives amply demonstrate. The most spectacular result of this rigidly defined, male-centred power system is the intolerable deal meted out to women, a crucial issue that a series of feminist and womanist

45. Bal, *Death and Dissymmetry*, pp. 84–85, 88–93, 127, 156, 182–84, 186, 198.

46. This aspect is acknowledged by Schneider, *Judges*, p. 269.

47. Carole Fontaine, 'The Abusive Bible: On the Use of Feminist Method in Pastoral Contexts', in Athalya Brenner & Carole Fontaine (eds.), *A Feminist Companion to Reading the Bible* (Sheffield: Sheffield Academic Press, 1997), p. 93.

scholars have contributed to placing at the forefront of biblical scholarship in recent decades.

Are These Narratives Relevant for Liberation Theologies?

One of the causes for concern that has motivated my writing this essay, are the oppressive effects of the horror embedded in the Sodom and Gibeah narratives on the lives of lesbian, gay, bisexual and transgender people.[48] However, I hope my analysis will have a practical scope that will make it applicable to the situation of various oppressed communities.

To answer the above question I posit that it is necessary to deal with the basic question of the agendas pursued by the narrators of Genesis and Judges. Who wrote these tales and for what purpose? Jordan (*The Invention of Sodomy*, p. 30) establishes a comparison and finds that 'the incidents at Gibeah are more horrible than the events surrounding Lot's hospitality'. As Carden (*Sodomy*, p. 24) points out, 'the story of Gibeah can truly be said to be a horror story set in a nightmare men's world'. Likewise, Bal (*Death and Dissymmetry*) speaks of a 'horror story' (p. 237), which leaves us wondering whether this is simply a piece whose 'association with sadistic pornography is obvious' (p. 236), given 'the deliberation and detail characteristic of sadistic discourse' (p. 119). Exum (*Fragmented Women*) is in agreement as she points out 'the text's phallocentric ideology' (p. 177) and 'if ... it were portrayed in film today, we would label it pornographic' (p. 196). Schneider sums up her own feelings about the story by describing it as 'painful' (*Judges*, p. 262).

It is perhaps difficult to see in what way such a hair-raising story of cruelty and bloodshed can become a tool of liberation. Personally, I confess my inability to make the connection if only the sex/rape/horror approach is pursued. Indeed, from a lesbigay perspective I even find it unhelpful. For centuries Christians have been taught that the Sodom and Gibeah narratives are primarily about same-

48. I tend to use the term 'lesbigay'. I am aware of some of the challenges faced by transgender people in modern western society, but I will not attempt to speak on their behalf. For a transgender approach to biblical interpretation, see, for example, Victoria Kolakowski, 'Throwing a Party: Patriarchy, Gender, and the Death of Jezebel', in Robert Goss and Mona West (eds.), *Take Back the Word: A Queer Reading of the Bible*, (Cleveland, Ohio: The Pilgrim Press, 2000), pp. 103–14. Likewise, it is not for me to speak for feminist and womanist theologians, although I share many of their concerns.

sex relations, despite the fact that they clearly are not. More recently, the consensus among scholars has settled for attempted gang rape, but the gap between ancient and modern interpretations discussed above indicates that, in biblical times, the plot was read differently. The reason why this is so is well worth pondering. I attribute the discrepancy to the changes in exegesis that occurred in the early centuries of the Christian church, and which were far more consequential than most scholars seem to realize. However, the specific circumstances are too complex to be explored here.[49] Suffice it to say that the force of medieval church tradition has been such that, in the minds of millions of people, the sex/rape notion still takes centre stage, particularly with regard to Sodom as the better known of the two narratives. As we have seen, most commentators have cast the Gibeah of Judges 19 in a similar role.

The Politics of Gibeah and Sodom

To find a way out of what I perceive as an interpretative impasse, I have looked for inspiration from several quarters; one being the ancient political context. Bal excludes this kind of approach because she feels that too much has been said about the politics of the Bible: 'the political background has been over-emphasized in preceding exegeses' (*Death and Dissymmetry*, p. 236). While this may have been true in the 1980's, I find the opposite has been the case in recent years. At least for my part, it was not until I discovered the likely political agendas behind the two narratives in question that something clicked. Several scholars have noted that, throughout the Gibeah story, a number of inter-textual allusions to various books of HB seem to point to a verifiable political agenda that is pro-David and detrimental to Saul. Thus, it cannot be excluded that the story of the outrage of Gibeah and its aftermath was composed deliberately to denigrate Saul and his tribe Benjamin.[50] Read in this

49. For a more detailed discussion, see Derrick Sherwin Bailey, *Homosexuality and the Western Christian Tradition* (London: Longmans, Green & Co., 1955), pp. 8, 10, 25, 26, 53, 82, 153, 157; Jordan, *The Invention of Sodomy*, pp. 1, 3–4, 9, 29–30, 34–37; Carden, *Sodomy*, pp. 61–62, 77, 116, 123–28, 135–37, 141–42, 145–48, 154, 160, 164–66.

50. Several commentators have made similar observations, particularly Marc Brettler, *The Book of Judges* (London & New York: Routledge, 2002) pp. 90, 111–16. See also Carden, *Sodomy*, p. 44, and Schneider, *Judges*, pp. 169, 257, 269. The latter is inclined to think that 'the Israelites were seeking a pretext for a war, or at least a war with Benjamin' (p. 271).

light, the shocking fate of the *pilegesh* from Bethlehem of Judah (same hometown as David) is exacerbated in gruesome detail in order to stir up anti-Saul and anti-Benjamin sentiment. In this sense, the *pilegesh* was indeed, to quote Exum's expressive phrase, 'raped by the pen'. Denouncing one's enemies for alleged atrocities is a classic stratagem for writers of political and/or military propaganda. Viewed in this perspective, the horrified reaction that the Gibeah narrative is still capable of producing in modern readers bears witness to the literary talent and powerful style of the Hebrew narrator, who was also a master of textual manipulation.[51]

If Judges 19 is a well-crafted coded diatribe against Saul and his clan (and this is at least a realistic possibility), perhaps a similar situation can be appreciated in the case of Sodom. So far, the specific commentary on the politics of Genesis 18–19 that I have come across is negligible. Nevertheless, it seems to me that the various allusions in Genesis to Sodom's Canaanite origins are significant and appear to point in the same direction. Sodom is an evil place and has to be cast in the role of villain along with all other Canaanites to form a contrast with the righteous Abraham, chosen by God, and his descendants the Israelites. Within this framework, the Sodom story comes to play an important early part in the long history of Israelite antagonism to the original inhabitants of the land of Canaan, having thus become the first link in a long chain of anti-Canaanite propaganda. In a not-so-subtle way, the narrative can be seen as setting the tone for the Israel/Canaan conflict throughout the Hebrew Bible, particularly following the Exodus and subsequent Israelite invasion of Palestine.

Viewed impartially, that is, without any religious or ethnic bias, I believe there is good reason to assume that the picture of the ancient Canaanites presented by Genesis and other parts of the Bible is far from being 'accurate' in any modern sense. While HB consistently portrays the Canaanites—the colonized victims, as it were—in very negative terms, the people of Canaan presumably viewed the Israelites as unwelcome intruders, invaders and oppressors. This aspect of the narrative seems to have gone largely undetected. As noted, commentators writing on Sodom tend to

51. Brettler, *The Book of Judges*, describes Judges 19 as 'a very learned text, full of allusions to other biblical texts' (p. 84). Likewise he calls the narrative 'a created story' (p. 82) given that 'Judges 19 does not reflect ancient events; rather, it creates them' (p. 90).

focus on the issues described earlier, that is, patriarchal hospitality, gender, sex, and rape. However, the question of colonization, vilification and victimization remains, begging comparisons with similar approaches over the centuries regarding the invasion and conquest of different nations around the world. One telling example could well be the European conquest and domination of other continents, a process in which the European colonizers represented 'civilization' and the indigenous peoples were portrayed as 'savages'. The political and cultural manipulation at the heart of this process resonates in an essay by Robert Allen Warrior.[52] He compares the situation of North American Indians with that of ancient Canaan. In both cases the vanquished and colonized nations were vilified and stigmatized as well as systematically exterminated.[53] I would posit, therefore, that the Sodom story has the potential for being read as a powerful allegory when it comes to decolonizing and decontaminating history as well as theology.

I am tempted to take this point a step further. It seems fair to say that if the above political analysis is *not* applied to the Sodom and Gibeah texts, the interpretation process remains incomplete, and the risk of misinterpretation and misuse increases. Literary, psychological and gender-focused criteria are all important tools in biblical interpretation, and I am a strong believer in interdisciplinary approaches. However, when it comes to such explosive material as Sodom and Gibeah, I personally also need to be aware of the possible political contexts and agendas to be able to relate to the more distressing moments. In addition, if the political dimension is left out, I fear that the patriarchal essence of both narratives will continue to have the potential to function as a tool of oppression in several ways.

Perhaps the first victim is the Hebrew Bible itself? The widespread antipathy against HB in the modern world, particularly among Christians, is only likely to be reinforced by one-dimensional

52. Robert Allen Warrior, 'A Native American Perspective: Canaanites, Cowboys, and Indians', in R. S. Sugirtharajah (ed.), *Voices from the Margin* (London: SPCK, 1991), pp. 287–95.

53. This is how Warrior describes his approach: 'I read the Exodus stories with Canaanite eyes. And, it is the Canaanite side of the story that has been overlooked by those seeking to articulate theologies of liberation. Especially ignored are those parts that describe Yahweh's command to mercilessly annihilate the indigenous population' ('A Native American Perspective', p. 289).

interpretations of narratives in which horror and brutality are central ingredients. Another undesirable side effect may be the fomenting of anti-Jewish sentiment.[54] Likewise, it should not be forgotten that the violence embedded in the fictional events described has proved its efficiency for victimizing lesbian and gay people. Indeed, both Sodom and Gibeah are still employed in some circles as toxic proof-texts.[55] Hence, I suspect, in order to attain liberation, learning to decipher literary myths and debunk the politics of textual manipulation generated by oppressive forces is crucial. This is particularly true of the canonical writings of the Bible.[56] Patriarchy may be a major villain, but it is certainly not the only one. Becoming aware of the political context of ancient narratives can enable us to unmask some of its more recent manifestations and repercussions, whether they take the form of colonialism and neo-colonialism, sexism, or homophobia.

Conclusions

The interpretative gap between the Hebrew Bible and a large number of modern scholars has been illustrated, particularly when it comes to identifying the villains of Sodom and Gibeah. The gap is largely to be attributed to the clash of two very different cultures based on different assumptions and values. While ancient Israel was mainly communal or group oriented, modern western culture tends to focus on the individual. A political analysis of biblical

54. This risk is recognized, among others, by Phyllis Trible, 'Feminist Hermeneutics and Biblical Studies', in Ann Loades (ed.), *Feminist Theology: A Reader* (London: SPCK, 1990), p. 24.

55. A large amount of anti-gay literature is being produced and promoted by influential Christian churches and scholars. Reviewing even a small fraction of this material would go beyond the purview of this study. Among the sources I have consulted I will limit myself to point to the writings of Robert Gagnon, who belongs on the erudite side of the homophobic spectrum, cf. his contribution to Via & Gagnon, *Homosexuality and the Bible*, notably pp. 56–60. See also Gagnon, *The Bible and Homosexual Practice*, primarily pp. 71, 72 (note 75), 73–78, 95. A useful list of anti-gay and 'ex-gay' literature is included in Tony Green, Brenda Harrison & Jeremy Innes, *Not for Turning: An Enquiry into the Ex-gay Movement*. Published jointly by the authors (Leeds: University Print Services, University of Leeds, 1966), p. 93.

56. Carole Fontaine's reflection on injustice in the Bible seems to apply to both narratives: 'Until we understand that injustice has been coded into the very text itself as it pursues the class interests of its authors and protagonists, progressive believers will be dumbfounded by the Bible's ability to support oppression' (*The Abusive Bible*, p. 94).

narratives such as Genesis 19 and Judges 19 is useful for detecting the likely agendas behind the events described, which may enable modern readers to identify this literature as politically motivated fiction or propaganda. The images of violence and horror may well serve the deliberate purpose of denigrating political opponents or entire communities, tribes or nations. A greater awareness of the agendas that generated the ancient narratives has the potential to make modern readers better equipped to confront the political fiction and manipulation in some modern narratives, particularly those that oppress women and lesbigay people as well as colonized communities and nations.

BIBLIOGRAPHY

Adler, Margot, *Drawing Down the Moon: Witches, Druids, Goddess-Worshippers and Other Pagans in America Today* (Boston: Beacon Press, 1979).

Akroyd, Peter, *Goddesses, Women & Jezebel* in A. Cameron and A. Khurt (eds.), *Images of Women in Antiquity* (London: Croom Hill, 1983).

Aldridge, Robert, *Colonialism and Homosexuality* (London: Routledge, 2004).

Alves, Ruben, *O Poeta, O Guereiro* (Petropolis: Vozes, 1992).

Althaus-Reid, Maria, *The Queer God* (London: Routledge, 2003).

Althaus-Reid, Maria and Lisa Isherwood (eds.), *The Sexual Theologian* (London: T. & T. Clark, 2005).

Alter, Robert, *The David Story, A Translation with Commentary of 1 and 2 Samuel* (New York: W.W. Norton, 1999).

Anzaldúa, Gloria, *Borderlands La Frontera: The New Mestiza* (San Francisco: Aunt Lute Books, 1999).

Atkinson, Clarissa Margare Miles, & Constance Buchanan, (eds.), *'Shaping New Visions: Gender and Values in American Culture'* (Ann Arbor: University of Michigan Press, 1987).

Bach, Alice, *Women in the Hebrew Bible* (New York & London: Routledge, 1999).

— 'Rereading the Body Politic' in Alice Bach (ed.), *Women in the Hebrew Bible* (New York & London: Routledge, 1999).

— 'The Pleasure of her Texts' in Athalya Brenner, *A Feminist Companion to Samuel and Kings* (Sheffield: Sheffield Academic Press, 1994).

Bailey, Derrick S., *Homosexuality and the Western Christian Tradition* (London: Longmans, Green & Co., 1955).

Bal, Mieke, *Death and Dissymmetry: The Politics of Coherence in the Book of Judges* (Chicago: The University of Chicago Press, 1988).

— 'A Body of Writing: Judges 19' in Athalya Brenner (ed.), *A Feminist Companion to Judges* (Sheffield: Sheffield Acadaemic Press, 1993).

Bechtel, Lyn, 'A Feminist Reading of Genesis 19: 1–11' in Athalya Brenner (ed.), *Genesis: A Feminist Companion to the Bible, Second Series* (Sheffield: Sheffield Academic Press, 1998).

Ben Ami, I., *Saint Veneration Amongst the Jews in Morocco* (Jerusalem: The Magnes Press, 1984).

Berlin, Adele, 'Characterization in Biblical Narrative: David's Wives' in David J.A. Clines and Jamara C. Eskanazi (eds.), *Telling Queen Michal's Story* (Sheffield: Sheffield Academic Press, 1991).

Bernard of Clairvaux, On the Song of Songs, Books 1–4 (Michigan: Cistercian Publications, 1979).

Bird, Phyllis, 'Images of Women in the Old Testament' in Rosemary R. Ruether, *Religion and Sexism* (New York: Simon and Schuster 1974).

Boer, Roland, 'Yaweh as Top' in Ken Stone (ed.), *Queer Commentary and the Hebrew Bible* (Sheffield: Sheffield Academic Press, 2000).

Braidotti, Rosi, *Metamorphoses: Towards a Materialist Theory of Becoming* (Oxford: Polity, 2002).

— *Nomadic Subjects: Embodiment and Sexual Difference in Contemporary Feminist Theory'* (New York: Columbia University Press, 1994).

— *'The Body as Metaphor: Seduced and Abandoned: The Body in the Virtual World'*, Video recording (London: ICA, 1995).

— *Patterns of Dissonance: A Study of Women in Contemporary Philosophy* (Cambridge: Polity Press in association with Basil Blackwell, 1991).

Brettler, Marc, *The Book of Judges* (London & New York: Routledge, 2002).

Brenner, Athalya (ed.), *A Feminist Companion to Judges* (Sheffield: Sheffield Acadaemic Press, 1993).

Briffault, Robert, *The Mothers: A Study of Origins and Institutions of Marriage* (London: Allen & Unwin, 1927).

Brodie, Thomas, *Genesis as Dialogue* (Oxford: Oxford University Press, 2001).

Brueggeman, Walter, A Commentary on Jeremiah: Exile and Homecoming (Grand Rapids: Eerdmans).

Butler, Judith, *Gender Trouble: Feminism and the Subversion of Identity* (London: Routledge, 1990).

Califia, Pat, *Public Sex: The Culture of Radical Sex* (San Francisco: Cleis Press, 2000).

Capra, Frijof and Charlene Spretnak, *Green Politics* (New York: Dutton, 1984).

Carden, Michael, *Sodomy* (London: Equinox Publishing, 2004).

Carroll, Robert, *Jeremiah: A Commentary* (Philadelphia: WJK, 1986).

Christ, Carol P., *Rebirth of the Goddess – Finding Meaning in Feminist Spirituality* (Reading, Massachusetts: Addison Wesley, 1997).

— 'Why Women Need the Goddess: Phenomenological Psychological and Political Reflections' in C.P. Christ & J. Plaskow (eds.), *Womanspirit Rising: A Feminist Reader in Religion* (San Francisco: Harper Collins, 1979).

— *She who Changes: Re-Imagining the Divine in the World* (New York: Palgrave 2003).

Downing, Christine, *The Goddess: Mythological Images of the Feminine* (New York: Crossroad, 1990).

Comstock, G.D., *Gay Theology Without Apology* (Cleveland, Ohio: The Pilgrim Press, 1993).

Cook, Roger, *The Tree of Life* (London: Thames and Hudson, 1974).

Cross, F.M. *Canaanite Myth and Hebrew Epic* (Harvard: Harvard University Press, 1973).

Culler, Jonathan, *Framing the Sign: Criticism and its Institutions* (Oxford: Oxford University Press, 1988).

Culpepper, Emily, 'Contemporary Goddess Thealogy: A Sympathetic Critique' in H. Danby, *The Mishnah* (Oxford: Oxford Press).

Daly, Mary, *Beyond God the Father: Toward a Philosophy of Women's Liberation* (Boston: Beacon Press, 1973).

— 'After the Death of God the Father: Women's Liberation and the Transformation of Christian Consciousness' in Carol P. Christ and Judith Plaskow (eds.), *Womanspirit Rising: A Feminist Reader in Religion* (San Francisco: Harper Collins, 1979).

Davies, W.D. *Paul and Rabbinic Judaism: Some Rabbinic Elements in Pauline Theology* (London: SPCK, 1965).

De Veaux, Alexis, *Warrior Poet* (New York: W.W. Norton, 2004).

Dube, Musa, *Postcolonial Feminist Interpretation of the Bible* (St Louis: Chalice Press, 2000).

Edemanl, Diana, V. (ed.), *The Triumph of Elohim: From Yahwisms to Judaisms* (Kampen: Pharos, 1995).

Eller, Cynthia, *Living in the Lap of the Goddess: The Feminist Spirituality Movement in America* (Boston: Beacon Press, 1993).

Exum, Cheryl, *Fragmented Women* (Valley Forge: Trinity Press International, 1983).

— 'Mother in Israel: A Familiar Story Reconsidered' in Letty M. Russell (ed.), *Feminist Interpretation of the Bible* (Oxford: Basil Blackwell Ltd, 1985).

Farmer, Penelope, *Eve, Her Story* (London: Victor Gollancz, 1985).

Fontaine, Carole, 'The Abusive Bible: On the Use of Feminist Method in Pastoral Contexts' in Athalya Brenner & Carole Fontaine (eds.), *A Feminist Companion to Reading the Bible* (Sheffield: Sheffield Academic Press, 1997).

Gagnon, Robert, *The Bible and Homosexual Practice* (Nashville: Abingdon Press, 2001).

Goldingay, John, *After Eating the Apricot Men and Women with God* (Carlisle: Solway, an Imprint of Paternoster Publishers, 1996).

Grigg, Richard, *When God Becomes Goddess: The Transformation of American Religion* (New York: Continuum, 1995).

Gimbus, Marija, *The Language of the Goddess* (San Francisco: Harper & Row, 1989).

Goodenough, E.R., *By Light. Light: The Mystic Gospel of Hellenistic Judaism* (New Haven, CT: Yale University Press, 1935).

— *Jewish Symbols in the Greco-Roman World* (Toronto: Pantheon, 1965).

Goss, Robert, *Queering Christ* (Cleveland, Ohio: The Pilgrim Press, 2002).

Goss, Robert and Mona West, (eds.), *Take Back the Word: A Queer Reading of the Bible* (Cleveland, Ohio: The Pilgrim Press, 2000).

Greenberg, Steven, *Wrestling with God and Men* (Madison: The University of Wisconsin Press, 2004).

Gunn Allen, Paula, *The Sacred Hoop* (Boston: Beacon Press, 1986).

Gunn, David, *The Story of King David* (Sheffield: Journal for the Study of the Old Testament, 1978).

— 'Reflections on David' in Athalya Brenner, *A Feminist Companion to Reading the Bible* (Sheffield: Sheffield Academic Press, 1997).

Halevi, Shimon, *The Tree of Life* (Bath: Gateway Books, 1991).

Halevi, Shira, *The Life Story of Adam and Havah* (Northvale: Jason Aronsen Inc., 1997).

Hanks, Thomas, *The Subversive Gospel* (Cleveland, Ohio: The Pilgrim Press, 2000).

Haraway, Donna, 'A Manifesto for Cyborgs: Science Technology and Socialist Feminism in the 80s' in Graham Harvey, *Listening Peoples: Speaking Earth* (London: Hurst & Co, 1997).

Hengel, Martin, *Judaism and Hellenism* (London: SCM Press, 1974).

Henry, Matthew, *Commentary on the Whole Bible,* http://www.ccel.org/ccel/henry/mhc.i.html

Herschel, Abraham, *God in Search of Man* (New York: Farrar Strauss and Giroux, 1955).

— *The Prophets: An Introduction* (New York, Harper & Row, 1962).

Heschel, Susannah (ed.), *On Being a Jewish Feminist* (New York: Schocken Books, 1983).

Heyward, Carter, *Staying Power* (Cleveland OH: The Pilgrim Press, 1995).

Howarth, Henriette, *The Breaking of Her Dawn* (Hyderabad: YWCA, 2000).

Hucks, Tracey E., 'Burning with a Flame in America: African American Women in African-Derived Traditions,' *Journal of Feminist Studies in Religion* 17/2 (fall 2001), pp. 89–106.

Isherwood, Lisa, *Liberating Christ* (Cleveland, Ohio: The Pilgrim Press, 1999).

— The Power of Erotic Celibacy: Queering Heteropatriarchy (London, T. & T. Clark, 2006).

Janson, H.W. and Dora Jane Janson, *The Picture History of Painting from Cave Painting to Modern Times* (New York: Harry N. Abrams Inc., 1957).

Jeremias, J. *The Parables of Jesus* (London: SCM Press, 1972).

Jewett, Robert, *The Captain America Complex* (Philadelphia: WJK, 1973).

Jewett, Robert and J.S. Lawrence, *The Myth of the American Superhero* (Michigan: Eerdmans).

Jordon, Mark, *The Invention of Sodomy in Christian Theology* (London & Chicago: The University of Chicago Press, 1997).

— *The Ethics of Sex* (Oxford: Blackwell, 2002).

Jung Mo, Sung, *Desejo Mercado e Religiao* (Petropolis: Vozes, 1995).

Kamuf, P., 'Author of a Crime' in Athalya Brenner (ed.), *A Feminist Companion to Judges* (Sheffield: Sheffield Academic Press, 1993).

Keefe, A., 'The Female Body, the Politic and the Land: A Sociological Reading of Hosea 1–2' in Athalya Brenner (ed.), *Feminist Companion to the Latter Prophets* (Sheffield: Sheffield Academic Press, 1995).

Keller, Catherine, *From a Broken Web: Separation, Sexism and Self* (Boston: Beacon Press, 1986).

King, Ursula, *Women and Spirituality: Voices of Protest and Promise* (London: Macmillan Educational, 1989).

Korsak, Mary P., *At the Start: Genesis Made New* (Louvaine: Leuvense Skrijversaktie, 1992).

Laffey, Alice, *Wives, Harlots and Concubines: The Old Testament in Feminist Perspective* (Philadelphia: Fortress Press, 1998, London: SPCK, 1990).

Lazaro Covadlo, E *En Este Lugar Sagrado* (Buenos Aires: LH, 1970).

Long, Asphodel, 'Anti-Judaism in Britain', *Journal of Feminist Studies in Religion 7/2* (Fall 1991).

— 'The Goddess in Judaism: An Historical Perspective' in A. Pirani (ed.), *The Absent Mother: Restoring the Goddess to Judaism and Christianity* (New York: Harper Collins Publishers, 1991).

— *In a Chariot Drawn by Lions: The Search for the Female in Deity* (London: Women's Press, 1992).

— 'The Goddess Movement in Britain' Feminist Theology No. 5 (Jan. 1994), pp.11 – 39.

— 'The One or the Many: The Great Goddess Revisited', *Feminist Theology* No. 15 (1997).

— *Asherah, The Tree of Life and the Menorah* (Neath: BISFT, 1998).

Mantin, Ruth, *Thealogies in Process: The Role of Goddess Talk in Feminist Spirituality* (unpublished, Southampton, 2002).
McKay, Heather, 'Old Wine in New Wineskin, The Repositioning of Male Hebrew Bible Characters in New Testament Texts in Athalya Brenner (ed.), *A Feminist Companion to the Hebrew Bible and New Testament* (Sheffield: Sheffield Academic Press, 1996).
McKenna, Megan, *Not Counting Women and Children: Neglected Stories from the* Bible (Kent: Burns & Oates, 1994).
McKinlay, Judith, *Gendering Wisdom The Host: Biblical Invitations to Eat and Drink* (Sheffield: Sheffield Academic Press, 1996).
Mellor, Enid, 'The Literatures of the Ancient Near East' in Enid Mellor (ed.), *The Cambridge Bible Commentary: The Making of the Old Testament* (London: Cambridge University Press, 1972).
Meyers, Carol, *The Tabernacle Menorah* (Missoula, Mt: The Scholar's Press, 1976).
— *Discovering Eve: Ancient Israelite Women in Context* (Oxford: Oxford University Press, 1988).
Moore, Gareth, *A Question of Truth* (London & New York: Continuum, 2003).
Morton, Nelle, *The Journey is Home* (Boston: Beacon Press, 1985).
Moser, Charles and J.J. Madeson, *Bound to be Free: The S/M Experience* (New York: Continuum, 1996).
Neusner, Jacob, T*orah Through the Ages: A Short History of Judaism* (London: SCM Press, 1990).
Niehr, Herbert, 'The rise of YHWH in Judahite and Israelite Religion: Methodological and Religio-Historical Aspects' in Edelman, *The Triumph of Elohim.*
Nissinen, M., *Homoeroticism in the Biblical World* (Minneapolis: Fortress Press, 1998).
Norris, Pamela, *The Story of Eve* (London: Picader, 1998).
Noy, Dov, *Folklore in Talmudic and Midrash* (Jerusalem: Universita ha-ivrit birusalyaim, 1968).
Olyan, S.M. *Asherah and the Cult of Yaweh in Israel* (Atlanta: Scholar's Press, 1988).
Patai, Raphael, *The Hebrew Goddess* (Detroit: Wayne State University Press, 1990).
— *Sex and Family in the Bible and the Middle East* (New York: Dolphin Books, 1959).
Pettey, Richard, *Asherah, Goddess of Israel* (New York: Lang, 1988).
Plaskow, Judith, *Standing Again at Sinai: Judaism from a Feminist Perspective* (San Francisco: Harper & Row, 1991).
Propp, V., *Morphology of Folktales* (Austin, Tx: University of Texas Press, 1968).
Raphael, Melissa, *Thealogy and Embodiment: The Post-Patriarchal Reconstruction of Female Sacrality* (Sheffield: Sheffield Academic Press, 1996).
– *Introducing Thealogy: Discourse on the Goddess* (Sheffield: Sheffield Academic Press, 1999).
– *Introducing Thealogy* (Sheffield: Sheffield Academic Press, 2000).
– '*Monotheism in Contemporary Feminist Goddess Religion: A Betrayal of Early Thealogical Non-Realism?*' in Sawyer & Collier (eds.), *Is There a Future for Feminist Theology?*
Rigoliosso, Marguerite, 'Interview with Starhawk', *Feminist Theology* 13/2, (2005), p.178.
Rosenberg, Martha, 'Debate Primer Panel' in J. Fernandez *et al, Cuerpos Ineludibles Un Dialogo a partir de las Sexualidades* (Buenos Aires: Aji de Pollo, 2004).
Rountree, Kathryn, *Embracing the Witch and Goddess* (London: Routledge, 2004).
Sawyer, Deborah & Diane Collier (eds.), *Is There a Future for Feminist Theology?* (Sheffield: Sheffield Academic Press, 1999).

Rowlett, Lori, 'Violent Femmes and S/M: Queering Samson and Delilah in Ken Stone, *Queer Commentary of the Hebrew Bible* (Sheffield: Sheffield Academic Press, 2001).
Ruether, Rosemary R., *Sexism and God Talk : Towards a Feminist Theology* (London: SCM Press, 1983).
Sallberg, Kam Rose, *Their Stories, Our Stories* (New York: Continuum, 1995).
Sawyer, Deborah & Diane Collier (eds.), *Is There a Future for Feminist Theology?* (Sheffield: Sheffield Academic Press, 1999).
Scanzoni, L., and V. Mollencott, Is the Homosexual My Neighbor? (San Francisco: HarperSanFrancisco, 1994).
Schneider, Tammi, *Judges* (Collegeville: the Liturgical Press, 2000).
Scholem, Gershon, *The Kabbalah and its Symbolism* (New York: Schoken, 1969).
Shargent, Karla, 'Living on the Edge: The Luminality of Daughters in Genesis to Samuel' in Athalya Brenner (ed.), *A Feminist Companion to Samuel and Kings* (Sheffield: Sheffield Academic Press, 1994).
Smith, Carol, 'Challenged by the Text: Interpreting Two Stories of Incest in the Hebrew Bible' in Brenner & Fontaine, *A Companion to Reading the Bible* (Sheffield: Sheffield Academic Press, 1997).
Smith, Mark, *The Early History of God: Jaweh and the Other Dieties in Ancient Israel* (San Francisco: Harper and Row, 1990).
Snaith, John G., *Eccliasticus or the Wisdom of Jesus, Son of Sirach* (Cambridge: Cambridge University Press, 1974).
Sojourner, Sabrina, 'In the House of Yemanja: The Goddess Heritage of Black Women,' in Gloria Wade-Gales (ed.), *My Soul is a Witness* (Boston: Beacon Press, 1995).
Starhawk, *The Spiral Dance: A Rebirth of the Ancient Religion of The Great Goddess* (San Francisco: Harper & Collins, 1979).
—*Webs of Power* (British Columbia: Gabriola Island, 2003).
Steinsaltz, Adin, *Biblical Images* (New York: Basic Books, 1984).
—*The Strife of the Spirit* (Northvale: Jason Aronsen Inc., 1988).
Stern, D, 'Midrash and Midrastic Interpretation', in Adele Berlin and Marc Zvi Brettler, *The Jewish Study Bible* (Oxford: Oxford University Press, 2004).
Stone, Ken, Practicing Safer Texts: Food, Sex and the Bible in Queer Perspective (London: T. & T. Clark, 2005).
Sturge, Mark, 'Don't Dis Me if You Don't Know Me' in *Black Theology in Britain*, 4.1 (Nov. 2001).
Stuart, Elizabeth, *Spitting at Dragons: Towards a Feminist Theology of Sainthood* (London & New York: Mowbray, 1996).
Taylor, Christopher S., *In the Vicinity of the Righteous: Ziyara and the Veneration of Muslim Saints in Late Medieval Egypt,* (Leiden, Boston, Koln: Brill, 1999).
Teish, Luisah, *Jambalaya* (San Francisco: HarperSanFrancisco, 1985).
— *Carnival of the Spirit* (San Francisco: HarperSanFrancisco, 1994).
Tomassi-Rogers, Sara, *Journeys Out of the Victim Role: A Feminist Theologians Personal Reflections on Male Violence* (Plymouth: College of St Mark and St John, 2000).
Trible, Phyllis, God and the Rhetoric of Sexuality (Philadelphia: Fortress Press, 1978).
— 'Feminist Hermeneutics and Biblical Studies' in Ann Loades (ed.), *Feminist Theology: A Reader* (London: SPCK, 1990).
— *Texts of Terror Literary-Feminist Readings of Biblical Narratives* (London: SCM Press, 1992).

Valler, S., 'King David and His Women: Biblical Stories and Talmudic Discussions' in Athalya Brenner (ed.), *A Feminist Companion to Samuel and Kings* (Sheffield: Sheffield Academic Press, 1994).

Von Rod, Gerhard, *Wisdom in Israel* (London: SCM Press, 1972).

Van Setters, John, 'The Pentateuch' in M. Patrick Graham and Steven L. McKenzie (eds.), *The Hebrew Bible Today and An Introduction to Critical Issues* (Louisville KY: Westminster John Knox Press, 1998).

Via, Dan & Robert Goss, *Homosexuality and the Bible* (Minneapolis: Fortress Press, 2003).

Wallace, Howard, *The Eden Narrative* (Missoula, Mt: The Scholar's Press, 1985).

Warrior, R.A., 'A Native American Perspective: Canaanites, Cowboys and Indians' in R.S. Sugirtharajah (ed.), *Voices from the Margin* (London: SPCK, 1991).

Weems, Renita J., *Just a Sister Away: A Womanist Vision of Women's Relationships in the Bible* (San Diego CA: Allan Boesak: LauraMedia, 1988).

Whybray, R.N., *Wisdom in Proverbs* (London: SPCK, 1965).

Witting, Susan, 'Theories of Formulaic Narrative' in *Semeia 5* (1976).

Wright, G. Ernest, *Biblical Archaeology* (London: Butler and Tanner Ltd., 1962).

Yarden, L., *The Tree of Life: A Study of the Menorah* (Ithaca, N.Y.: Cornell University Press, 1971).

Young, Robert, *Postcolonialism: A Very Short Introduction* (Oxford: Oxford University Press, 1995).

Index of Biblical References

Old Testament

New Testament

Index of Authors

Printed in the United Kingdom
by Lightning Source UK Ltd.
121650UK00001B/187-228/A